T0290131

DESIGN
YOUR
THINKING

PRAISE FOR *DESIGN YOUR THINKING*

'Dr Soni has delivered a lucid treatise on the "how to" of design thinking. A must-read book'—Vijay Govindarajan, Coxe Distinguished Professor, Tuck School of Business, Dartmouth College

'A fresh perspective on design thinking with important added elements, namely inspiration and scale. As new opportunities in a dramatically different world are explored, one will be able to draw on unique insights from the multitude of case studies peppered throughout the book. A thorough and sincere effort by Dr Pavan Soni'—Dr R.A. Mashelkar, National Research Professor and former Director General, CSIR

'An amazing read from Dr Pavan Soni. Rich in literature on design thinking and insights from Indian examples, the book guides the evolution of the thinking process systematically and systemically'—Dr K. Radhakrishnan, former Chairman, ISRO

'Pavan Soni's thought-provoking book reminds us of the critical importance of design thinking to deliver on strategy. A great read for both start-up entrepreneurs and corporate leadership teams'—Kiran Mazumdar-Shaw, Executive Chairperson, Biocon

'Design thinking has become a mainstream topic for businesses over the last few years. While digital natives have embraced design thinking as a way of life, traditional companies have lagged behind. This book is a very useful guide, as most companies will benefit from the transformation that design thinking can bring'—G.V. Prasad, Co-chairman and Managing Director, Dr. Reddy's

'I have known Dr Pavan Soni as an innovative thinker, and he brings this capability to the fore in this book. He combines real-world examples along with theory behind various phases of design thinking to facilitate learning and to transform you into a design thinker'—Ashok Soota, Executive Chairman and Co-founder, Happiest Minds Technologies

'Pavan demystifies design thinking and shows how any individual and organization can systematically practice it and unleash creativity and innovation, turning problems into opportunities'—Dr Manish Gupta, Director, Google Research India

'Dr Soni's book brings the design-thinking method and mindsets into action, supported by experience, evidence and examples. This book emphasizes the importance of starting with empathy and finding problems worth solving. These mindsets, skill sets and tools could be key to our individual and collective success in solving the most important business and social problems of the future'—Dr Vishal Sikka, Founder and CEO, Vianai Systems

'As technology becomes an integral part of every industry, human-centric solutions that are inspired by empathy will become increasingly important. Innovation will need a design-thinking mindset. This book is an excellent primer to build your mental muscle for creative problem-solving' —Dr Rohini Srivathsa, National Technology Officer, Microsoft India

'Industries must graduate from solving problems to identifying and framing the problems worth solving, and this is a skill that doesn't come organically. More than brilliant ideas, we need genuine customer insights and disciplined execution. In *Design Your Thinking*, Dr Soni offers a framework based on design thinking and shows us how one can become a more disciplined problem-solver'—Soumitra Bhattacharya, Managing Director, Bosch Limited, and President, Bosch Group in India

'A fascinating and insightful book, about something that has not yet been simplified to the extent of driving innovation. There have been many purists and theorists explaining divergent and convergent thinking, design methodology and the need to humanize work, but not many have translated the concepts into something tangible and meaningful for organizations. *Design Your Thinking* does that. Worth reading several times'—Kalyan Ram Madabhushi, CEO, Global Chemicals, Aditya Birla Group

'As Dr Pavan Soni says, design thinking is to innovation what Six Sigma is to quality. This book will show you how to become a master design thinker and therefore an expert innovator. It provides a clear framework, plenty of techniques and tools, and lots of relevant examples. A must-read: an excellent and timely book on an important topic'—Jaideep Prabhu, co-author of *Jugaad Innovation*

'From *samvedana* to *srijansheelta*, as I often put it, summarizes the design zig-zag that Pavan so lucidly describes in this book. It helps in situating an unmet need of people, potential customers and, in some cases, co-creators in the centre of the problem-solving process. I hope this book helps many readers to recognize the need for developing sensitivity and not just the skills for designing affordable solutions'—Professor Anil K. Gupta, Founder, Honey Bee Network

'Dr Soni's book adds two unique stages of inspiration and scale to the product-development process of design thinking. It also provides practical wisdom from around the world. *Design Your Thinking* is a much-needed book for aspiring product developers and business leaders alike' —Dr Gopichand Katragadda, Founder and CEO, Myelin Foundry, and former Group CTO, Tata Sons

'Dr Pavan Soni, in his book *Design Your Thinking*, urges you to think innovatively and adopt a human-centric approach towards modern-day problem-solving. This book is set to be an essential read for the new-age leaders of tomorrow'—Kulmeet Bawa, President and Managing Director, SAP Indian Subcontinent

'Pavan Soni does an incredible job of framing design thinking (DT) as a mindset rather than merely as a toolkit. He demolishes the myth that DT is all about empathy and customer service. Empathy needs to blend with expertise in order to yield sustainable business. If you need to understand what DT is all about and how you can fire up innovation at your work, you came to the right place'—Charles Dhanaraj, Piccinati Endowed Chair Professor of Strategy, Daniels College of Business, University of Denver

'Design thinking is more about thinking than just designing, and in *Design Your Thinking*, Dr Pavan Soni offers a research-backed and practically relevant primer on how to foster a systematic approach of thinking and problem-solving'—Dr Rajendra Srivastava, Dean, Indian School of Business

'India needs innovation at scale. *Design Your Thinking* endeavours to offer the proven tools and methods to unearth problems, develop ingenious ideas and solve the problems effectively, so that you create impact at scale. A much-needed and timely treatise on how to bring discipline into our otherwise chaotic approach towards creativity'—Major General Anil Khosla, former Military Secretary to the President of India

'Pavan's book couldn't be more timely, given the challenges the corporate world is facing. Being part of one of the world's most innovative companies, I can fully relate to the fact that innovation is not a one-off eureka moment or a one-time event but a structured, repeatable process that must be embedded into an organization's DNA. *Design Your Thinking* would help you do the same, systematically'—Ajay Nanavati, former MD, 3M India

'Extremely well-written book. Highly readable, lucid and with relevant Indian examples having the right connect to the global context. Introduces design thinking to every lay person and professional! Loved it!'—Girish Paranjpe, former Joint-CEO, Wipro

'In *Design Your Thinking*, Dr Pavan Soni, has brought alive the fact that a journey towards breakthrough must be conceptualized, strategized and embarked upon in a structured manner. A must read for leaders, entrepreneurs and executives who aim to nurture a culture of innovation, by design'—Deepak Chopra, Group CEO, ANAND

'As Bill Gates famously said: "Never before in history has innovation offered promise of so much to so many in so short a time." Design thinking is that approach to innovation. Through *Design Your Thinking*, Pavan offers key insights on practising design thinking and fostering an innovation culture at scale'—Rajiv Bhalla, Managing Director, Barco India

'Are you a student? A teacher? An entrepreneur? A manager? A thinker? Does the question "Can thinking be patterned?" interest you? Go and read Pavan's book. You will be convinced that the answer is "Yes"' —Professor S. Sadagopan, Director, IIIT Bangalore

'As we move from efficiency-centric world to experience-centric world, the design paradigm shifts from system-centric to customer-centric model. This book offers the framework to ideate, evaluate and converge on our creative efforts to reframe the problem and build a solution which is desirable, deployable and scalable'—Vijaya Kumar Ivaturi, Co-founder and CTO, Crayon Data, and former CTO, Wipro

'The terms design and design thinking are mistakenly used interchangeably. In this book, Pavan has very lucidly explained, with a lot of examples, how and why design thinking is a disciplined approach to solving problems— the outcome of which may lead to innovations!'—Ravi Arora, author of *Igniting Innovation* and *Making Innovations Happen*

'In this book, Dr Pavan Soni has quoted numerous real-life business scenarios which provide the reader with an opportunity not just to understand the concepts but also to practise those. *Design Your Thinking* is a must-read for anyone who is interested in questioning the status quo' —Sreenath Narayanaiah, Director, Shared Business Services, Merck

'Design thinking can be viewed as an analytic and creative process that engages a person in opportunities to experiment, create and prototype models, and to gather feedback and redesign. Dr Pavan Soni's book is an excellent working example of this philosophy and pedagogy of learning. A must-read for all involved in design and learning in all spheres' —Professor Parameshwar P. Iyer, Chairman, IP TeL, and Principal Research Scientist, Indian Institute of Science

'*Design Your Thinking* is a rare blend of academic depth and business practicality, written in a way that would appeal to broader audiences. It amplifies the power and impact of earlier design-thinking frameworks and shows how individuals can embrace the design-thinking mindset of "clear head, deep heart, thick skin". This book is a must-read for all those who want to "perceive, pivot or persist" in this new age' —Dr Madanmohan Rao, Research Director, YourStory, and Charter Member, TiE Bangalore

'*Design Your Thinking* provides a great inside look at creative problem-solving. It is a must-read for designers, entrepreneurs and managers involved in innovation'—Professor Klaus Lang, University of Applied Sciences Neu-Ulm, Germany

'*Design Your Thinking* provides practitioners with insights into how design thinking can be utilized, as well as a philosophical base on which design thinking stands. A great gift from the country of wonderful frugal innovations'—Professor Norio Tokumaru, Nagoya Institute of Technology, Japan

'Leading brands worldwide have made design thinking a part of their organizational DNA, and for good reason. Design thinking enables you to zoom out and view the big picture, which could be the magic ingredient behind breakthrough ideas. This book will enable novices to explore the world of design thinking and help readers get a deeper understanding of the subject'—Vikas Gupta, Managing Director, Talent, Deloitte

'Dr Pavan Soni's book on design thinking couldn't be more timely and relevant. Replete with wonderful case studies and best practices from across a range of companies, *Design Your Thinking* will not only make you think but inspire you to act'—Sripada Chandrasekhar, Clinical Professor, Organisational Behaviour, Indian School of Business

'Time has come that design thinking be applied beyond products, beyond customers and beyond specific functions. We at Bigbasket try that every single day, and I wish you do the same. This book would serve as a definitive guide in your journey to embrace design thinking in totality'—Hari Menon, Co-founder and CEO, Bigbasket.com

DESIGN
YOUR
THINKING

THE MINDSETS, TOOLSETS AND SKILL SETS
FOR CREATIVE PROBLEM-SOLVING

PAVAN SONI

PENGUIN
BUSINESS

An imprint of Penguin Random House

PENGUIN BUSINESS

USA | Canada | UK | Ireland | Australia
New Zealand | India | South Africa | China | Singapore

Penguin Business is part of the Penguin Random House group of companies
whose addresses can be found at global.penguinrandomhouse.com

Published by Penguin Random House India Pvt. Ltd
4th Floor, Capital Tower 1, MG Road,
Gurugram 122 002, Haryana, India

First published in Portfolio by Penguin Random House India 2020
Published in Penguin Business 2022

ISBN 9780670094097

Typeset in Adobe Garamond Pro by Manipal Technologies Limited, Manipal
Printed at Replika Press Pvt. Ltd, India

www.penguin.co.in

Dedicated to my wife, Nimisha,
who taught me the virtues of humility,
empathy and discipline

Contents

Introduction

'I still believe that sitting down and reading a book is the best way to really learn something.'

—Eric Schmidt, former CEO, Google[1]

Non-linear growth necessitates non-linear ways of thinking. This maxim is as true in our personal lives as in the professional spheres. While we face multifaceted problems, we must bear in mind that such complex problems require simple approaches, often leading to counter-intuitive solutions that are scalable and enduring. The rapid proliferation of communication and computation technologies, rising affordability of devices and emergence of new business models have offered us more choices than we can meaningfully make sense of, and this further accentuates the importance of honing a systematic approach of thinking.

When was the last time you were *taught* how to think? Do you even believe that thinking can be taught? While growing up, we all intuitively assumed that only by gaining experience can we think more clearly. But as John Dewey reminds us: 'We do not learn from experience, we learn from *reflecting* on experience [italics mine].'[2] Just because you have solved a problem numerous times does not mean that you are adopting the best approach of solving it, or that you *know* the best approach. In our endeavours of engineering solutions and crafting our careers, we often miss out on the important skill of *designing our thinking*. A pattern of thinking that can help us break away from set patterns in a disciplined manner. Does such a pattern of thinking even exist? Can thinking be disciplined? Yes, very much, and this book is a humble attempt in that direction.

The book builds on the rich literature of design thinking and offers a systematic approach of problem-solving, which could be adopted in situations ranging from new product development to meaningfully addressing your everyday problems. The pioneering work on design thinking by IDEO, Stanford d.school, LUMA Institute and MIT Media Labs has helped introduce this idea to the popular imagination. The biggest contribution of design thinking to the discourse on creative problem-solving and innovation has been to bring to prominence the significance of empathy, experimentation and iteration, and the imperative of embracing ambiguity, instead of fearing it. However, this discourse has also led many to perceive design thinking as an approach exclusively suited to technology product development, especially in the fast-paced start-up world. While tech companies tend to benefit immensely from the approach, design thinking is by no means limited to the world of hi-tech, as many of the tenets and methods of this approach to problem-solving have a wide application.

The primary intent of writing this book is to enable a broad-based adoption of design thinking as a human-centric approach to problem-solving, which helps bring discipline to this otherwise chaotic process. The method is as useful for new product development as for everyday problems, including accounts receivable, customer service and employee engagement. If employees can embrace a more systematic posture towards problem-solving, they would greatly be benefited and so would the organizations. The same can be said about personal lives, where a deeper understanding of other people's motivations can greatly help improve relationships.

The second objective of the book is to discuss, celebrate and draw insights from numerous innovations and acts of creativity from a wide array of Indian organizations. The discourse on creativity in general, and design thinking in particular, is disproportionately oriented towards the Western audiences and industries that practitioners find it difficult to draw meaningful inspirations and insights from. India, with its cultural and economic context, offers a unique opportunity to embrace systematic approaches to problem-solving, and I deem that examples from India would immensely help in moving us in that direction.

Finally, my aim in writing this book is to help managers, entrepreneurs, students and enthusiasts adopt design thinking by learning useful toolsets and skill sets, and cultivating the appropriate mindsets. As a teacher and corporate trainer, I have always believed that true learning happens when the participants adopt the tools, practise the skills and hone the right mindset, and throughout the book I have attempted to offer those three, so that the readers can learn design thinking on their own. The real proof of this book's effectiveness would be measured in terms of a reader's ability to solve a complex problem systematically, without the help of an external consultant or a coach of design thinking.

The book includes case studies and practical lessons on creativity, innovation and design thinking from companies like 3M, Accenture, Amazon, ANAND Group, Apple, Aravind Eye Hospitals, Asian Paints, Bain & Company, Bigbasket, Biocon,

Booking.com, Bosch, Café Coffee Day, DMart, Dr. Reddy's, Disney, Flipkart, Future Group, Google, Hero MotoCorp, Hewlett-Packard, Honda, IDEO, iD Fresh Food, IIM Bangalore, IndiGo, Infosys, Intel, Intuit, ISRO, ITC, Johnson & Johnson, Lemon Tree Hotels, Mahindra, Maruti Suzuki, McKinsey & Company, Microsoft, Netflix, Ogilvy, Ola Cabs, Oyo Rooms, Paytm, PepsiCo, Pixar, Reliance, Royal Enfield, Samsung, Sony, Tata Group, Tata Motors, Titan, Twitter, Unilever and Wipro. There are over thirty books and twenty-five research articles that have gone into the writing of this book, presenting the most relevant and contemporary in design thinking. Each concept is supplemented with relevant examples so that the learning could be reinforced.

The book has ten chapters, each addressing a specific aspect of creative problem-solving, through the lens of design thinking. The first chapter, 'What is Design Thinking?', offers a primer on design thinking, as a philosophy and an approach, and delves into how the approach is different from other popular practices of creativity, such as critical thinking, lateral thinking and lean thinking. The chapter also presents an overview of the design thinking process model, comprising these stages: inspire; empathize and define; ideate; prototype and test; and scale. Each of these stages is presented in a separate chapter in the book. The second chapter, 'Why Design Thinking Now?', explains the relevance of design thinking to the current times and why our traditional models of problem-solving need to be more human-centric, prototype-driven and iterative, so that we can elegantly solve more complex, multifaceted problems. The third chapter, 'Key Tenets of Design Thinking', lists a set of principles and the mindsets that characterize design thinking, with relevant cases where remarkable outcomes have been achieved by solving problems in a human-centric manner.

The fourth chapter, 'Inspire', delves into the first stage of design thinking—inspiring, getting a brief, bringing in diversity—and looks at how leaders can set in motion the practice of design thinking in their teams. The fifth chapter, 'Empathize and Define', argues why traditional market research approaches fall awfully short of getting to the real insights and how one could build better channels and means to get to a richer understanding of the customers. The chapter also shares methods of narrowing down one's focus to the most significant problems to be solved and sheds light on how to frame a problem worth solving.

The sixth chapter, 'Ideate', offers the principles of effective ideation while presenting techniques to increase the quantity and quality of ideas. The seventh chapter, 'Prototype and Test', presents the significance of prototyping and explores the means of idea validation and improvement, including the practices of storytelling, storyboarding and scenario building. The eighth chapter, 'Scale', delves into what happens to a validated concept and how it can be scaled to realize the desired impact. The chapter also offers ways of measuring the progress on design thinking and important leadership attributes to enable the ramping up of validated ideas.

The last two chapters aim to bring the discussion back to the general context of corporate and individual problem-solving and offer practical insights on adopting design thinking. The ninth chapter, 'Design Thinking in Action', starts with an overview of a typical two-day design thinking workshop, and shares practical advice on how to manage such programmes in your organization without relying on external experts. The tenth chapter, 'How to Be a Design Thinker', shifts the focus towards individuals and presents a set of practices one could adopt to become a better design thinker, in both personal and professional milieus.

There are three supplementary segments towards the end of the book. Appendix A summarizes the key skill sets, toolsets and mindsets that support each of the five stages of design thinking. Appendix B answers a set of frequently asked questions that you might find useful in furthering your pursuit of practising and propagating design thinking. The chart attached at the end presents a summary mind map of the entire book, which would serve as a ready reference during your learning and execution journey.

This book is an exercise in design thinking, with all of its key elements in action: human centricity (I have tried to keep the language simple); visual thinking (the book is replete with relevant figures and charts); iterative thinking (all chapters have gone through extensive revision); and prototyping mentality (several of the concepts were validated through workshops before being included in the book). I sincerely hope that my readers find this work informative, inspiring and practical, and that after reading it they echo what Eric Schmidt, as quoted in the epigraph, thinks about reading books.

1

What Is Design Thinking?

'Design is a user-focused prototype-based development tool that can make our organization adapt to the fast-changing external environment. Building a design-led organization requires creativity, a deep understanding and empathy of human behaviour. It also requires the skill to synthesise different and often conflicting trends and ideas . . . Communication, customer experience, logistics, organisation structures, and even strategy can be tangible outcomes of design-led thinking.'

—Kishore Biyani, CEO, Future Group[1]

You are born in a middle-class business family and in one of the most remote parts of the country. You could barely manage to get to school, and you knew in your head that completing your education would not be feasible, or even wise. However, you have had the knack for coding from a very early age, and you like to travel. Between the ages of seventeen and twenty, you get to stay at over 100 bed-and-breakfasts, guest houses and hotels across the country, see for yourself the massive dearth of affordable and good-quality budget hotels, and moot an idea of offering affordable stay. A college dropout by now, and much before turning twenty, you have already failed six times. Then, the legendary Peter Thiel spots you (because you dropped out of formal education), and the rest, as they say, is history. I am not talking about any Silicon Valley fantasy story but about Ritesh Agarwal, who founded Oyo Rooms at age twenty. Today, he stands atop an empire that spans over 23,000 hotels across 800 cities in eighteen countries around the world.

Agarwal's story has all the elements of what it takes to solve a thorny problem elegantly: empathy (he stayed at all sorts of hotels himself, instead of just hiring a market research agency); iteration (he failed some six times before getting the business mix right); being hands-on (he started coding at age eight and used to sell SIM cards in local markets); prototyping mentality (he pivoted his initial foray, Oravel Stays, into Oyo as he gathered deeper insights); and scale (Oyo is well set to become the world's largest hotel chain by 2023). What we are looking at is design thinking in action, except that when Ritesh was in the thick of the action, he did not think of it this way. For him, thinking and acting were simultaneous, and as the young, college-dropout billionaire puts it, 'It was a combination of insights from my own travel experiences and a deep desire to do something meaningful . . . For me, it is about having a passion for solving a big problem and leaving a huge impact. Once you have that, everything else falls into place.'[2]

This book intends to help you learn how to solve important problems systematically, so that you create solutions that your customers desire, are technically feasible and remain viable for your business in the long run. Welcome to design thinking.

Prior to understanding design thinking and taking a deep dive into its principles, process model and key techniques, it would be helpful to discuss the shortcomings with the traditional approaches of creative problem-solving and innovation.

The traditional model of innovation is inadequate

Problem-solving is the cornerstone not only of scientific and technological progress but also of successful commercial endeavours. At times, the problem is known and well-articulated, such as 'How to manage Bangalore's traffic situation?' And then there are those thorny issues—like 'How to ensure women's safety on public transport?'—where no single or clear answer exists. Well-solved problems often result in products and services, and in upsides for the solvers in terms of businesses. For something to qualify as innovative, it must be new, surprising and radically useful.[3]

One of the most widely adopted models of new product development and innovation is the stage-gate process, which has been in existence for a very long time. Some form or shape of this model has been adopted in the software development space and dubbed the 'software development life cycle' or the 'waterfall model'. Figure 1 presents a stage-gate process of new product development which you might be practising in your organization, knowingly or unknowingly.

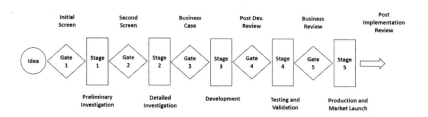

Figure 1: Stage Gate process of problem-solving or new product development (Courtesy: Robert Cooper)

The stage-gate process looks intuitive, with its key checkpoints and stages of further investment. The intuitiveness of the model is only matched by its extent of adoption, across organizations of all sizes. The model is neat, except that it does not work all that well at high levels of ambiguity. It assumes that the problem is well known, the internal and external environments are relatively stable, and that there are only finite possibilities that one has to choose from. But that is hardly the luxury most problem-solvers would have.

Some of history's most glorious product failures have all allegedly gone through the grind of this stage-gate process. Impeccably executed and with no dearth of funds, products like Apple Newton, Sony Betamax, Microsoft Zune, Iridium satellite phone, Segway, Toshiba HD DVD, Google Glass, Amazon Fire Phone and Samsung Galaxy Note7 failed miserably. The problem was not in execution but lay somewhere outside the zone of control of the innovating organization: customers, stakeholders, ecosystem, timing, regulators, etc. Perhaps the firms were too keenly following an out-of-sync process to marshal their ideas.

In India, too, we can find products, with a lot of heart and money pumped into them, that couldn't excite customers. Ambitious and well-executed projects—such as Tata Nano, Mahindra two-wheelers, Maruti Suzuki Kizashi, Godrej Chotukool compact fridge, Tata Swach water purifier and Aakash tablet—failed to solve problems profitably. One must only look at the graveyard of failed start-ups in India and of flop Bollywood movies, purportedly the world's largest production house in terms of sheer volume, to appreciate how many ideas fail. Nothing wrong with their approach of product development or problem-solving, except that it was, perhaps, too insular.

The stage-gate process, or its variants, suffer from the following key challenges. Firstly, it all starts with an idea, and there lies the seed of trouble. An idea for what? For whom? What problem does it address? Starting with an idea, and not a problem, is the cardinal sin most entrepreneurs are guilty of and, resultantly, their enterprises fall victim to the not-so-surprising high mortality rates. Idea cannot be a starting point; it should rather be a problem or an opportunity. Ideas ought to come later in the game, once the insights are gathered and the scope is firmed. In fact, for a problem which is fully understood, ideas can come from anywhere, including from partners and customers.

Secondly, the concept testing and validation happens late in the journey—of a product, process or problem—and by then a lot of investment has already been made. Such a delayed validation does no good because, by now, the stakes are already steep and an escalation of commitment ensues. The situation worsens when managers, suffering from confirmation bias, dismiss the weak signals that might jeopardize their logic. That is where good money gets thrown behind bad money, especially if the idea is a brainchild of a senior executive.

The third major concern with the stage-gate logic is that it necessitates a business case well ahead of even a rudimentary investment and market validation. Think of it, if the opportunity is so new and the problem so ill-defined, how valid would your numbers be? It is all GIGO (garbage in, garbage out), and yet corporates swear by such dense, often rigorously evaluated, presentations. What if an idea does not clear the funding threshold of the company on the day of the presentation? It has got no chance.

This brings us to the fourth concern with the model, and it is to do with the gates. These are go/no-go gates where an idea *must* qualify on certain pre-defined parameters before it gets further funding. What if a promising idea does not make the cut due to limited information available with the product team or the evaluation committee? It is lost forever. And then the idea that seems okay on all parameters keeps getting funded before it turns out to be a Segway. The gates deprive more ideas of a chance, let alone doing any good to the promising ones. The truly radical ideas get heavily discounted in such straight-jacketed models.

Lastly, as you can make out, the process is linear. Once an idea is out, it is out forever. There are hardly any means of iteration, course-correction, skipping a stage, recursion to a previous one, accelerating through some and pausing at others. The model works for efficiency and not effectiveness. Statistically speaking, the process tries to contain *type-A error* (failed innovations) at the cost of *type-B error* (missed innovations).[4] As you, a practising manager or an aspiring entrepreneur, would know, type-B errors are costlier and yet difficult to ascertain.

A type-B error is when you miss out on a great opportunity and your competition laps it up, and, in the process, seals your fate in that market. As a case in point, Bill Gates calls missing out on Android as his career's biggest mistake. That is your type-B error. Ironically, it turns out that the only way to contain the type-B error is to allow for more type-A errors, which is to say, 'Fail faster to succeed sooner.'

Stefan Thomke, from the Harvard Business School, and Donald Reinertsen, of Reinertsen & Associates, identify six key fallacies with the traditional approaches of product management.[5] They tell us that a 'waterfall model' or stage-gate approach of innovation has the following mistaken assumptions: 1) High utilization of resources will improve performance; 2) Processing work in large batches improves the economics of the development process; 3) Our development plan is great, we just need to stick to it; 4) The sooner the project is started, the sooner it will be finished; 5) The more features we put into a product, the more customers will like it; and 6) We will be more successful if we get it right the first time.

An efficiency-maximizing mindset is suitable only for continuous improvement or production but is highly counterproductive when it comes to innovation. Hailing an experimental mindset as the most essential attribute for complex problem-solving or new product development, Thomke and Reinertsen note: 'Experimenting with many diverse ideas is crucial to innovation projects . . . The faster the experimentation cycle, the more feedback can be gathered and incorporated into new rounds of experiments with novel and potentially risky ideas.'[6]

We need a model that is flexible, closer to the users, open to feedback on an ongoing basis, lowers type-B errors, contains the cost of type-A errors, does not swear by the business plans, and is fast. Design thinking can just be the approach.

The model of design thinking

Design thinking is a systematic, human-centric approach of problem-solving. With its origins in industrial design, product design and architecture, design has, for long, been very narrowly associated with the tangibles. 'Because design has historically been equated with aesthetics and craft, designers have been celebrated as artistic savants,' says Jon Kolko, the founder of Austin Center for Design.[7] That limited view is fast giving way to a broader application of the tenets of design to a wider set of problems and contexts. The evolution of design to design thinking is the graduation from thinking about the product or service to thinking about the relation between the product and the humans, and the relation between humans. According to Kolko, a design-centric culture transcends design as a role, imparting a set of principles and practices to anyone keen to bring ideas to life.

In design thinking, the emphasis is on thinking and doing, and not just on designing. The outcome may be a product, or a process, or a service, but more significantly, an experience. Experiences, not just at the level of the company-customer interface but for the entire business ecosystem. The element of design in design thinking draws inspiration from Confucius's famous quip, 'I hear and I forget. I see and I remember. I do and I understand.' It is as much about doing as about thinking, if not more so.

Tom Kelley, the long-time general manager of the Silicon Valley-based product design firm IDEO and younger brother of IDEO founder David Kelley, defines design thinking as, '[An approach that] involves applying the creative tools and mindset that designers have used for decades to new challenges going well beyond what has traditionally been thought of as design.'[8]

He further identifies the prime ingredients of design thinking as *empathy*, *experimentation* and *storytelling*. IDEO founder, David Kelley, who also established the Stanford d.school, offers: 'Design thinking relies on the natural – and coachable – human abilities to be intuitive, to recognize patterns, and to construct ideas that are emotionally meaningful as well as functional.'[9]

Tim Brown of IDEO provides a more elaborate definition of design thinking: 'A human-centered approach to innovation that draws from the designer's toolkit to integrate the needs of the people, the possibilities of technology, and requirements for business success.'[10] The simultaneous pursuit of human desirability, technical feasibility and business viability keeps the efforts of problem-solving earnest. In an insightful TED Talk, Brown traces the evolution of design as a profession and argues why it is imperative that the principles of product design be broad-based to solve more complex social and business problems.[11]

IDEO has contributed significantly in popularizing the construct of design thinking. Founded in 1978, IDEO has truly grown beyond a design company to an innovation and creativity consultancy. A brief history of IDEO is presented by Tom Kelley in his book, *The Art of Innovation*.[12] The company has evangelized the notion of 'design with a small "d"', nudging people to think beyond designing objects with aesthetics and functionality to an approach of holistic problem-solving.

However, the event that popularized IDEO and its contemporary approach to (product) design was a programme that aired in 1999 on ABC News' *Nightline*. Titled 'The Deep Dive into IDEO', the documentary offered a peek into IDEO's design philosophy and into the methods adopted by an eclectic team as they redesign a shopping cart in just five days. The video, which is available on YouTube, is a good starting point to appreciate a systematic approach of problem-solving and the environment that enables such an endeavour. It is informative at multiple levels: the process of design thinking, the right mix of people, the ideal workplace design, empathy, humour and creativity at play, and the role of a leader.

Along with specific tools, techniques and principles, design thinking could be viewed as a method that introduces discipline into the otherwise chaotic process of creativity. The two most popular models of design thinking are from IDEO and the Stanford d.school.

Shown below is the six-stage design thinking process as practised and preached by IDEO.[13]

1. Frame a question: Identify an anchor question that motivates the team.
2. Gather inspiration: Get to the field to generate fresh insights.
3. Generate ideas: Go for a high number of ingenious ideas.
4. Make ideas tangible: Build crude prototypes to see your ideas in action.
5. Test to learn: Put your prototypes to test with a real audience.
6. Share the story: Inspire others through emotional narratives.

The process might look linear, but as David Kelley likes to say, 'Design thinking is not a linear path. It's a big mass of looping back to different places in the process.'[14] It is a system of overlapping spaces and not a neat sequence of orderly steps. Tim Brown identifies these overlapping spaces as *inspiration, ideation* and *implementation*. In the inspiration space, insights are gathered from all possible sources; the ideation space aims at translating insights into ideas; and, finally, the implementation space is where the best ideas are scaled to create the ultimate impact, in the form of products, services or customer experiences.

The Stanford d.school, founded by David Kelley in 2005, adopts a similar approach. The process clearly marks out *empathize* as a significant and primal phase of the design thinking journey. Shown next is the five-stage design thinking process, as adopted by the Stanford d.school.[15]

1. Empathize: Learn about and from your audience about their real concerns.
2. Define: Sharpen your focus on the most important problems to be solved.
3. Ideate: Generate a high volume of ideas around your problem.
4. Prototype: Convert your ideas into quick and dirty mock-ups.
5. Test: Subject your prototypes to real-world validation.

In the two models of design thinking as discussed above, the problem-solving journey starts with the users (through empathy) and culminates with the users (through validation). At its very core, the design thinking process is a series of divergent and convergent steps. So, instead of thinking linearly from a problem to a solution, the notion is to first generate choices and then make choices. The difficult part is to think divergently, and design thinking necessitates that you go broad before you go narrow.

The models from IDEO and Stanford d.school have been widely adopted and adapted. However, for design thinking to effectively address real-world problems, we still need to add two more stages to the process: inspire and scale. Inspire addresses the question of 'Why design thinking?'; and scale aims at ensuring that the 'impact is realized to the idea's truest potential'. Hence, by supplementing the stages of inspire and scale to the models of IDEO and Stanford, design thinking becomes a more comprehensive process.

The five-stage model, presented in Figure 2, elucidates the design thinking, or creative problem solving, process that forms the basis of this book.

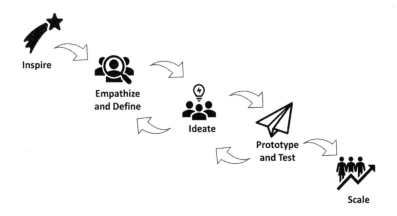

Figure 2: A design-thinking or creative problem-solving model

Following is an overview of each of the five stages, which are later detailed in separate chapters of the book.

Inspire

What often remains unclear is, 'Why innovate?' And even if one has to innovate, 'Why bother about being systematic?' A problem can be solved without going through the rigours of design thinking, or through any other systematic technique of creativity. Then why design thinking?

The inspire stage is critical in establishing a purpose of the problem-solving exercise and a rationale for embracing a systematic approach such as design thinking. If the leader, or the project sponsor, falls short in setting the right purpose, what follows is highly inconsequential. The purpose of purpose can never be overemphasized.

Empathize and define

The cornerstone of design thinking is empathy, and as you would get to know along the course of this book, this demand for empathy can make the very difference between a failed start and an early success. Empathy does not come effortlessly, especially in a context where a problem needs to be solved fast and the access to customers is limited. However, empathy can be engineered, and there are specific toolsets and skill sets available to stimulate an empathetic mindset.

The flipside of empathy is the tendency of getting lost in a myriad of problems and concerns about customers, or fellow humans, and that is why sharpening the focus is valuable. Design thinking mandates you to pick the most acute of the problems to be addressed, keeping in mind that not every problem is worth solving and not every problem can be solved.

Ideate

Right in the middle of the journey is ideation, where the pendulum swings from convergence to divergence, in favour of quantity over quality of ideas. Quantity over quality might be the most counter-intuitive principle in ideation, and yet scores of managers want that one breakthrough idea that can revolutionize everything. The emphasis in the phase is to be systematic and adopt a set of time-honed methods of generating ideas without bringing one's biases into play. The ideas are only as good and useful as the ingenuity of the insights and the sharpness with which the problem is defined.

Prototype and test

Once there are enough candidate ideas, it is time to pick the most promising ones and to scale some of those. Here again, design thinking brings discipline to the entire approach. Other than encouraging us to focus on empathy, a major contribution of design thinking is the extensive value it lends to prototyping and testing the concepts rigorously.

Because prototyping and testing happen iteratively and often even simultaneously, as you build to learn and validate, the two stages are clubbed into one. Though the IDEO and Stanford d.school models treat prototyping and testing as separate stages, the boundaries between prototyping and testing are more blurred as compared to the boundaries between other stages, such as ideation and prototyping. Hence, the two stages are discussed together.

Scale

Finally, all meaningful ideas must scale to the real-world context. It is only through scale that impact is created. At this stage creativity translates into the realm of innovation and creates a lasting impact. The element of scale was embedded in both the Stanford d.school and IDEO models. Bringing it to the fore highlights the significance of this stage. Even if a prototype works and the customers love it, only through scale an idea's impact is realized.

On the importance of scale in solving real-word problems, Peter Thiel, the co-founder of Paypal, notes, 'If you could scale incredibly fast, on the one hand you have to race really hard to scale fast, but the benefit is that you're achieving escape velocity from the black hole that is hyper competition.'[16] It is the scale that offers the ultimate validity to your idea, whether it is in the start-up milieu or that of an enterprise.

For each of the aforementioned five stages, the relevant mindsets, toolsets and skill sets can be identified and can guide us as to how design thinking could be brought into action to solve specific real-world problems. Think in terms of the toolsets, skill sets and mindsets as the *what, how* and *why* of design thinking, as depicted in Figure 3.

Figure 3: Toolsets, skill sets and mindsets of learning and practising design thinking

The toolsets elucidate the tangible models and frameworks to structure an interview, or generate ideas, or create a quick and dirty prototype, and the relevant skills are those of interviewing, ideation and validation, respectively. The mindset comprises the temperaments and quintessential behaviours required to effectively practise a skill or master a tool. For instance, deferring judgement and building on the ideas of others are vital mindset-level changes required for creative problem-solving. In fact, building on the ideas of others is the most salient way by which the quantity and quality of ideas can be driven up, and this warrants both good listening skills and empathy.

Further, there are a host of tools, frameworks and methods to learn and practise design thinking available at IDEO U[17] and at Stanford d.school[18]. The intent of this book is not to replicate such dense methods, or to add to those, but rather to weave the methods and practices around a conducive mindset, so that almost anybody could start solving problems more methodically and creatively.

Design thinking is not old wine in a new bottle

An important question remains: 'Is design thinking new, or is it just a rehash of some old concepts of problem-solving?' There are some elements that the approach of design thinking borrows from the extant practices of problem-solving. And then there are a few specific features, such as empathy, prototyping and the iterative nature of problem-solving that design thinking brings to prominence.

To answer the question of what is new in design thinking, let us look at a two-by-two matrix, as shown in Figure 4.

On one axis you have the problem, the extent to which it is known or unknown; and the other axis is the solution, which could be known or unknown. We do not typically understand the problem as much as we think we do, for what we usually get to see are the symptoms of the underlying problems, and getting to the root cause is significant. Similarly, whether the solution is known or unknown is determined by the degree of novelty and utility of the idea, and not by its presence or absence.

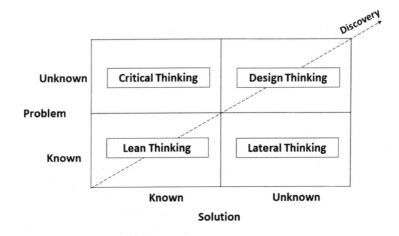

Figure 4: Design thinking vis-à-vis other models of problem-solving

This leads us to the four quadrants: from known problem and known solution, to unknown problem and unknown solution. As we move from the known-known to the unknown-unknown, the degree of ambiguity increases, and hence the diagonal denotes discovery. The intent of this representation is to identify the techniques from the stable of creative problem-solving which are most suitable to each context, and to highlight the uniqueness of design thinking.

Lean thinking

The starting point is the domain of reasonably well-articulated problems and a set of well-known solutions. This is largely the realm of lean thinking, which is about doing tasks cheaper, faster, better and with minimal waste or rework. Since the problem and solutions are relatively well known, the emphasis here is on efficiency and reducing variability of the outcome. Techniques such as Six Sigma, Kaizen, Lean, Agile, Scrum, root cause analysis, five-whys analysis and other variants of the lean philosophy, notwithstanding their subtle differences, generally deal with lower levels of ambiguity. Most problems around product manufacturing (and not design) would fall under lean thinking. For instance, Six Sigma is a time-tested method for improving a product or process performance but not so much when it comes to new product development, because in the latter case there is a clear need for introducing variance, which is something lean thinking is at odds with.

For instance, if you look at the parking issue in a city like Bangalore, the problem will fall under the lean thinking quadrant. The root causes are reasonably known: too many cars, too few parking spaces, lack of information on parking availability and low discipline. As for the solutions, these have also been well-adopted (elsewhere), such as multilevel parking, taxes on driving during peak hours, odd-even policy and the like. It would be relatively easy to solve the problem with well-tested solutions.

Critical thinking

As we move from well-known and well-articulated problems to the realm of complex, ambiguous problems, we get into the domain of critical thinking. Largely understood as a way of analysing facts to form a judgement, critical thinking aims at getting to the root cause of a situation and then solving the constraints. The Japanese and the Germans are particularly good at critical thinking, as exhibited by their above-par engineering performance. The Japanese term *genchi genbutsu*, which literally means 'go and see for yourself', exemplifies their comfort with and penchant for going to the root of the problem before attacking it. Not just that, Japanese companies also insist that identifying problems and solving those is the responsibility of *every* employee.

One of the powerful techniques of critical thinking is the 'Theory of Constraints', which was pioneered by the management guru Eliyahu Goldratt as a systematic approach to identifying and eliminating constraints in a system. The notion is that once a constraint (read problem) is identified, the process of constraint elimination (read solution) is straightforward. The premium is on discovering the problem or the root cause, and the solution is to be found in a relatively well-documented set of methods.

Another powerful technique in this quadrant is TRIZ, a Russian acronym for 'Theory of Inventive Problem-Solving'. TRIZ frames a problem in the form of a (physical) constraint and offers a host of solutions to resolve the contradiction. Here, the effort is in discovering and framing the problem, and the solutions are relatively known. Problems around process improvement, product improvement and even system betterment could be addressed using this approach.

Picking from the previous case of car parking issues in Bangalore, the core concern on addressing the issue of 'discipline' can be a domain of critical thinking. Why is discipline missing at large? A thorough investigation and some introspection can lead us to the causes, such as improper law enforcement, lack of role models, inadequate monitoring and corruption.

Lateral thinking

The next in line is a zone where the problem is reasonably clear but the solutions are not, and that is the domain of lateral thinking. A term coined by Edward de Bono, lateral thinking has come to stand for all those techniques that suspend logic momentarily to get to an inspiration that could solve a problem in ingenious ways. To de Bono, creativity involves breaking out of established patterns of thinking in order to look at things in a different way.

Apart from the host of methods ranging from lateral thinking to 'Six Thinking Hats', some useful techniques that help solve well-defined problems include mind mapping; SCAMPER technique; inventive triggers; methods from the book *Blue Ocean Strategy*, such as 'Buyer Utility Map', 'Three Tiers of Noncustomers' and 'Six Path Framework'.[19] These methods are particularly useful in addressing problems that call for non-linear ways of thinking.

Going on to the problem of traffic in Bangalore, one of the concerns around safety is that bikers are not willing to wear helmets. Any improvement in the safety of bikers straightaway leads to savings for the exchequer. Why do bikers and pillion passengers prefer not to wear helmets? A critical thinking-based view would lead us to explanations ranging from the concrete—like the inconvenience of carrying the helmet, the discomfort of wearing it, storage issues—to the hedonic—such as the style and fun of riding a bike.

Lateral thinking can be a useful approach in addressing this issue. As a case in point, a few petrol pumps in Bangalore have put a condition that you get to buy petrol only if you come wearing a helmet. The 'no helmet, no petrol' experiment in Bangalore did help nudge the commuters to some extent.[20] In fact, lateral thinking can be the most effective way of solving low-hanging problems.

Design thinking

Finally, we come to the realm of design thinking, where both the problem and the solution are relatively less understood. The approach of design thinking assumes that the first set of problems that meet the eye are no more than symptoms, and that it is critical to delve deeper into people's mindsets and contexts to get a better understanding of the real issues. The element of discovery, led by empathy, is the cornerstone of design thinking, and once the problem is well-understood, ideas flow systematically. Design thinking is best suited for problems characterized by high levels of ambiguity, which by their nature would involve human emotions and context fluidity.

A growing concern, worthy of being addressed by design thinking, is women's safety on roads. No Indian city is immune to this problem. The fact that women feel and are unsafe on the roads is a cause for great concern and embarrassment for all of us. It can have far-reaching consequences for our country, socially, economically and morally. For this problem, both the root causes and a clear set of solutions are not available. The core causes can range all the way from improper street lighting to a lack of gender sensitization. It is difficult to nail down specific reasons, as they mostly work in concert and in unpredictable ways. As for solutions, we have tried technology, vigilance, social policing, awareness campaigns, self-defence training, harsh punishments and the like, but to little avail. Since design thinking engages with human emotions and motivations, it could be the most suitable approach towards addressing this issue. There won't be one silver bullet addressing the challenge. A multiplicity of ideas must be generated, prototyped, tested and then scaled for an effective redressal.

In summary, the two most salient contributions of design thinking to the discourse of creative problem-solving are, firstly, bringing to prominence the role of empathy and human-centricity; and secondly, highlighting the value of prototyping and user-testing in an iterative manner. At a broader level, design thinking could be equated to systems thinking, which subsumes each of the other three modes of thinking, as laid out in Figure 4. The stages of 'empathy' and 'define' could be folded into critical thinking; that of 'ideation' builds on a lot of methods from lateral thinking; and the 'prototype' and 'test' stages can be rolled into lean thinking. This bucketing might be a slight leap of faith but would hopefully help drive home the point that design thinking is indeed not old wine in a new bottle.

Design thinking is to innovation what Six Sigma is to quality

Imagine you are in the 1950s and 1960s, and someone proposes to you that quality can be institutionalized. What would be your reaction? You might laugh it off. Back then, people weren't too conscious of product quality, services or experiences. If quality was at all a parameter of consideration, it was mostly limited to select individuals and management styles. Making quality embedded in the processes and institutions was unthinkable. But not so much in Japan. Japanese automakers and consumer electronics companies taught the world, much to the dismay of their Western competitors, that quality can indeed be engineered right into the processes and systems, and that it is a matter of discipline.

Thanks to companies like Toyota, Sony, AlliedSignal, Motorola and General Electric, terms like Six Sigma have got into our vocabulary, and our overall understanding of quality, beyond products, has improved. Most sincere companies have quality departments. They boast of having employees trained as 'Black Belts' and 'Green Belts' in Six Sigma, follow TQM (Total Quality Management) and TPM (Total Productive Maintenance) techniques on a regular basis and even audit the quality of their policies and processes. However, Six Sigma is not a particularly effective tool for innovation. 'Methodologies like Six Sigma are all about reducing risk, but they are not effective for innovation because innovation by definition is risky,' says Mauro Porcini, PepsiCo's chief design officer. [21]

Quality has moved from being an art to a science. But sadly, innovation remains limited to the realm of art, if not magic. We need to regularly invoke the spirits of Thomas Edison, Steve Jobs, Nikola Tesla and refer to the deeds of Elon Musk, Jack Ma and Jeff Bezos to stir people into thinking about innovation and creativity. We still seek inspiration somewhere to churn out creativity but often do not realize that we all are creative and that we just need to *unleash* our creativity. In the words of Sir Ken Robinson, 'Creativity is as important as literacy.'[22] Except that creativity has not been treated with the sincerity and respect it merits.

The state of innovation today is akin to that of quality in the 1960s. Innovation ought to move from the preserve of the select few, the artists or the geniuses, to a larger audience, and for that to happen design has to move away from the design community to almost everybody. Design thinking could well be the catalyst of this mass-scale diffusion of the systematic practices of creative problem-solving. The approach is intuitive, systematic; it has a lot of methods in case you get bored of one; it helps you bring your whole body to work; and, above all, it is fun. As Jon Kolko likes to put it, 'Design thinking is an essential tool for simplifying and humanizing.'[23]

Jeanne Liedtka from the University of Virginia's Darden School of Business claims that design thinking has the potential to do for innovation exactly what TQM did for manufacturing. Her seven-year study of fifty projects across sectors, including business, healthcare, and social services, reveal that adopting design thinking has benefits in terms of unleashing people's full creative energies, winning their commitment and radically improving processes. Liedtka further notes, 'The structure of design thinking creates a natural flow from research to rollout . . . Along the way, design-thinking processes counteract human biases that thwart creativity while addressing the challenges typically faced in reaching superior solutions, lowered costs and risks, and employee buy-in.'[24]

The move towards design thinking is certainly not at the cost of quality, or of the disciplined pursuit of perfection. But as IDEO's Tim Brown puts it, 'The trick is to do this without sucking the life out of the creative process – to balance management's legitimate requirement for stability, efficiency, and predictability with the design thinker's need for spontaneity, serendipity, and experimentation.'[25] For solving problems elegantly, we need to embrace design thinking as a yin-yang of chaos and order, divergent and convergent thinking, structure and fluidity, because if left on their own, most organizations would like to reduce variance and increase predictability instead of getting comfortable with greater variance and ambiguity. Design thinking is a humble nudge urging you to be comfortable with ambiguity and yet being in control of the proceedings, as you now have a well-defined pathway, a set of tools that have been shown to work and a guiding philosophy which is highly suited to being practised across a wider canvas of creative problem-solving.

Can design thinking help large, established organizations to innovate better? Yes. The Defense Advanced Research Projects Agency (DARPA) in the United States of America is a case in point. Established in 1958 with the mission 'to prevent and create strategic surprise', DARPA has been instrumental in giving the world some of the most useful technologies in recent decades. DARPA created the computer mouse, RISC computing, GPS, micro-electro-mechanical systems, Siri, drones, Roomba robot, autonomous cars and the Internet. DARPA is nothing like how you would expect a government-funded research agency to function. There are no permanent teams, projects have minimal staff and they have no labs. They operate on a shoestring budget, and often their project leaders are in their mid-30s. What DARPA follows is a very lean, agile, design thinking-led model of conducting practical research.

Regina Dugan and Kaigham Gabriel, former DARPA officials, identify some of the defining features of DARPA and why the institution has remained meaningful for over sixty years.[26] At any given time, DARPA would have close to 200 programs under an estimated budget of $3 billion, with contributions coming in from 100 performers from various partner organizations and about 120 staff members, in functions like finance, contracting, HR, security and legal. Dugan and Gabriel point out three salient characteristics of DARPA projects: *ambitious goals*, *temporary project teams* and *independence*. The ambitious goals, which are of strategic importance, create focus and inspire genius. Temporary project teams attract the best and brightest talent from across institutions and nations and keep the endeavour focused and energized. Finally, independence in terms of selecting and running project teams allows for bold and timely decisions, which might often be unpopular.

Dugan and Gabriel note that most projects at DARPA fall under the Pasteur's Quadrant—a framework developed by the scientist Donald Stokes to classify research on the basis of 'quest for fundamental understanding' and 'consideration of use'. The kind of research that falls under the Pasteur's Quadrant, named after the French chemist and microbiologist Louis Pasteur, aims at both expanding basic science and solving society's problems, such as developing navigational aids or autonomous vehicles.[27] Drawing parallels with design thinking, the researchers note, 'Projects in Pasteur's Quadrant require different techniques. They involve fast iterations. Planning should be light and nimble. Progress can be assessed by tracking iterations to see if they are converging on goals, revealing dead ends, uncovering new applications, or identifying the need for unforeseen scientific advances.'[28] If DARPA can benefit from a user-centric, iterative approach to problem-solving and innovation, there would hardly be a setting where design thinking will not be useful.

The sweet spot of design thinking

From the above discussion it might seem that design thinking is the holy grail of creative problem-solving. But that is not true. As the philosopher Karl Popper reminded us, 'In so far as a scientific statement speaks about reality, it must be falsifiable . . .' We must identify the boundary conditions of design thinking to make the approach valuable. It would be useful to mark out the contexts where design thinking serves its best and where it might lose its effectiveness.

Design thinking, at its core, involves humans: their desires, emotions, pains, aspirations, behaviours, kinesthetics and other dimensions of being, and a problem that does not involve such elements is best not approached with design thinking. By this argument, there could possibly be three contexts in which design thinking might not be very effective: fundamental research, disruptive innovation and pure improvisation.

As far as fundamental research goes, there are no customers to begin with, and typically the endeavour is technology push, and not market pull. In the words of Wernher von Braun, 'Basic research is what I am doing when I don't know what I am doing.' Because design thinking starts with empathy, there is no avenue to gain insights on what works and what does not, and you are at best looking at probabilities. Design thinking comes in when some of the more fundamental questions have already been answered. It would be hard to see scientists and engineers working at CERN adopting design thinking for solving their problems, or even those contemplating the thorny issues around quantum computing. Many of these efforts are far removed from where design thinking would start adding value.

The second avenue where design thinking may not be handy is in disruptive innovation, which, by definition, destroys the incumbent practices and preferences. Harvard Business School's Clayton Christensen cautions companies against listening to their customer too intently because the existing customers do not want disruptions; they are rather happy with incremental improvements. Many of the insights gathered through customer interactions, observations, empathy maps or other techniques of problem discovery might be misleading for a company attempting to disrupt the current market. Not listening to the *happy* customers typically goes against the grain of design thinking, and hence, the approach might not be a suitable starting point for those attempting truly disruptive innovations. Once the innovation is introduced, the customer would be happy to propose incremental improvements, as the associated risk of adoption is lowered.

Improvisation or jugaad, which denotes frugality, in both approach and outcome, does adopt a part of design thinking, namely prototyping and testing, and not so much empathy and systematic ideation. Those who improvise and create *good enough* solutions to their (own) problems do not bother to adopt the design thinking methods, let alone being disciplined. They think, tinker, test, fail, iterate and then produce, though without often achieving the desired scale. They might have intuitively followed design thinking, but to call this approach of improvisation design thinking would clearly be a stretch.

It would suffice as of now to reiterate that we must respect the boundaries of design thinking, so that we can pick the projects worth the discipline that design thinking demands. As a reminder, design thinking is apt when engaging with a complex, multifaceted problem involving human emotions, and such humans need not be customers alone. One also needs to have sufficient time to get through the motions of divergent and convergent thinking. For other contexts, parts of design thinking, such as ideation or prototyping and testing, might be useful on a standalone basis.

2

Why Design Thinking Now?

'The balance of power is shifting toward consumers and away from companies. The right way to respond to this if you are a company is to put the vast majority of your energy, attention and dollars into building a great product or service and put a smaller amount into shouting about it, marketing it.'

—Jeff Bezos[1]

How is it that you remember your last vacation in detail but not so much about your breakfast last weekend? Our mind tends to store experiences which are unique and even short-lived more acutely than those which are routine and longer in duration. As a result, it is hard to forget a near-death experience or the experience of falling in love for the first time. As the Nobel laureate Daniel Kahneman explains: 'We actually don't choose between experiences, we choose between *memories* of experiences. And even when we think about the future, we don't think of our future normally as experiences. We think of our future as *anticipated memories* [italics mine].'[2]

If our bodies react to new experiences differently and our minds treat such episodes with a lot more care, should it not be wise, then, to design such experiences with far greater intent? It does not suffice for companies to offer better experiences through their products or services; individuals themselves should be more mindful of the experiences they accumulate and transfer over a lifetime. The designing of experiences is no longer limited to those with more knowledge, power or access. It's everyone's responsibility.

To add to this, the tools of creation are rapidly getting diffused, owing much to the democratization of knowledge, ideas, capital and talent. No longer can it be said that the next big breakthrough would come from a well-endowed organization or from a person with a high IQ. Increasingly, brilliant ideas are hiding right around the corner, waiting for a connection to happen, and as much as fortune favours the prepared mind, creativity favours the connected mind. Further, the boundaries between B2B (business to business) and B2C (business to consumer) are fast getting blurred and so are the artificially created chasms between buyers and sellers. The customers, employees and investors have more choices than ever before, and the cost of experimentation has come down radically, thanks to pervasive and affordable means of computation and communication.

A 2005 survey of the world's most innovative companies by the Boston Consulting Group (BCG) mentioned these as the top ten names: Apple, 3M, General Electric, Microsoft, Sony, Dell, IBM, Google, Nokia and P&G.[3] In the 2019 BCG survey, the top ten companies were: Alphabet/Google, Amazon, Apple, Microsoft, Samsung, Netflix, IBM, Facebook, Tesla and Adidas.[4] Only four names from 2005 remained in the top ten—Apple, Microsoft, IBM and Google—while Nokia, General Electric and Sony were not even in the longlist! That is the relentless pace of change and disruption. The upstarts have triumphed over the incumbents in their own game, and so we have Tesla ahead of BMW and Daimler, and Vale ahead of the venerable Rio Tinto.

Not surprisingly, almost 50 per cent of companies in the S&P 500 would be replaced in the next ten years. It means, almost 250 new companies on the chart and a bigger number out. If the esteemed General Electric can be dropped from the S&P after over a century of its listing, do you think your company can survive change? The Indian IT services industry is already facing the heat of artificial intelligence and unrelenting customers, even though this sector is, by far, one of the largest employers in India and a huge source of foreign exchange. The value propositions of being cheaper, faster or better no longer excite customers. The customers, for the most part, are not fully aware of the extent of their own problems and the opportunities lying ahead, and so they are looking for someone who can help them discover and define the problems before these could be solved, a skill that does not come organically.

This harsh realization is what Microsoft CEO Satya Nadella captures when he observes, 'Our industry does not respect tradition – it only respects innovation.'[5] The statement is as applicable to low-tech industries anywhere as to the high-tech industries in the West.

Here are a few key reasons why design thinking deserves to be adopted more seriously and pervasively.

Products and services have blurred into experiences

Whether you are buying a product or hiring a service, at the end of the day you are consuming an *experience*, and in this experience economy, a lot more of your senses are involved. The traditional products have become more like services, and services have become experiences. In today's marketplace, customers are shifting from passive consumption to active participation. Memorable experiences are not scripted by leaders or marketing departments but are delivered at the *moment of truth* by the customer-facing executives. And such experiences must be crafted and delivered with the same precision as the products. We are all seeking authentic experiences and even the most mundane task can be made into a cherishable experience. Such authentic experiences often take shape by allowing for spontaneity, and, paradoxically, this spontaneity must be designed beforehand, and technology is only a small part of that desirable experience.

Do you wonder why people spend such huge amounts to attend TED Talks, when all of these are available for free on the Internet? Because people want to 'experience' being in the company of thinkers and doers, and get inspired. That is the same reason that thousands of Indians queue up every summer to watch Indian Premier League matches in their cities. Many of them travel across cities, stand in lines for well over four hours, often in scorching heat, when they could have watched their favourite players from the comfort of their living rooms. They seek genuine experiences, and they are ready to pay anything, risk anything to seek that involvement.

People, rich and poor, are going beyond amassing stuff to seeking experiences, and that is visible among a wide cross section in India and in several other emerging economies. Abhijit Banerjee, co-recipient of the 2019 Nobel Prize in economics, notes, 'Generally, it is clear that things that make life less boring are a priority for the poor.'[6] He offers a counter-intuitive explanation of why the poor spend more on festivities, marriages and other social functions, even if they are often deprived of material goods, such as televisions, bicycles or radios. Another explanation is to do with social equity and collateral, but equally, there is the desire to seek an experience and make life *less boring*.

Is it possible to infuse experience through design in the most commoditized and undifferentiated products? Yes, and the Indian watch brand Titan has made an empire doing so.

In December 1987, when Titan opened its first retail outlet at Bangalore's Safina Plaza, watches were perceived as functional products, dominated by HMT Watches and Allwyn Watches and a few international brands whose watches were smuggled into the country. It was Titan that made us think about watches as pieces of adornment and even collectables. (The same was done later for jewellery, accessories, perfumes and, more recently, sarees.) Since its formative days, Titan has paid special attention to how its watches are displayed and to the overall buying experience. Notwithstanding the award-winning designs of its watches, the company's focus has largely been on designing the buying and gifting experiences. Not just these, Titan has also invested in the product repair experience, setting up repair centres within showrooms to win customers' trust.

On how Titan went about improving customer experience, Bhaskar Bhat, the company's former MD, notes, 'Formalising an informal sector and transforming it for the benefit of the consumer is what we have done best. We are sort of bringing order from disorder. We create elevating experiences for the customers.'[7] As Titan demonstrates, designing experiences could be an enduring competitive advantage.

Problems are becoming multifaceted

With the levelling of the playing field and a desire for standing out, companies are realizing that their problems are increasingly becoming multi-dimensional, and so should the thinking of the problem-solvers. The products, services and experiences have become part of a complex system where there is a simultaneous pursuit of differentiation at the front end and standardization at the back end. It is out of tune to think of any problem as being purely a constraint of science or technology, which was, incidentally, the fundamental premise of the Russian problem-solving technique TRIZ. Every problem would have an element of usability, and not just functionality or aesthetics. Much along the lines of what Steve Jobs professed: 'Design is not just what it looks like and feels like. Design is how it works.'[8] When you focus on how humans interact with a solution, be it a product or a service, design thinking takes prominence. While design was mostly about solving specific problems, design thinking elevates the discussion to the systems level where one needs to understand how different problems interact with each other to shape experiences.

'Sometimes the problem being tackled is itself multi-faceted', says Jon Kolko.[9] He continues, 'Think about how much tougher it is to reinvent a health care delivery system than to design a shoe. And sometimes the business environment is so volatile that a company must experiment with multiple paths in order to survive . . . Specifically, people need their interactions with technologies and other complex systems to be simple, intuitive, and pleasurable.'

Take for example the two-wheelers market in India. For a long time, the dominant parameter of interest and, hence, competitive differentiation, was mileage. The likes of Hero Honda, Bajaj and TVS Motor Company, were in an arms race to offer better mileage and styling for their bikes. And then, in 2001, came the Honda Activa, a two-wheeler that threw the caution of mileage to the wind and offered an entirely new parameter of interest: convenience.

The increasing urbanization, greater participation of women in the workforce and growing congestion in cities made a perfect case for gearless scooters, and Honda, with its continued focus on quality and technology, made the most of that trend. The gearless scooter has an appeal for both the young and the old, the male and the female, and makes for a good family vehicle. Its large floorboard, broad seats, under-seat storage and sturdy grab rail makes it a convenient and safe vehicle for city commute. By October 2019, over 22 million Honda Activa two-wheelers were sold in India. Over the years, Honda Activa has beaten Hero Splendor, which was among the world's top-selling bikes, and has secured an enviable 14 per cent share in the Indian two-wheelers market.[10]

What do you think worked in favour of Honda and to the dismay of traditional bike manufacturers? The incumbents defined the problem too narrowly, as technical in nature, while Honda Activa managed to disrupt the very framing. That necessitates a redesign of thinking (and not the product), which rival bike-makers learnt the hard way.

All companies are fast becoming B2C

A critical trend is the morphing of B2B industries into B2C. There is a growing realization that all industries, regardless of their traditional affiliations, must think in terms of the end-consumers and end-users of their products and services. Along these lines, Harvard Business School's Clayton Christensen proposes that customers *hire* products and services to get a job done. He says, 'When we buy a product, we essentially "hire" it to help us do a job. If it does the job well, the next time we're confronted with the same job, we tend to hire that product again. And if it does a crummy job, we "fire" it and look for an alternative.'[11] He does not distinguish between a B2B company and a B2C company, and maintains that the 'job to be done' must be everybody's prerogative. This kind of an approach calls for adopting a vocabulary laden with emotions, and not just logic. Here, emotionally charged language is not considered thin, silly or biased.

Intel learnt this fact long back and launched its famous 'Intel Inside' campaign, bringing its core technology products to the consciousness of its consumers and, in turn, creating an enviable brand. The customers do not see the product, but it is the *experience* of using an Intel microprocessor that the company wants to impress upon their minds and continues to draw a premium from. Even the most science-driven industries, such as pharmaceuticals, are increasingly focusing on their end-consumers and the milieu in which their lives can get better. One such example is Dr. Reddy's.

The Hyderabad-based pharma major, Dr. Reddy's has its own innovation and design thinking centre, called Studio 5B. Located in Mumbai, the studio has an inspiring purpose: 'To use design thinking to inspire and create solutions that make a difference to the health and everyday lives of people.'[12] It has an eclectic set of employees, with educational and work background. They are a mix of UI (user-interface) and UX (user-experience) designers, copyright specialists, consumer researchers, product designers and architects among others. Going well beyond the medicines that Dr. Reddy's discovers and manufactures, the lab prides itself in deeply engaging with the patients and their contexts, including family members, medical-care providers and the healthcare community at large.

Adopting a design thinking-led approach, Dr. Reddy's launched a new corporate identity in 2015. Their new heart-shaped logo is an expression of empathy and dynamism, which helps keep patients at the centre of everything that Dr. Reddy's does. The heart symbolizes empathy and care, while the circles that make up one-half of the heart connote dynamism and responsiveness. As Dr. Reddy's managing director,

G.V. Prasad, says, 'The belief "Good Health Can't Wait" lends new meaning to our core purpose of accelerating access to affordable and innovative medicines.'[13]

In my recent visit to the Biocon headquarters, I noticed the same movement from product-centricity to patient-centricity, and not just in corporate slogans or artefacts at the offices but also in some of their people practices. In one of Biocon's offices, I saw a huge poster mapping out the entire patient journey, and Biocon employees would put their names against the stages where they contribute to the patient experience. By toggling the view from the journey of a medicine to the journey of a patient and involving employees—from across the functions of drug discovery and development, manufacturing, sales and marketing, and even finance and HR—Biocon is nudging its employees to realize that they are all *hired* by the patient and her family to help them get better.

If a pharma company realizes the importance of empathy towards end-consumers and the need for having dynamism in their responses, organizations at large can no longer afford to ignore the fact that the approaches of the past fall painfully short in addressing today's multifaceted challenges. All companies are B2C today. For systems-level challenges, we need a systems-level thinking, which integrates the desires of the customers with what is technically feasible and viable for the business.

Widespread digitization of human engagements

The pervasive computation, communication and the adoption of general-purpose artificial intelligence in businesses have made machines an important intermediary in human-to-human interactions. Leaders have begun to realize, often to their dismay, that digitization is not a natural extension of the analogue world. Squeezing in a machine between erstwhile human-to-human interactions necessitates paying close attention to the issues of trust, reliability, privacy, convenience and economics. Digitization of both customer interactions and employee engagements requires deep levels of empathy and intuition—not typical of how problems are solved in the corporate milieu.

Take, for instance, Paytm. When was the last time you called a Paytm call centre and spoke to an employee or an agent? Perhaps never, or rarely, if at all. And yet you are comfortable transacting money over your mobile in an almost habit-like manner. Not just you, many people—including cobblers, street hawkers, vegetable vendors and small storekeepers—seem to be comfortable embracing online transactions without having any human intervention.

One of the main breakthroughs in the journey of the massive and rapid adoption of digital payments was the Paytm QR code. Launched in October 2015, the Quick Response code was a frugal exaptation of an existing technology to a novel context, whereby a user does not have to key in a ten-digit mobile phone number while making a payment. This takes away the labour, the associated errors, and it soon gets into people's habits. All other players had to eventually adopt the QR code-based payment systems. But as they say, habits die hard, and Paytm continued to build on the habits it had once helped cultivate. When the QR code-based payment picked pace, Paytm launched the feature 'Scan any QR code to pay using Paytm' to further keep the customers from leaving the platform.

On the employee front, there are applications like Yammer, Slack, Dropbox and G-Suite among others which have found their place alongside the venerable Microsoft Office productivity tools, symbolizing a large-scale transition from the analogue to the digital means of employee engagement. Of the several platforms and applications that get created and pushed, only a few survive, owing to their human-centric designs that offer more benefits than perceived losses.

The necessity is to carefully design the digital experiences, and with the digitization wave far from having reached its crest, there is a lot to learn about human interactions. Design thinking offers the right temperament and the associated skills and tools to enable a digital transformation, which is inevitable in all walks of business and life.

Customers are growing knowledgeable and restless

When problems and opportunities become multifaceted, the bargaining power shifts more towards the customers, as witnessed in the case of the Indian two-wheelers market or that of low-cost airlines. The proliferation of computation, communication, cheap data and affordable end-user devices has ensured that information can no longer be monopolized. While this reduced information asymmetry is desirable from the standpoint of customers, it often means a sense of loss for the producers. As a producer you must realize that the user is no longer waiting for your genius solution; she is getting a job done already, with or without you, and you'd better learn to work *with* her rather than *for* her.

On the growing involvement of customers in designing their own experiences, IDEO's Tim Brown observes, '[Design] migrates from designers creating for people to designers creating with people to people creating by themselves through the application of user-generated content and open-source innovations.'[14]

As an example, consider TEDx, the independently organized TED conferences. In 2019 India hosted many TEDx events, averaging a staggering four events every week and numbering among the highest globally.[15] These events were held at locations such as Virudhunagar, Sarigam, Majitar, Varikoli, Sirukalathur, Alandi and Bapatla—places you would struggle to locate on a map of India. These are not your Mumbai, Bangalore, New Delhi or Chennai, where customers are spoilt for choices, but locations which were far below the radar for all these years. How did this happen? TED did not do it all by itself. Their users pulled it off, and so very brilliantly at that. As a result, we have several amazing stories from those unheard, unsung change-makers. All made possible because someone somewhere was connected and was offered a chance.

As the head of TED, Chris Anderson, opines, 'India might be the most active country on the planet in terms of the TEDx events . . . There's a beautiful spirit of optimism here. It's a country that believes in learning and self-improvement.'[16] TEDx is also an example of what happens when information asymmetry starts to disappear. If customers only have the right tools to create, they can do wonders, and their reliance on experts reduces as a result.

The tools of experimentation are becoming widespread

With knowledge comes the courage to experiment, for now the fear of the unknown is replaced by the excitement of exploration. As Peter Thiel likes to put it, 'Brilliant thinking is rare, but courage is in even shorter supply than genius.'[17] Remember the power the printing press offered to people at the time of Gutenberg? It is what Google is doing today with its Google Maps and Search. For free. A mass adoption of these tools of creation and experimentation changes everything. They almost become *general-purpose technologies*, much like the steam engine or electricity.

An unmistakable phenomenon demonstrating the power of widespread, low-cost experimentation is the massive online open courses (MOOC) movement. These affordable, widely accessible and, mostly, high-quality courses have been embraced by students and senior executives alike. The online platform MIT OpenCourseWare, which started in 2001, had hosted over 2,400 courses and 285 million visitors by August 2019.[18] Another prominent platform, Coursera, has over 40 million learners and 190 university partnerships and offers fourteen-plus degree programs, in just eight years since its start. Several of these courses are offered by working professionals who would otherwise miss out on a large audience benefiting from their knowledge and skills. There are, of course, concerns regarding monitoring progress, evaluation and personalization, but with enough AI pumped in, these are solvable problems.

With such models in place, both the supply and the demand sides of the learning equation have opened up to an unprecedented level. This mandates new ways of thinking about engagements, as the online experience is not as controlled as a classroom setup. The beneficiaries are mostly working executives, students in the long tail of access or affordability, or even aspiring leaders. Today, working professionals no longer need to make the hard choice of leaving a job for pursuing education. Learning and working can happen concurrently. As Satya Nadella says, 'I buy more books than I can finish. I sign up for more online courses than I can complete. I fundamentally believe that if you are not learning new things, you stop doing great and useful things.'[19] And guess who might be teaching Satya? Perhaps a nerd sitting somewhere in India. Would this have been possible a couple of years back? Unlikely.

Why dwell only on educational content? YouTube now allows almost anyone to display talent at a next-to-nothing cost. Thanks to novel licences, like Creative Commons, content creation, distribution and value appropriation has become more convenient. You regularly see participants from tier-2 and tier-3 cities of India showing up on the stages of *Indian Idol, India's Got Talent* and *Sa Re Ga Ma Pa*, among other reality shows, because now the discoverability of talent has gone up. They learn, they improvise, they make mistakes, they demonstrate, they partner, and then they get spotted. This opens up the playing field like never before and necessitates enterprises to create new engagement models within their ecosystems.

The clash of business models is here to stay

Among the seminal developments over the past couple of years, thanks to the pervasive influence of the Internet, is the evolution of new business models. One of the pioneers of the lean start-up movement, Steve Blank defines a business model as how your company creates, delivers and captures value.[20]

It is no longer the case that a superior product wins in the market; instead, a superior business model goes on to make profit, and it could well be wrapped around an inferior product. The first movers can be dislodged by the late entrants, provided the latter spin a new business model, as shown by Netflix over Blockbuster, or Ola Cabs over Meru Cabs.

When competition shifts from product or service superiority towards that of the overall business model, businesses must look at customer interactions more holistically, and this mandates an integrative approach to thinking. With the advent of new business and revenue models, the playing field opens up radically, for now the customers have greater choices not only in terms of offerings but also of payment methods and other complementary aspects.

Let's look at the movie industry. There are several competing business models and each with an array of companies. You can watch a movie in a multiplex, at a no-frills theatre, on television with ads, on Netflix, buy it on YouTube, buy a DVD, rent a DVD or watch a film on Amazon Prime Video or any other content streaming application. The product is the same—the movie—but the way it is rendered is entirely different. With such a wide range of choices, the players must now elevate the discussion from what (is offered) to how (it is consumed), for now there is truly little to differentiate beyond experience management.

In sectors ranging from travel to groceries and healthcare, the incumbents are facing the heat from the disruptors, who barely have to circumvent the traditionally steep entry barriers, because now they are equipped with newer business models. This trend gets further fuelled by a wider access to risk capital, well-built ecosystems and high disposable incomes on the consumer side. Online food delivery is a case in point, where different players with competing business models co-exist, while consumers typically have the last laugh.

Competition among business models means two things for your enterprise. Firstly, do not just think of delivering a better product, but instead think more broadly in terms of offering a better experience. Secondly, you do not have to do everything by yourself; instead, tap into the ecosystem for complementary assets. And if you do not have a ready ecosystem to tap into, develop one, much the way Elon Musk is doing for his electric vehicles venture by giving away his hard-earned patents for free. Remember, the first versions of electric cars were built in the mid-1800s, and yet they have not become commonplace. This could be owing to missing business models and underdeveloped ecosystems, and the genius of Tesla is not in building a better car, but in fostering a virtuous business model. Musk, who is no stranger to design thinking, observes, 'You have to match the convenience of the gasoline car in order for people to buy an electric car. They don't want to feel as though their freedom [is] curtailed in buying electric cars. They want to be able to do a cross-country trip, visit friends and family, go on vacation. These kinds of things.'[21] Hence, the product is a mere piece of a larger puzzle. The real focus is on the customer and on how various parts of the ecosystem must come together in service of the customer.

Markets are throwing new surprises at you

Let us look at some of the interesting developments in the Indian consumer market over the past few years.

More Indian men are donning beards these days. The phenomenon picked pace over the last few years, triggered by the likes of Indian cricket star Virat Kohli going for a sharply groomed beard, and then by the scores of Bollywood stars, prominently Ranveer Singh and Shahid Kapoor, turning beards into style statements. The male grooming market, which, for long, was limited to shaving creams, razors and lotions, is now getting dominated by moustache- and beard-grooming products, with as many as 177 new male grooming brands and variants launched between April 2018 and March 2019.[22]

The near monopoly of the 115-year-old Gillette has been challenged in the last few years, resulting in the parent company, P&G, taking an $8 billion write-down on its Gillette shaving business.[23] How many more blades, which all brand ambassadors and what price points would motivate men to shave in India and elsewhere? Who saw that coming? That is how markets take you by surprise, even if you are endowed with the best technologies, brands, market access and enjoy a captive customer base. Perhaps one solace for Gillette is that more men are moving away from hiding a receding hairline to shaving their heads. The likes of Jeff Bezos, Satya Nadella, Vin Diesel, Bruce Willis, Andre Agassi and Dwayne Johnson have given balding men, as Malcolm Gladwell would say, the 'permission' to take on the blade. Research has only bolstered the trend suggesting that men with shaved heads are perceived as more dominant, taller and stronger than their counterparts.[24]

The growth story of the SUV market in India is also illustrative in this respect. Despite the bad road infrastructure, extremely high traffic density and prohibitive costs of fuel and maintenance in India, 2019 became the 'Year of SUVs'.[25] Alongside the robust product portfolio of Tata Motors, Nissan, Mahindra, Fiat Chrysler Jeep, Maruti Suzuki and Hyundai, the Indian SUV market saw the entry of Korea's Kia Motors and China's MG Motors. In fact, in 2019, fifteen out of twenty new cars launched were SUVs. The sales of SUVs seemed to beat the overall recessionary trends in the automobile space, with the world's largest car maker, Volkswagen, declaring that every new Volkswagen car in India will henceforth be an SUV.[26] How did India become a hot favourite for off-road and sports utility vehicles? Also, it is a common observation that most of these vehicles are still used within city limits, each typically carrying a sum total of one occupant. Again, who would have expected this trend?

Consider another statistic. Though Indians seem to be ever hungry for entertainment and infotainment content, between January and June of 2019, over 20 million DTH and cable TV subscribers cancelled their subscriptions.[27] The monthly tariffs for DTH connections are often prohibitive as compared to the price points of other sources of content, such as on-demand video streaming. This surge in online consumption of content is fuelled by pervasive and affordable data services, mass-produced content for specific audience segments across languages and genres, and new content formats, like live streaming of cricket matches.

This trend calls for new ways of thinking on the part of both media houses and advertisers on how to engage with an ever restless and mobile customer base.

Such trends can be best explained by resorting to the 'tipping point' theory proposed by Malcolm Gladwell. Gladwell says, 'Ideas and products and messages and behaviours spread just like viruses do.' He characterizes a tipping point with three features: 'One, contagiousness; two, the fact that little causes can have big effects; and three, that change happens not gradually but at one dramatic moment.'[28]

What should be appreciated, however, is that such developments indicate that our traditional approaches of understanding market forces and changing customer preferences are reactive at best. There is a need for a fundamental relook at the way problems are framed, communicated and solved. And design thinking, with its principles, methods, tools, frameworks and temperaments, could offer a panacea. In the next chapter, we look at some of the important tenets of design thinking, which are essentially the mindset changes required to effectively practise this systems-oriented way of problem-solving.

3

Key Tenets of Design Thinking

'At the end of the day a successful, focused enterprise is one that has developed a deep understanding of its customers' needs, its competitive environment, and economic realities.'

—Louis V. Gerstner, former CEO of IBM[1]

When you search for a book on Amazon, these are the options you would be presented with: paperback, hardcover, Kindle, Audible audiobook, mass-market paperback, audio CD, CD, unabridged and unknown binding. Amazon does not mind if you buy a book from Amazon Publishing or a used book from a fellow enthusiast, or from a corner bookstore in your own city, as long as you buy it *at* Amazon. The company wants to manage your book-browsing and buying experience and does not bother inviting competition to the mix.

Likewise for the Amazon Fire TV Stick. Can you watch Netflix using the Amazon Fire TV Stick? Yes, of course. You can watch almost anything that you would on the Internet. Amazon does not care about what you watch as long as you allow Amazon to manage your experience. What matters to the company is *how* you experience content and not *what* you watch, per say.

Witnessing the surge of e-books, Jeff Bezos was quick to initiate a cannibalization of his book business with the introduction of Kindle. The practices of having a competitor sell books on Amazon and e-books on Kindle, and letting Netflix stream on Fire TV Stick might seem business as usual but that is not so, for most companies fiercely shield their customers from the competitors, becoming more product-focused and competition-obsessed than customer-obsessed. In this regard, Bezos is clear. As he notes, 'If you're competitor-focused, you have to wait until there is a competitor doing something. Being customer-focused allows you to be more pioneering.'[2] That is what explains the trillion-plus-dollar market capitalization that Amazon has accrued and why Bezos is the richest man around. It is the mindset that matters.

In this chapter, we discuss key mindset elements that must be cultivated not only to design your thinking but also to practise design thinking more effectively. Such mindsets provide the scaffolding for skills and tools to become useful.

Bring the human to the centre of your work

Amazon is famous for being *customer-obsessed* and for having an empty chair at every meeting—where the proverbial customer sits and demands your attention. But do not mistake the customer only as a consumer or the end user. It is the human-centricity that translates into customer-centricity, and one must look at the customers rather widely. The customer is not always the one who pays for your products or services. Think of the customer as the one whose problem you wish to solve.

At Amazon India, things go one step further towards bringing the customer perspective, literally, to the table. According to

Amit Agarwal, a longtimer at Amazon and the firm's India head, every weekly review meeting with his leadership team starts with a customer call. They are literally hearing the 'voice of the customer', except that it is seldom pleasant.

Having been through several such calls, Agarwal reflects, 'You can see people bristling, recoiling in their chairs because the customer is going on and on about how the service was bad. It sets the tone for what the meeting is about.'[3] That is how Jeff Bezos and 'Jeff Bots' (those who have internalized the way Bezos thinks)—Agarwal being a famous one—keep most of the organization tuned towards the true north.

Citing the remarkable success both Amazon and Renault enjoyed in India, Vijay Govindarajan, of Dartmouth College's Tuck School of Business, and Ravi Venkatesan, former chairman of Microsoft India, identify three patterns of developing customer-centricity in an Indian context.[4] Firstly, the leaders must display a strategic and long-term commitment to the Indian market, much like what Amazon CEO, Jeff Bezos, and former Renault CEO Carlos Ghosn demonstrated through their several visits and stays at India. Secondly, creating strong local teams and shifting resources and decision-making authority to India, as exemplified by Amazon's India CEO Amit Agarwal, who has been successfully leading the office for a long time. Thirdly, creating offerings which are appealing, affordable and accessible to the emerging middle class, and thinking of new business models. The way Renault's Duster and Kwid took on the Indian market is a case in point, illustrating how local innovations can be driven by a keen understanding of Indian consumers.

In another local innovation, in 2016, Amazon rolled out a vendor outreach programme—Amazon Chai Cart. These tea carts would move around on the busy, narrow streets of urban India and educate small shopkeepers about the benefits of starting an online business. The tagline of the campaign—'*Chai toh hai bahana, maksad hai aapka vyapar badhana* (The tea is just an excuse, our objective is to further your business)'—was widely accepted, and in a period of four months, the team travelled 15,280 km across 31 cities and engaged with over 10,000 sellers.[5]

Another initiative was Amazon Tatkal, which enables local businesses from tier-2, -3 and -4 towns to go online and sell products on Amazon in less than sixty minutes. This studio-on-wheels speeds up the business launch process through easier registration, imaging and cataloguing services.[6]

Against the backdrop of these sensitization programmes, Amazon India launched the 'I Have Space' (IHS) initiative in 2017, under which local *kirana* stores, or people with storage facilities, could partner with Amazon to deliver products within a 2–3-kilometre radius of their stores. By mid-2019, the company had tied up with 18,500 stores across 225 cities in India.[7] These are some of the initiatives by which Amazon overcame a late entry into the Indian market, and it is now giving tough competition to Flipkart and other domestic retailers.

Do not limit yourself to thinking of the customer as the one who writes a cheque for you; instead, look at her as someone who offers you a genuine insight. Interventions in design thinking could be aimed at the vendors, employees and partner community, and not necessarily at the end customers. Design thinking advocates looking at human-centricity in a broader manner, and not just towards those whom you serve.

It is not about designing as much as about thinking

The origins of design thinking from the disciplines of industrial and product design, and from architecture, lead one to very narrowly associate the field with designers. In fact, it was very much the case for a long time, but today design thinking has come to represent an approach of problem-solving which is rooted in the principles of useful design. The emphasis is increasingly on *thinking* than on *designing*.

Instead of thinking about what to build, one must learn to build in order to think. The imperative is to think holistically and systematically and not just to design a clever product. The outcome can well be a great piece of design but it seldom is, for people are consuming experiences more than ever. It is often quite easy to get lost in the act of designing, given the fun the activity offers with its art, craft and storytelling elements, and lose out on the bigger picture. Even in design thinking, if there is not a genuine thought given to the fundamental questions and the contexts thereof, the result may not at all be creative. The approach is only as good as the thinking applied.

Take, for instance, the case of Tata Nano, the 'People's Car', which was the dream project of Ratan Tata and was built by the team that had delivered the wildly successful Tata Ace. From conceiving the very notion of building a one-lakh-rupee car to the final product launch in 2009, the engineering team was largely focused on product design and manufacturability, and not so much on 'thinking' about the product-user equation. A great piece of design, even by contemporary standards, the product symbolized frugal engineering but failed where it mattered: commercialization. Not sufficient thought was given to the parameters beyond the engineering and cost of the car, such as maintenance and repair, fuel prices, availability of parking space and the perception value. It was almost labelled as the 'poor man's car'—certainly not desirable from Ratan Tata's or even the common Indian's point of view. The reason could well be that it all started with *sympathy* and not empathy, as Ratan Tata *felt* for the 'Indian families riding on scooters, four or five on a scooter, maybe the child sandwiched between the mother and father . . . often on slippery roads in the dark'.[8] Eventually, the Tata Nano project had to shut down. It must be noted here that a good innovation starts with empathy and not sympathy, with a focus on thinking and not just on designing.

Focus on the subject, not the object

A significant contribution of the design-thinking tribe is to bring to our consciousness the notion of human-centricity, or in a commercial context, customer-centricity. The movement away from the object (the stuff) to the subject (the user) requires a significant cerebral shift. Almost all the previous approaches of problem-solving, ranging from the Russian TRIZ to de Bono's lateral thinking, or triggers like SCAMPER, start with the object that needs to be worked upon. However, in design thinking, the starting point is always the subject, while the object remains largely in the background.

Let us take an example of adding value to a pen. In the traditional approach, you would start with the pen and try improving it with more features, less waste, broader variety, more functionality or whatever else a creative approach suggests. Whereas in design thinking you would start with the question: 'Why does the user need the pen?' The answers could be well beyond the obvious one: for writing. Someone might need a pen for adornment, or just for signing purposes, or, perhaps, as a matter of habit. Armed with these new insights about the user and the usage, you may meet the desire for adornment or address a user's habit with something other than the pen—an outcome not even remotely entertained in the traditional approaches of problem-solving because they would start and end with the pen. In design thinking, function matters more than form, just as the purpose matters more than the product, and this stems from the ethos of user-centricity. Take the case of one of the most significant innovations in healthcare, the incubator, which has been radically transformed over the years by keeping the subject in mind.

The world over, more than 15 million low-birthweight and premature babies are born annually, of which over a million die.[9] Most such deaths are in poor countries, including India, where often there are no hospitals with proper incubators. Traditional incubators could cost anywhere around $20,000, not including the costs involved in the supply of electricity and oxygen, the need for trained staff, maintenance, spares and conducive environmental conditions. Most developing countries cannot afford this, leading to thousands of avoidable deaths. But there have been several innovations in this sphere, led by large enterprises and start-ups alike.

In 2010, the GE Healthcare division in Bangalore designed the Lullaby baby warmer and priced it at 30 per cent the price of traditional incubators.[10] With features such as pictorial warnings and colour coding, the device consumes less power, requires low maintenance and is ideal for a rural setup. Even then, such medical devices remain out of reach of most parents, who do not have access to a hospital and need local support during those crucial few hours after the birth of a child. So it is not just the cost or convenience that is an issue, but also access. Further, the cold reality remains that as much as 96 per cent of the total medical equipment donated to developing nations become non-functional within five years.[11] How do you solve the repair problem?

Timothy Prestero and Neil Cantor run an NGO called Design that Matters, which, in 2008, launched NeoNurture, an incubator made entirely of automotive parts: headlights provide the warmth, motor blowers and dashboard fans give out filtered air for heating or cooling, and indicator lights serve as alarms for health workers.[12] The insight of using auto parts to make an incubator emerged from a deep understanding of resources available in most rural parts of the world. The 'car incubator' is powered by motorcycle batteries, is portable, easy to repair and removes the dependency on traditional incubator spares, repairs and expertise.[13]

In both these cases—of the Lullaby and the NeoNurture—the focus largely remained on the object, but the case of the Embrace Baby Warmer takes the conversation further, on how an acute attention on the subject (the baby and the family) can offer new insights and bring about a radical solution that was previously unthinkable.

The idea of Embrace took shape at the Stanford d.School as a part of the Design for Extreme Affordability class of 2008. The team, comprising Rahul Panicker, Jane Cen, Linus Liang and Naganand Murty, started with the following brief: 'How might we create a baby-warming device that helps parents in remote villages give their dying infants a chance to survive?' Adopting a design-thinking approach, the team went about conducting an intense first-hand market research, staying with families in Nepal and India, visiting several hospitals in rural areas and identifying key challenges in keeping newborns warm at home. With an unwavering focus on the child (the subject), adopting a clear-slate design and questioning the assumptions behind the classic incubators (the object), the team created the Embrace warmer. The final product, based on the technology of a heat-retaining device, looks much like a quilt and costs just under 1 per cent of the price of traditional incubators. It has already impacted the lives of over 300,000 babies in twenty-two countries.[14] The wide adoption was possible because of the 99 per cent cost reduction and enhanced convenience, which happened because the designers had started with the basics—adopting a human-centric approach and challenging some of the long-held assumptions.

So, if you really want to disrupt the status quo, start with the subject, and not the object of your fascination.

Solve the problem 'with' the customer, and not for the customer

The traditional division of labour in the product market has been that the customer has a problem which, hopefully, is well articulated and is to be solved by some experts who, in turn, would get paid for the solution. The expertise was supposed to be concentrated with the seller, while the consumer just had the choice of purchase or payment. That is no longer true, especially with the democratization of ideas and talent. You need to create a conversation with your customer to understand the problem and then solve it jointly. As IDEO's Tim Brown puts it, 'Design thinking is about creating a multipolar experience in which everyone has the opportunity to participate in the conversation.'[15]

Why solve the problem *with* the customer? There are at least two explanations. Firstly, a problem may not always be apparent or known; and secondly, the customer may already have a working solution. So, instead of outguessing the customer about the problem and then trying to foist your pet solution on her, why not create the solution with the customer? If the suitable tools, insights, avenues and confidence are given to the customer, she might surprise you with a genuine creation. We are getting into an age of co-creation and co-design, and the producer of this age need not always be the expert. The key is to engage with those who are facing the problems most acutely and may have some insights on how to address those, and, in many cases, may even have devised a means of alleviating the pain. The boundaries between creators and consumers blur as a result, and pervasive and affordable technology makes this possible more than ever before.

With pervasive technology and connectivity, the cost of prototyping has radically come down. You need not build a full-scale version of your idea to put it to test. You are good enough even building a digital mock-up of your *leap of faith* concept and putting it to test in a controlled setting. Instead of investing in designing clever user interfaces for your application, you may use graphics, or better still, sticky notes, to seek concept validation. The low cost of prototyping means you can pack far more learning in a given time frame and budget and move towards your end objective faster and with fewer blind spots. Technology also helps in getting the customer involved, physically or virtually, in a non-intruding manner.

Designers at IDEO practise something called the Boyle's Law (named after one of IDEO's master prototypers, Dennis Boyle), which states: 'Never go to a meeting without a prototype.' A prototype would give the customer something tangible to offer feedback on and help the project's progress. Approaches like customer clinics are powerful means of engaging the customers in bringing certain problems to the surface, developing possible coping mechanisms and validating those, all in collaborative setting.

Consider how the renowned neurosurgeon Dr V.S. Ramachandran solved the problem of phantom or amputated limbs. Dr Ramachandran's Mirror Box Therapy involves a vertical 2x2-foot mirror in a box. The patient places his residual limb, or stump, on one side of the mirror and the intact, normal limb on the other, so that when he looks at the reflection of the latter in the mirror it seems visually superimposed on the phantom, thereby creating the illusion that the phantom has been resurrected.[16] First tried on patients in 1993, the Mirror Box Therapy has since been improved and has facilitated remarkable recoveries in several severe cases. The simple method, created *with* the patients, has shown to offer relief from many chronic neurological disorders that have long been regarded as intractable, such as phantom pain, hemiparesis from stroke and complex regional pain syndrome. Think of the cost of the mirror box as against that of a neurosurgery, besides the risk associated with going under the knife. That is how elegant solutions can be systematically co-created with the customers.

Building on a similar approach, Mileha Soneji, an industrial designer, developed a staircase illusion for her uncle who was suffering from Parkinson's disease. In her TEDx Talk, Mileha narrates that by observing and interacting continuously with her uncle she could understand the challenges of and the solution to her uncle's mobility problems and devise a deceptively simple solution.[17] The *staircase illusion*, as the solution is called, has shown to significantly correct the walking difficulties of that one patient (subject) and could be scaled to several such patients, because the solution was developed *with* the customer and not for the customer.

Design thinking aims to take away second-guessing from the efforts of problem-solving. Here, the problem is *co-discovered* with the customer before it is *co-solved* with the customer, and all this while a continuous line of feedback ensures that you never run the risk of over-engineering your solution or overwhelming your customers. As Eric Schmidt notes, 'Giving the customer what he wants is less important than giving him what he doesn't yet know he wants.'[18]

Think beyond products

One of the biggest misconceptions about design thinking is that it is primarily about designing new products. Though design thinking is a powerful approach to new product development, there is a wider array of contexts which benefit from adopting this structured approach of problem-solving, one that keeps customers at the centre of attention.

A company that has captured an enviable market position without necessarily having a winning product is Maruti Suzuki. Though Maruti Suzuki, over the years, has delivered blockbuster products, such as Maruti 800, Alto, Wagon R, Swift and Dzire, the above 50 per cent market share that the company enjoys could well be attributed to its activities beyond the realm of new product development. Maruti Suzuki exemplifies the idea that it takes more than a winning product to win in the market.

Maruti Suzuki, formerly Maruti Udyog Limited, was born of a market research conducted in 1980 which identified the need for a fuel-efficient, reliable and affordable car that would serve the typical family of four, for commuting within city limits. The benchmark price was Rs 50,000, which was about twelve times the typical starting salary of a government employee.[19] After much deliberation with global auto majors, the executives in the Indian government settled for Japan's Suzuki Motors Corporation, which specialized in making small cars. The joint venture led to the production of three automobiles: Maruti 800 (1983), Maruti Omni (1984) and Maruti Gypsy (1985). These vehicles continue to sell to date, except for Maruti 800, which was discontinued in 2014 after being the first car for millions of Indians.

In his address to the employees in 1987, Dr V. Krishnamurthy, founding CEO and chairman of Maruti Udyog Limited, said, 'We simply cannot forget that we are not in the business of selling cars. We are selling to our customer a long-term commitment to take care of their needs for transport efficiently and economically.'[20] Remember, this was a time when Maruti was a public sector undertaking (PSU), subject to the most draconian of government rules and regulations, and with negligible competition either from Calcutta's Hindustan Motors or from Bombay's Premier Padmini. Why should a government unit with over 80 per cent market share worry about customers, let alone customer service? But the very spirit of looking beyond the product helped the company face the onslaught of multinationals, especially Hyundai Motors, entering the Indian market, and fight back for the lion's share.

From the company's very inception, Maruti's leadership focused on high-quality after-sales services. The company followed a strict 'no sales without service' rule for all its dealers. A dealership would get activated only after all the servicing facilities were in place and certified by Maruti. As early as 1985, the company had set up the Maruti Authorized Service Stations (MASS), which by August 2019 grew to a service network of 3,600 workshops across over 1,800 towns and cities.

To hasten the service response time, the company introduced a series of firsts in the Indian market. In mid-2000s, the company launched its Maruti On-Road Service (MOS) to attend to vehicle breakdowns, and this rapidly grew to 415 MOS installations across the country. To further crunch the response time on car services, in August 2018, the company introduced 24/7 on-road assistance with 350 quick response teams on bikes in 250 cities.[21] The latest introduction on the service front is Maruti's Service on Wheels workshop, for servicing, repair and overhauling jobs at customers' doorsteps.[22]

In 2001, the company introduced Maruti True Value, a marketplace for pre-owned cars, which would soon become a reliable avenue for Maruti to upsell its products to existing customers. The cars sold at the outlets undergo a 376-point check, quality evaluation, refurbishment and certification process, and the customers are offered up to one-year warranty and three free services. By August 2019, there were 250 True Value centers across 151 cities in India.[23]

To make it easier for customers to purchase new cars, Maruti joined hands with leading Indian banks in 2003, offering car finance through Maruti Suzuki Finance, which further helped both customers and dealerships get better value from the company. Around the same time, the company entered car insurance services through a host of leading insurance providers and launched Maruti Insurance.

In another move towards customer-centricity, the company, in 2007, started the Maruti Driving School, another first by an automobile manufacturer in India. By July 2018, over a million drivers were trained by the 450 Maruti Driving Schools across 212 cities in India.[24] There's little doubt that when somebody learns to drive on a Maruti, it is a Maruti that comes home.

With all these service-related introductions, Maruti Suzuki inched closer to its former glory and retained its ground amid stiff competition from Hyundai Motors. But the company was still perceived as an economy-segment leader and never considered a serious player in the fast-growing and profitable premium segment, dominated by the likes of Honda City and Hyundai Verna. As a response, one of the most daring and timely steps by the company was to launch the Nexa, Maruti's premium car showroom.

Introduced in June 2015, against the backdrop of a network of 1,650 dealerships across India, Nexa would offer Maruti Suzuki a gateway into offering the experience customers desire while buying a premium car—an experience that cannot be managed by the dealership that also sells the Maruti Alto. The idea was to apply the practices of hospitality to the purchasing of cars, pamper the customers and offer the experience of a lifetime by enhancing both the digital and human touch.[25] The first car launched exclusively through Nexa was the S-Cross, and soon it was followed by the Baleno, Ignis, Ciaz and XL6, which offered a significant facelift to the brand. As of November 2019, with 300 outlets across 200 cities, Nexa contributes to 20 per cent of the company's sales, having added a million new customers.[26]

It is hard to beat a company that has sold over 20 million cars—one that took twenty-nine years to reach the 10 million mark and another eight years to add another 10 million to that figure.[27] That is how you both create the market and lead it. But it was not the car alone that worked. It was well beyond the four-wheelers—it was services, network, trust and convenience. The story of Maruti Suzuki demonstrates that too narrow a focus on the product, even when the customer is primarily paying for it, may leave little to differentiate.

Strike a balance between desirability, feasibility and viability

One of the questions that often surfaces in design thinking discourse is: 'Does every type of creative problem-solving qualify for design thinking?' The answer is no. Design thinking is different in a way that it focuses extensively on human beings whose problems are to be solved and whose lives must be impacted. But it does not stop with what is good for humans. The approach also takes into consideration the technical possibilities and business requirements of growth and sustainability. As Tim Brown notes: 'The willing and even enthusiastic acceptance of competing constraints is the foundation of design thinking.'[28]

This deliberate balance between desirability, business viability and technical feasibility makes design thinking a far more robust and well-rounded approach to problem-solving. Instead of getting skewed towards making customers happy at all costs, design thinking encourages you to also keep in mind the practicality of the solution and its impact on the business.

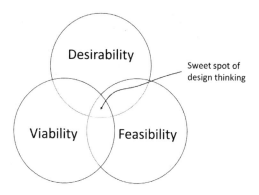

Figure 5: Design thinking calls for achieving a balance between desirability, feasibility and viability

Desirability is about the *human factors:* 'What does the human really desire and not just need or want?' The human in question need not always be the customer. It could be a buyer, a user, a channel partner, an employee, a supplier or almost anybody whose problem needs to be addressed. If the idea is not desirable and does not lead to a 'wow factor' for your intended audience, even if you can do it well and do it profitably, it is a false start. An understanding of true desire comes with empathy, where you cut through the clutter of what is said and known to get to people's motivations and core beliefs. Most desires are unarticulated, and it takes skill to unearth what is often not known to the customers themselves. Steve Jobs could create remarkable products because he focused on what the customer desired and not on what she needed or wanted. This was possible only because of Jobs's extremely good observation and probing skills.

Technical feasibility is a set of *technical factors:* 'Does the idea really deliver what it promises?' Far too many ideas have failed because they could not be executed within the right time frame and budget. As ideas take shape through rounds of technical evaluations and pass through the proverbial innovation funnel, they are left as a pale shadow of their original self. With the dimension of technical feasibility, the design-thinking process grounds the pursuit of innovation and minimizes wasteful efforts. The constant cycle of iterations and a prototyping mentality ensure that the outcome is closer to what really works rather than being merely wishful thinking. Desirability aside, it takes a lot of tinkering for an idea to see the light of day, and hence the importance of technical feasibility. It took the prodigious James Dyson fifteen years and over 5,000 prototypes to perfect the breakthrough bagless vacuum cleaner. As Nassim Nicholas Taleb says, 'A country's assets reside in the tinkerers, the hobbyists, and the risk-takers'[29]—a trait successful companies cultivate painstakingly.

Business viability is about *economic factors*: 'Does the idea make business sense?' A clever idea is only as good as somebody's willingness to pay for it, so that the business can deliver value in a sustainable manner. The start-up world is replete with glorious ideas that did excite customers but could not continue to do so, as they were often built on false economic assumptions and poor business logic. The constraint of business viability is not just for the for-profit side of the world, but also for non-profits and government agencies that must, at the least, ensure sustainable operations. The Internet economy offers a wide array of business model choices that relieve customers of the burden of paying directly for the goods and services they consume. (Google is a case in point.) However, business viability cannot be an afterthought. In fact, the high mortality rate in the start-up arena could often be traced to the unwillingness of the founders to treat business viability with the same rigour as desirability or technical feasibility.

Between desirability, technical feasibility and business viability, what should be your starting point? On this question, David and Tom Kelley of IDEO offer, 'Human factors aren't necessarily more vital than the other two. But technical factors are well taught in science and engineering programs around the world, and companies everywhere focus energy on the business factors. So we believe that human factors may offer some of the best opportunities for innovation, which is why we always start there.'[30]

Further, a primacy of desirability over feasibility or even viability ensures that organizations gravitate towards ideas which are high on novelty. Otherwise it is quite easy to get lost in an ocean of trivial ideas. The way managers evaluate the efficacy of an idea is significantly different from the way customers do. Jennifer Mueller of the Wharton Business School, and her co-researchers Shimul Melwani and Jack Goncalo, propose that while customers look for high levels of novelty in an idea, managers deem feasibility as an important determinant of good ideas.[31] Through a series of experimental studies, the researchers identified that under high levels of uncertainty managers often gravitate towards more feasible ideas, while they continue to seek novelty. By bringing in the importance of desirability into the mix of technical feasibility and business viability, managers could ensure that they do not subconsciously weed out radical ideas.

At a broader level, the balance between desirability, feasibility and viability translates into the emerging concept of the Triple Bottom Line, or 3Ps, where 'people' represents desirability, 'planet' indicates adoption of sustainable and feasible technologies, and 'profits' come from astute focus on financial viability. ITC, one of India's largest conglomerates, is an exemplar organization in its adoption of the Triple Bottom Line into the manner in which it conducts its business, social and environmental engagements.

A case in point is ITC's e-Choupal, a rural farming initiative that connects farmers directly to the markets and provides information regarding weather forecast, crop pricing and other insights on effective farming techniques. Since its launch in June 2000, the service has touched over 4 million farmers in some 35,000 villages through its 6,100 kiosks.[32] The initiative has helped ITC make a successful entry into the branded atta market (through the launch of Aashirvaad), branded food (through Sunfeast) and packaged juices (with the B Natural brand). That is how a focus on people and planet makes business sense. We need to think of business in terms of *compassionate capitalism*, where empathy meets possibilities and profitability.

Think broad before you go narrow

Design thinking relies on the divergence of thought process, before convergence sets in. In other words, you need to create choices in order to make effective and non-obvious choices; otherwise, there is no creation. A premature convergence would leave too many possibilities unexplored and lead to the same old ends. The risk of divergent thinking is having a lot of false starts, but that is entirely acceptable and rather encouraged in creativity. That is what the British educationalist Sir Ken Robinson constantly reminds us: 'If you're not prepared to be wrong. You'll never come up with anything original.'[33]

Between creating choices and making choices, what do you think comes more intuitively to us? Typically, making choices is far more effortless than thinking of options. Through millennia of evolution, the human mind has been tuned to rule out a large set of factors in favour of a few. This is not only more efficient but also less risky—for what if some of the options you generate are outrightly crazy? Well, in design thinking, we encourage such wild ideas, by design. We allow for multiple ideas to compete with each other, organically, and by corollary, we need a good base to start with if we need some of these ideas to survive. So long as the ideas fall under the ambit of the design brief or the objective statement, there is no need to press the panic button. As they say, let a million flowers blossom (and then you can prune them). As shown in Figure 6, design thinking is a rhythmic exchange between divergent and convergent thinking, or between analysis and synthesis.

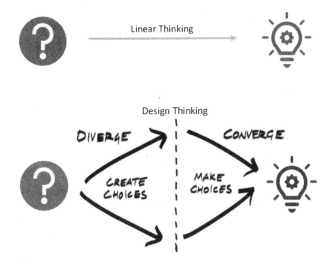

Figure 6: Learn to think broad before thinking narrow

A research by Robert McCrae, of the US National Institutes of Health, offers that creativity is particularly related to the personality domain of openness to experience and to one's ability to have divergent thinking. On the basis of scores of tests on divergent thinking obtained between 1959 and 1972, and correlating those with a variety of personality measures administered since 1980, the author proposed that 'creative people are adjusted, sociable, and productive as well as open', and that 'open people may have developed intellectual and especially divergent thinking abilities through a lifetime of practice. By exercising their cognitive faculties, they may have discovered or retained skills that were lost to closed individuals.'[34] In summary, divergent thinking can be cultivated with practice.

Yet divergent thinking is not a natural way to approach problems in work and life. To get to understand how difficult divergent thinking is, consider this thought experiment. If you have to devise means of getting more bike riders to wear helmets, what will you be more comfortable doing: A) generating ten ideas, or B) choosing among ten ideas? I reckon it would be option B. Making choices is mostly effortless, logical and straightforward, whereas generating choices is painful, often illogical and calls for an entirely different approach of thinking. Though the psychologist Barry Schwartz offers that a greater number of choices makes us more anxious and taxes our cognitive abilities, not having enough choices does not lead us to new pathways either. As for creativity, more is always better, and that is why there is a premium on the quantity of ideas. In fact, as Wharton professor and psychologist Adam Grant says: 'The hallmark of originality is rejecting the default and exploring whether a better option exists.' He further adds that, 'Originality is not a fixed trait. It is a free choice.'[35] So, you can choose to make more choices, before settling in.

How does one cultivate the ability to think broad? This crucial ability of thinking could be shaped with a few practices. Firstly, learn to park your judgement, so that you allow nascent ideas to take some shape under cover. Secondly, push yourself to work in a diverse setting, to allow for pattern-breaking and newer stimuli. Thirdly, be rigid about the outcome but flexible about the approach, so that you can allow for a genuine sense of surprise. All these practices are equally applicable to a group setting and to individuals. The groups thrive amid diversity, while individuals gain from honing multiple affiliations and fostering a T-shaped personality (more on these later).

The ability of one person to be adept at both divergent and convergent thinking is what author and academic Roger Martin calls *integrative thinking*. In his book *The Opposable Mind*, Martin defines integrative thinking as, 'The ability to face constructively the tension of opposing ideas and, instead of choosing one at the expense of the other, generate a creative resolution of the tension in the form of a new idea that contains elements of the opposing ideas but is superior to each.'[36] Integrative thinkers do not mind the messy problems; they actively seek less obvious but potentially relevant factors and are not afraid to question the apparently obvious links or to consider multilinear relationships. Martin offers that integrative thinkers tend not to break down problems into their constituting pieces; rather, they like to look at it in entirety, as they embrace holistic instead of segmented thinking and are willing to park their judgement in the light of fresh insights.[37]

A good example of going broad before going narrow is *biomimicry*, the science of learning from nature. When architects and engineers had to design and build more eco-friendly infrastructure, they resorted to nature and studied the commonplace termite houses. These tall and ordinary-looking structures can maintain reasonably constant temperatures, humidity and oxygen supply all through the year, and in the most non-disruptive manner. Equipped with these insights from the world of termites and ants, the architects are now infusing more nature into their synthetic designs, by going broad for inspiration before going narrow for application. In the words of the prestigious Pritzker Architecture Prize-winning Indian architect, Balkrishna V. Doshi, who, among other things, designed the IIM Bangalore campus: 'Design is nothing but a humble understanding of materials, a natural instinct for solutions, and respect for nature.'[38]

So the next time you are faced with a daunting problem, de-focus before you re-focus.

Learn to compartmentalize your thinking

Creative problem-solving requires discipline more than anything else. Being systematic is the only way you can bring your creativity to fruition. Even breaking away from a pattern can be a matter of being disciplined. To paraphrase the leadership coach Andy Stanley, the great challenge is how to marry creativity with discipline so that discipline amplifies creativity without destroying it. We, most often, err on the side of chaos than order when it comes to creativity, to destructive ends. But that needs to be checked, for being disciplined about creativity is not natural or easy.

A good practice is to think in compartments, separated by time and intent. Think of creative problem-solving as a three-stage process: 1) problem exploration; 2) solution generation; and 3) solution validation. These three compartments are shown in Figure 7.

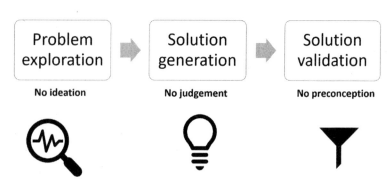

Figure 7: Three compartments of thinking systematically

Problem exploration

What is your typical first reaction when somebody comes to you with a problem? Most would quickly jump to a solution or offer a recommendation. This reaction is common in both professional and personal life. And how many times does the other person really get wowed by your genius solution? Seldom, I reckon. Yet we cannot resist the temptation of hopping to a solution given the first sight of a problem.

To understand a problem like never before you need to develop the curiosity and the eye of a child, and the ability to postpone your judgement, coupled with the courage to ask some apparently dumb questions and to not be satisfied with the most obvious explanations. A useful reminder is that a problem fully understood is half-solved.

For effective problem-solving, it is critical to stay with the problem for as long as possible. Almost always, what you see at first is not the problem but a symptom, and by attacking the symptom you are going nowhere. Staying with a problem, or as some say, *sleeping on a problem*, does not happen easily but is critical for effective problem-solving. Learn to hold on to your ideas, for by offering that one solution you might be short-circuiting the very vital process of problem exploration.

As the saying goes, 'Give me six hours to chop down a tree and I will spend the first four sharpening the axe.' In the realm of creativity, if you have six hours to solve a problem, spend four hours exploring the problem and getting to its root cause.

Solution generation

What is your first reaction when somebody comes up with an idea to your problem? You most likely dismiss the idea, stating that you have tried it before or that it does not work this way. It is human to dismiss ideas, for we are historically engineered to play safe. But when there is a licence, and need, to be creative, you have to learn to throw caution to the wind. While you are at the ideation stage, validation of those ideas should be avoided at all cost. You must cerebrally and temporally separate idea generation from idea validation.

In the solution-generation stage, it is crucial to be comfortable with ambiguity. Too much urgency to bring an order to the proceedings, or to converge prematurely, could lead to suboptimal idea generation, or to the generation of routine solutions. Not being judgemental about others starts with not being judgemental about yourself. If you are in the realm of ideation, let quantity thrive over the quality of your ideas. By cutting loose, you allow for radical ideas to come to the fore, both for yourself and for others in the team.

It is worth reflecting on what Malcolm Gladwell says on being judged, 'The older I get, the more I understand that the only way to say valuable things is to lose your fear of being correct.'[39] Only when you are being non-judgemental will the dots start to connect, often subconsciously and to surprising effects. And, when we have enough ideas on the table, we look at picking the finest.

Solution validation

Once you have thought through the problem in sufficient detail and have left no stone unturned while ideating, you can start to converge to the most meaningful ideas. The third and final compartment is about culling the ideas, and here too we need to invoke science.

A disproportionate number of decisions, in corporate and personal life alike, are based on common sense and gut feeling, rejecting rational approaches. Daniel Kahneman, an expert in the field of behavioural economics, warns us about this, saying, 'Clearly, the decision making that we rely on in society is fallible. It is highly fallible, and we should know that.'[40] The Nobel laureate urges us to adopt 'System 2' (slow and deliberate thinking) over 'System 1' (fast and automatic thinking) while making critical decision, such as which ideas to pursue and spend scant resources on. That is why relying on hunch and gut feeling is not the best approach for picking the most promising ideas.

If you were to pick two out of ten ideas for further investment, how would you typically do that? Most managers would resort to conventional wisdom (an oxymoron in itself) to pick the most trusted bets. Most decisions are made on the basis of optimism and over-confidence, rather than on the basis of sound logic or due diligence, and nothing can be more tragic if an idea emerging from a genuine insight gets killed by a senior leader just because 'it doesn't sound right'.

Instead of resorting to pure guts, now is the time to invoke a few tried-and-tested methods. A host of techniques for concept prototyping and validation are discussed in Chapter 7. As of now, it must suffice to establish the importance of thinking in compartments while solving a problem creatively.

From symptoms to problems to the root causes

A useful practice in design thinking is to assume that every problem is a symptom. The real problem is almost always buried deep under, and it takes a lot of effort and patience to get to the core problem before it could be solved meaningfully, except that most people do not want to put in the required effort. As a result, they attack symptoms to no avail and see the problems resurfacing in uglier manifestations.

Let us take the example of a visit to a doctor. Suppose there are two doctors, Doc A and Doc B. Both are equally qualified and are used to seeing a good number of patients daily. As you make your way to the chamber of Doc A, she asks you: 'So, tell me. What is your problem?' You start with, 'I have a serious headache from the past few days, I have lost my appetite, I feel weak all day long, I find it difficult to concentrate . . .'—and you go on. To a question on your own problem, the language you chose is of symptoms. For your own body, you have no inkling as to what your problem is—whether it is bacterial or viral, internal or external. You are not sure. Without even letting you finish, Doc A interrupts and prescribes a few medicines. She says, 'I got it. Take these medicines for the next two days and you should feel better, and if you don't, come and see me again.' You look at the prescription and walk out, thanking the doctor. And lo and behold, you take those medicines and feel better in the next two days, while you still have no understanding of your problem.

Doc B starts with the same question: 'So, tell me. What is your problem?' You go on with the same answer, narrating your symptoms. Except this time, the doctor lets you finish your explanation and asks some probing questions to get a better understanding of the 'root cause' of the problem, carries out some routine checks and declares: 'Nothing much is wrong. You have got too worked up. Just go home, take some rest, eat light food and you will feel better over the next two days. If you don't, come and see me again.' You walk out without medicines, but now with an understanding of your problem and, possibly, an awareness of how to prevent it from happening again.

Which of the two doctors would you trust? Doc A, who did not listen to you, gave you medicines, and you are fine? Or Doc B, who did listen to you, did not give you medicines, and you are fine? I reckon it would be Doc B. And if you still feel it is Doc A who did a fine job, answer this: 'Which of the two would you trust your child with, Doc A or Doc B?' Usually, the answer is Doc B. The difference between the two is empathy. As Daniel Goleman, one of the strongest proponents of emotional intelligence and empathy, puts it, 'Relationships [between doctors and patients] would be fostered more readily if medical education included some basic tools for emotional intelligence, especially self-awareness and arts of empathy and listening.'[41] And we have all encountered these two types of doctors in our lives.

How do you usually behave at office or in front of a customer? Like the one who knows all the answers and does not let the customer or colleague finish? Or like the one who helps move from symptoms to problems to the root cause, before suggesting a remedy? It is important to listen and make others understand the problem before proposing a solution. The ability to go from symptoms to problems can make the difference between a failed start and a timely finish.

Are we so poor at problem diagnosis? Research suggests that getting to the real problem is not a well-developed skill in most people. In a survey of 106 C-suite executives from ninety-one private and public-sector companies in seventeen countries, Thomas Wedell-Wedellsborg, an executive coach, learnt that around 85 per cent found their organizations bad at problem diagnosis, and 87 per cent thought that this flaw carried significant costs.[42] The reason, cites Wedell-Wedellsborg, is that people often lack simpler problem-diagnosis tools and frameworks which can be applied almost on a daily basis and with visible results. What he proposes is an approach of reframing the problem in a manner that it triggers a different line of thought. For instance, instead of asking 'Why is the elevator so slow?' you may reframe the problem as, 'How to make waiting less annoying?' The new framing opens up more possibilities, such as putting mirrors in the lift, playing music, installing wall displays and transparent lifts, among others.

In any customer engagement, it is only fair to assume that what the customer is narrating is a symptom and not the real problem. Seeking the 'voice of the customer' does not always lead you to the core issues, because, as Tom Kelley observes, customers often lack the vocabulary to explain what is wrong, especially with new-to-the-world products and services. You would need to ask the right questions, listen with intent and observe with purpose to get to what the customer *meant* and not what she *said*.

Getting to the root cause can yield surprising insights, as demonstrated by Tata Ace, the mini truck from Tata Motors that created an entirely new segment in the highly competitive Indian commercial vehicles industry. In early 2000s, the commercial vehicles division at Tata Motors was experiencing stagnation. The higher end of the market was seeing competition from the likes of Ashok Leyland, while the lower end, the sub-four-tonne category, was getting lost to three-wheeler transport carriers from Bajaj Auto, Mahindra & Mahindra and Piaggio. To address the stagnation, Tata Motors formed a cross-functional team of young engineers, led by Girish Wagh, to get into the trenches and conduct first-hand market research. Their investigation led them to some valuable insights. They found that goods carrier customers were looking at greater stability, safety, comfort, all-weather protection, more load-carrying capabilities over short hauls and prestige in their vehicles—features that traditional three-wheelers lacked. There was a general trend towards a rise in the demand for small trucks that could easily navigate city streets, village roads as well as highways, much in line with the emerging hub-and-spoke model of logistics. Further, some of the state and national highways, such as the Mumbai–Pune Expressway, did not allow three-wheelers to ply, which further lowered the business potential of three-wheeler goods-transport vehicles.

Equipped with these insights, the small team set out to design an entirely new offering in the small-commercial-vehicle category, instead of repositioning its existing offerings, or getting into a direct competition with the three-wheeler makers. The first task was to design and develop a two-cylinder engine, which would offer better fuel efficiency than the engines commonly used in three-wheelers, while meeting the BS II and BS III emission norms. To further save on the development time and cost, the team raised the extent of parts co-creation with vendor partners to 80 per cent, much higher than the industry norm.[43] This also led to highly innovative designs and features for the new mini truck. After a development period of four years, the mini truck, named Tata Ace, and marketed as '*Chhota Haathi* (Mini Elephant)', was launched in 2005 at a price tag of Rs 2.25 lakh. By 2019, Tata Motors had sold over 2 million Tata Ace trucks, dominating the market, which picked pace with the action in the e-commerce industry. Today, a Tata Ace, or its variant, is sold every three minutes, and Tata Motors enjoys a market share of above 70 per cent in the sub-two-tonne segment.[44]

Apart from creating an entirely new category, Tata Ace has helped thousands of entrepreneurs, especially in rural India, to fulfil their business aspirations in the emerging transport and logistics industry. It could happen because the team understood the psyche of the customers who wish to earn prestige within the community, make a decent earning, while being able to afford a four-wheeler goods carrier. It is highly likely that a Tata Ace delivered groceries to you from Bigbasket or fulfilled your one-day delivery from Amazon. Perhaps the most crucial difference between Tata Ace and Tata Nano was that the former started with empathy while the latter with sympathy. A genuine sense of empathy allows deep insights to trigger new ideas and helps create 'Blue Oceans'—uncontested marketplaces based on radically new value propositions. So, never settle for symptoms, get to the root causes and seek fresh insights.

It is about 'what less' and not 'what else'

If you study the Embrace baby warmer on its functioning or aesthetics, you will realize that it is nothing like a traditional baby incubator. And yet it manages to serve the very core function of keeping the baby warm and that too with minimal training required for the operator. That level of breakthrough would not have been possible if not for the clean-slate approach the team adopted and the immersive learning they painstakingly gathered while situating themselves right in the context of the problem. But their core philosophy was minimalism. Instead of asking *what else* can be done with the incubator, they looked at *what less*, and this approach helped get rid of the non-essentials, which were not questioned for all these years. The classic incubators are very much in business, but Embrace addresses a significant niche.

Steve Jobs, practitioner of the Zen philosophy and minimalist to the core, observed that innovation is saying no to a thousand things. He could well have added so many more functions to Apple's original MP3 player, the iPod, but he abstained from doing that, and this led to the creation of a cult. By starting with the subject and not the object, you can truly reduce your thinking to the bare essentials and then build on top, only if needed. Design is not to delete from what already exists, but to add to the basics.

An example would further help convey the nuances. Do you remember the VCR or VCP remotes of the 1980s and '90s? Those bulky gadgets, with no less than forty buttons and then some more hidden beneath a cover within the remote, are good examples of bad design. These were designs where an engineer did not want to leave an inch of silica or plastic to waste, embedding all conceivable functions into the product. It was design by the philosophy of *just in case* (the user wants to get up in the middle of the night and watch a movie from a precisely timed frame).

Compare that with the Amazon Fire TV Stick remote, which does even more with just about the bare essential buttons. That is the approach of 'what less' instead of 'what else'. The 'one-click checkout', pioneered by Amazon, and now a commonly available feature in online transactions, was conceived to reduce the customer's efforts to the minimum and let her focus on the shopping. The idea clicked for its simplicity. The company continues to ride the minimalism wave, avoiding the fatal trap of 'feature creep' or 'category creep'. So, learn to press the delete button often.

Sell the problem before you sell the solution

Let us revisit a familiar office situation. You have a great idea (at least in your head) on which you have worked for weeks, and now it is the time to unveil the prototype to a large audience, including your sponsors. Your exhausted enthusiasm is met with some stony and confused faces and then some questions on the very purpose of the idea. Have you been through this ever? Wait till you do.

If people are not interested in your idea, it is not *their* problem. It is *your* problem. The idea is great in your head and unless you make it sound great in their heads, they have no reason to pay attention. Before you work on solving the problem, it is critical to elevate the problem to an almost existential level so that your stakeholders *pull* the solution from you. Your audience and your customers need to be shown the problem, and then the solution almost becomes a by-the-way statement.

One of the best examples of being able to sell the problem before selling the solution is the cloud storage service provider Dropbox. The 2009 'Dropbox Intro Video' is a brilliant example of how the narrative elevates a seeming non-problem to the level of concern and then proposes a solution—all this in a fun-to-watch manner.[45] In fact, if you remember the commercials from the '80s and '90s, they typically started with a hook like this one: 'Do you feel too exhausted by the end of the day? Are you missing out on what all your life has to offer?' And you exclaim: 'Oh yeah!' What follows is almost inconsequential, for they have already caught your attention and you are yearning for the panacea.

Another case of selling the problem before selling the solution is to be found in the hand-sanitizer market in India. Till a few years back, you would see alcohol-based hand disinfectants at select places, like hospitals, emergency units, high-end restaurants and hotels. Today, it is a household item. How did this happen? The industry sold the problem of periodic outbreaks of avian flu, swine flu and SARS, and then with some creative advertisements and market push, the likes of Reckitt Benckiser and Unilever created this new and highly profitable category.

Most corporate presentations start with a solution and, in even worse cases, with the effort that has gone behind the solution. How do you draw your audience into your solution? You start by elevating the problem. Is there a method to it? Yes. A particularly useful tool comes from McKinsey's Barbara Minto. Minto's time-tested approach of SCQA Model offers a neat way of presenting solutions, in a consultative manner.[46] It starts with laying out the present *Situation*, followed by the *Complication* that warrants your attention, the key *Question* that needs to be addressed and then your genius *Answer*. All this in less than a minute, or in just about a few sentences.

Think with your hands

Design thinking focuses enormously on prototyping and iteration to arrive at the right answers quickly. David Kelley deems design as a verb and not a noun. It necessitates getting your hands dirty, giving shape to concepts and seeing to it that your well-intended ideas finally work. Thinking with hands does not just work for artists (who do it a lot) but also for scientists, and for practically anyone. In fact, we must try to retain the mind of a child in the body of an adult, because unlike adults, who think before acting, children think *by* acting.

On the importance of thinking with hands, Tim Brown notes, 'The shift from physical to abstract and back again is one of the most fundamental processes by which we explore the universe, unlock our imagination, and open our minds to new possibilities.'[47] Yet most people would rather delegate to others this seemingly dirty practice of try-outs while themselves staying comfortably behind the line of action.

This hands-on mentality is very eloquently discussed by David and Tom Kelley when they talk about prototyping in medical tech products, which are usually tricky to visualize.[48] The first set of prototypes, however crude they may look, allows the discussion to proceed at a rapid pace, and with the customers participating in the act, you come remarkably close to the desired result much before you run out of steam. David Kelley notes that 'you only have to prototype the unbelievable part [of the concept]', and that 'you are prototyping to answer a question to yourself'. Tom Kelley calls this 'build to think'. He adds, 'In history, the human brain and human hands co-evolved . . . [and] as you do this tactile expression in terms of the physical prototype, you learn in the process.'[49] That is what thinking with your hands means.

A research involving 120 students, including eighty with design backgrounds, demonstrated the utility of physical prototyping in overcoming design fixation. When asked to design new tools using a construction set, it was seen that students created better functioning designs when they worked with physical materials. Interestingly, the research also showed that groups design better than individuals, but only when physical materials are absent.[50] Does it mean that availability of physical materials to prototype can potentially compensate for a missing team? The findings remain inconclusive, but the importance of working with your hands cannot be overemphasized. Engaging in physical creation is critical for the evolution of ideas.

At the Stanford d.school creative studio called Creative Gym, trainers conduct a short two-hour class aimed at equipping the incoming participants with critical design-thinking skills. In quick succession, they take the class through hands-on exercises on a wide range of skills, including seeing, feeling, communicating, building, connecting, navigating, synthesizing and inspiring. These skills are aimed at heightening intuition levels of the students and making them more aware of their context. Indeed, it might take a lifetime to hone these skills, but an acknowledgement of what it takes to be able to think clearly and towards a creative end is humbling.

Shimon Peres, former president of Israel, identifies the kibbutz way of living in his country as one of the reasons for the scientific and technological temperament of its people. From an early age, the community members engage in farming and other industrious efforts aimed at achieving self-sufficiency, and in the process develop dexterity with tools, ability to improvise, frugality and resourcefulness. In fact, Israel would be one of the rare places where you would find junkyards in day-care facilities, pre-schools and kindergartens to encourage kids to tinker.

Malka Haas, a kindergarten teacher in Israel, observes that playing with junk involves the whole person: muscles and senses, emotion and intellect, individual growth, and social interaction.[51] From a very early age, thinking and doing is tightly coupled in Israelis. This is a reason why Israel is ranked among the most innovative countries and has the highest number of start-ups per capita anywhere in the world.[52]

Visualize your thinking

While design thinking emphasizes on thinking in a structured manner to break away from the structures, it is equally about *doing*. Being hands-on is one means of bridging the knowing–doing gap, which, according to American actor Richard Biggs, is life's greatest gap. And doing not just in the three dimensions but also in the dimension of time: past, present and future. One of the relevant skills that designers bring to the pursuit of creativity is their ability to visualize an idea and make it lifelike for others. It is a skill honed over years of learning and practising, which comes in very handy to solve complex problems.

The ability to visualize a problem and its solutions goes way beyond what words can capture and convey. Drawing mind maps, flow charts, box diagrams, stick figures, free-hand sketches, journey maps, scenarios, storyboards and other means of expressions makes the discussion lively. The ability to think visually brings out the functional characteristics as well as the emotional content of a problem or an idea, and is an immensely powerful way of both learning and exercising empathy. To paraphrase the Oscar-winning filmmaker and graphic designer Saul Bass: Design is thinking made visual.

Leonardo da Vinci was an expert in practising visual thinking. He would endlessly draw sketches, often to exactness, of things around him, and keep bridging the boundaries between art and science. His ability to observe minute details could only be matched by his ability to capture those minute details in his sketches.

In his biography of Leonardo da Vinci, Walter Isaacson tells us that Leonardo recommended to young artists the practice of walking around town, finding people to use as models and recording the most interesting ones in a sketchbook.[53]

The Codex Arundel, a 570-page notebook, dating from between 1480 to 1518, is where some of Da Vinci's most detailed work can be seen, and you would be at a loss to decipher the boundaries of art and science. The book is available in digital format, with annotations, at the British Library, and it shows how the great genius worked.[54]

In modern-day parlance, the creatives are more likely to doodle than to write, let alone type, and organizations are designing their workplaces to encourage that kind of visual expression. I saw this at the new office of Flipkart, where people often write and sketch at their desks, at conference rooms, at cafeterias—pretty much everywhere. There were colourful markers, tables you can write on and erasers all around. In such a setting you are never away from a medium for expressing your ideas, seeking instant feedback and taking the concept forward collaboratively. The same could be seen at companies like Titan, Bosch and Novartis, where this open expression of ideas goes a long way in fostering a climate of innovation and where you are not supposed to be secretive about your creative musings.

An effective design-thinking workshop offers people enough physical space, art-and-craft materials, time and psychological safety, so they can express themselves freely, and this leads to three essential outcomes. Firstly, it liberates the child inside you. It gets you to draw, sketch, doodle and do stuff that you would have most likely abandoned a long time ago. Secondly, it lowers your inhibitions and of those around you, allowing thoughts and questions to flow freely, so that you are not self-critical when addressing a problem. Thirdly, it gets your hands in action, which helps enormously while prototyping and validating ideas. Since our hands and brain co-evolved, it is necessary to use one to be able to effectively use the other. So, do not shy away from putting your thoughts out in the open, for it is the fastest way to validate those and to avoid getting into a rabbit hole of your own make-believe world.

Fail often to succeed sooner

Failure is an integral part of innovation, and design thinking teaches us how to manage failure systematically and systemically. By containing failure, the odds and speed of success can be greatly increased. A useful failure is one which happens early and offers lessons for further course of action. A prototyping mentality pushes you towards a good amount of learning in the shortest possible time and on minimal budget.

Elon Musk, one of the foremost innovators of the present generation, fondly says, 'Failure is an option here. If things are not failing, you are not innovating enough.'[55] The same sentiment is echoed by another legend, Jeff Bezos, who notes, 'If you want to be inventive, you have to be willing to fail.'[56] And yet failure does not come easy to most.

The notion of failing often to succeed sooner hinges on the *minimum viable product* (MVP), which is more of a mindset than an actual, tangible manifestation of an idea. Each iteration brings you closer to the *ideal final result* (a term borrowed from TRIZ), or even helps add new avenues of thinking. Improvisation takes precedence over improvement, and being right the first time gets replaced by being *wrong the first time*. This is certainly easier said than done, for most people find it exceedingly difficult to pull themselves up from the let-downs and give a problem another full-blooded shot. It is critical to continue building on failures, or, as the saying goes at IDEO, 'You could stumble, as long as you fall forward.'[57]

Thomas Edison was a master of improvisation and of failing faster and more often than most. The Wizard of Menlo Park, as he was known as, had, at one point in time, the largest industrial laboratory anywhere in the world, and he was thick into experimentation, improvisation and, unmistakably, imitation. He surrounded himself with gifted tinkerers, improvisers and experimenters, who would give shape to his ideas and build prototypes endlessly till the concepts would see the light of day. The years of tinkering made Edison reflect, 'Many of life's failures are people who did not realize how close they were to success when they gave up.' In a way, design thinking is more about *design tinkering*.

These were some of the useful mindsets required to understand and adopt design thinking in personal and professional contexts alike. In the next chapter, we delve into the first stage of the design-thinking process: inspire.

4

Inspire

'Forty years ago, I started Biocon with the vision of creating a business that would leverage science for the benefit of society. With just two employees, Biocon started making industrial enzymes in a 3,000 square feet shed in Bengaluru . . . In the next 40 years, we balanced scientific risks, capability risks, regulatory risks, financial risks and business risks to emerge as India's premier biopharmaceutical enterprise.'

—Kiran Mazumdar-Shaw[1]

The German philosopher Friedrich Wilhelm Nietzsche famously reminded us, 'He who has a *why* to live for can bear almost any how [emphasis mine].' The fate of a design-thinking workshop depends on how well a leader has set the *why* for a team. The why can range from learning the methods of design thinking all the way to solving a thorny problem or fostering a culture of innovation. As David Packard, co-founder of Hewlett-Packard, says, '. . . [P]eople work to make a contribution and they do this best when they have a real objective when they know what they are trying to achieve and are able to use their own capabilities to the greatest extent.'[2] To get the most out of design thinking, start by setting clear, ambitious objectives. In the absence of a well-laid-out purpose, the intervention loses its value.

On the basis of my experience of conducting design-thinking and problem-solving workshops over the years, I have witnessed three categories of organizations: the *curious*, the *adopters* and the *transformers*. Let me explain each in detail. I would encourage you to identify the state of your team or organization according to how well the purpose of adopting design thinking has been laid out there.

The *curious* category comprises companies that want to *learn* about design thinking, or about ways of creative problem-solving. The leaders there have heard or read about this concept and would like to know more. The driving factor is curiosity or the urge to belong to the tribe. Such sessions rarely move beyond a checklist for the learning and development departments, or for business sponsors. My endeavour remains to help such teams see the big picture and to connect the workshop with an ulterior motive, such as new product development, or process improvement, or getting through a tough client engagement. I do my best and I seldom hear from them again.

The *adopters* include the firms that have a clear mandate to *apply* design thinking, to solve some pressing problems or to create new opportunities. Most of these inquiries get triggered by the business, and often the learning and development leaders, or business leaders, directly reach out to discuss further. Such engagements do generate serious commitment on both the sides and go well down the productivity lane. The business sponsors are keen to know how the participants are applying the practices and whether the sessions have helped further the understanding of creativity in the workplace.

Among the more memorable engagements I have had involved a workshop I conducted for Biocon, where we attempted to invigorate their 'Branded Formulations' business with patient-centric ways of thinking and behaving. Likewise, at a workshop I conducted for Tanishq, the leadership team at the factory aimed at instilling creative thinking at the grassroots level and bringing about cost savings and process improvements. And at a workshop for Honeywell, the ask was to help the team by means of structured problem exploration and scoping. In most such engagements, the business leaders are the sponsors, and they are keen to see that the workshop helps raise the bar of performance and learning.

The *transformers* category is where the business leaders and the learning partners are keen to make a lasting impact on their organizations and to use design thinking as means of *cultural revival*. These hands-on workshops invariably lead to extensive mentoring sessions where the participants demonstrate the application of design-thinking concepts to real-world problems and seek continuous guidance. In certain cases, design-thinking projects are tied to the participants' appraisals, which makes them more sincere in their participation and the projects more impactful.

Some of my high-impact projects were those with cross-functional teams at Asian Paints, with category leaders at Flipkart and with product managers at NEC Corporation. The workshops followed long, disciplined mentoring sessions, where the teams demonstrated the application of what they have learnt, and the management took a keen interest in realizing the benefits of their investments. Professionally, nothing beats seeing your teachings translate into action, especially in organizations which are doing well. Personally, however, the sheer pleasure of teaching, regardless of the category of the audience, remains supremely crucial to me.

Set a design-thinking vision

On the basis of a study of design practices, at over 300 publicly listed companies across countries and industries, McKinsey identified four tenets of outperformance.[3] Firstly, the leading adopters of design thinking measure the business impact of design with the same rigour as when they track their revenues and cost. Secondly, they embrace the full customer experience by bringing down internal barriers between physical, digital and service design. Thirdly, the outperformers broad-base design thinking beyond a department or a group of individuals by nurturing cross-functional teams and engaging in interdisciplinary projects. Lastly, they lower the risk of getting to breakthroughs by encouraging users to learn, test and iterate by honing a prototype mentality.

The following note by Brad Smith, former CEO of Intuit, sums up what a design-thinking culture feels like:

> We did not limit our conversations to employees directly involved in developing our products—we tried to get everyone thinking about design. We asked people in the finance department to consider how easy it is to submit a purchase order and whether that process could be streamlined. In HR we talked about the overall design of the job application and interview process—from the time candidates first encounter the employment section of our website right up to the moment someone is hired. Intuit has 8,000 employees, and we want them all thinking about how to improve the design of products and services, even if those offerings are intended for internal support only.[4]

In summary, the leaders in design thinking treat it as more than a feeling, more than a department, more than a product and more than a phase. And knitting all this together is a solid customer insight backed by a design-centric vision crafted by the leadership team.

Create a stretch

A design-thinking workshop is a befitting occasion to do some bold, audacious thinking. It would be such a tragedy if you get your best and brightest for an offsite and still discuss operational issues. You need to look at new products, new customers, new markets, new business models, brand-new solutions for long-standing problems and bring in a fresh perspective. You need to set stretch goals for your design-thinking expedition.

Several stretch goals come from crisis, either natural or created by leaders. Effective leaders know how ambitious goals can catapult their teams into achieving the impossible. A master of setting stretch goals, the former chief of Intel, entrepreneur and author Andy Grove says, 'Bad companies are destroyed by crisis. Good companies survive them. Great companies are improved by them.'[5] When Grove famously noted that *only the paranoid survive,* he urged leaders to be unreasonable, so that employees cannot reach their goals by merely resorting to linear ways of thinking. At Google, they believe that if you do something 1.3X every quarter, you will hit 10X within three years, and that is a true moonshot.[6]

Samsung, the venerable South Korean chaebol, has moved from an imitator to a pioneer in a matter of just three decades. What drives the company? *A perpetual sense of crisis.* The company has knocked down pioneers like Toshiba, Sony, Intel, Nokia and, more recently, Apple—by adopting paradoxical approaches to product and people management. The following statement by Samsung's chairman, Lee Kun-hee, sums up the company's spirit: 'Change everything except your wife and kids.'[7]

Samsung has embraced the design-thinking approach by embedding the principles of empathy, prototyping and failure tolerance right into its business planning. Way back in 1971, the company established a design function, which was focused on product and process design. In the mid-'90s, the company made two major transitions: in 1993, from quantity-focus to quality-focus; and in 1996, from engineering to design. Later, in 2001, Samsung opened its Corporate Design Centre (CDC) in Seoul, aimed at infusing design-thinking philosophy across functions. Each business unit has a set of designers who work closely with the CDC, which in turn reports directly to Samsung's CEO.[8]

Samsung practises design in four horizons: *line-up design* (up to twelve months), *archetype design* (18–24 months), *next-generation design* (2–5 years) and *future design* (5–10 years).[9] The line-up design focuses on developing new products and user interfaces within a business unit. The archetype design requires the CDC to generate new platforms and concepts. The next-generation design aims at helping senior managers across business units to conceive new business investment plans and investigating new enabling technologies. Finally, the future design helps the C-suite of Samsung visualize the distant future and create technology road maps. Samsung remains one of the few companies globally which is among the top ten on the following important lists: of companies with highest patents granted by the United States Patent and Trademark Office (USPTO); of those with the highest R&D spending in absolute terms; and of the world's most innovative companies, as ranked by the Boston Consulting Group. Samsung has perfected a process to convert ideas into cash in a very predictable and reliable manner. And that happens by design.

One of the role models of setting up and delivering on stretch goals is Flipkart, India's first and largest unicorn. Within a decade since its start, Flipkart went from a valuation of just about a million dollars to over $20 billion, and the company has done well in the face of intense competition from Amazon India and players like Reliance and Future Group. The following statement captures the magnitude of Flipkart co-founder Sachin Bansal's strategic stretch: 'We believe India can produce a $100 billion company in the next five years, and we want to be that.'[10]

Such audacious goals push people's imagination, and, consequently, a new type of thinking emerges. Remember, non-linear growth comes from non-linear thinking. Just to cite an example, between 2011 and 2014 Flipkart grew in sales terms by a factor of 100 times, from a humble $10 million to over $1 billion.[11] One of the enablers of this jump was the exclusive tie-up for the sale of Motorola and, later, Xioami phones in India. In February 2014, when Flipkart launched Moto G, over 10,000 units were sold within five minutes, and within twenty minutes of the sale opening, the site crashed! In July that year, the Xiaomi 'flash sale' was another crowd-puller, setting a trend of scarcity-driven brand creation in the Indian mobile market. To get Motorola and Xiaomi to agree to sell exclusively on Flipkart needed courage and persistence, but more vitally, a push towards the outrageous. Who would have thought that the likes of Motorola and Xiaomi would settle for an exclusive deal with an upstart like Flipkart? But it happened, ushering in a new trend in the Indian e-commerce space.

From the e-commerce space to outer space. The Indian Space Research Organization (ISRO) stands out among the rest, refuting those who claim that India is not an original innovator and that Indians settle for improvisation. On 5 November 2013, ISRO launched its Mars Orbiter Mission (MOM), also known as Mangalyaan. With the MOM making a successful entry into the Martian orbit on 24 September 2014, India became number four in the world—after the United States, Russia and the European Space Agency—to have achieved this feat and the only one to have done so in the first attempt. The mission statement for MOM read, 'Exploration of Mars surface features, morphology, mineralogy, and Martian atmosphere by indigenous scientific instrument.' The key operative here is indigenous.

With a shoestring budget, severe paucity of time and limited international support, scientists and engineers at ISRO challenged some of the long-held assumptions of the space age and completed the mission successfully. Almost all of the technology and components adopted for the mission were developed indigenously. On the design front, the designers kept the payload of about five instruments at a meagre 15 kg, which was suitable for the Martian orbit, and opted for compact launch vehicles and space-saving satellites, such as the Microsat. A genius move on their part was that instead of the planned adoption of a Geosynchronous Satellite Launch Vehicle to launch the satellite, the team adopted a less-powerful Polar Satellite Launch Vehicle and placed the spacecraft into a highly elliptical Earth orbit. For about a month, six orbital manoeuvres would gradually increase the distance of the apogee and one final push would inject the spacecraft on to a path that will transfer it to Mars.[12]

MOM is the only Martian artificial satellite capable of capturing the image of full discs of Mars in one view frame as well as images of the far side of the Martian moon Deimos. Designed to be in the orbit for about six months, the Orbiter, by September 2019, had already clocked five years in operation, sending home thousands of pictures, totalling two terabytes.[13] Developed at a cost of about $74 million—it took Hollywood $100 million to make the movie *Gravity*—and at one-tenth the cost of NASA's Maven Orbiter, the MOM is an incredible example of how a genuine stretch, coupled with hard-earned capabilities can lead to groundbreaking innovations.

Leaders must, however, be careful in creating the stretch. They must understand the situations where constrains, especially of time, can lead to higher creativity, and they must know of occasions where constrains can hamper creativity. Harvard's Teresa Amabile, and her co-researchers Constance Noonan Hadley and Steven Kramer, have shared their findings on how stress negatively impacts the creativity of knowledge workers. In a qualitative study comprising 9,000 diary entries by 177 employees working at seven US companies, the researchers discovered that under intense time pressure and unrealistic deadlines, creativity suffers as employees feel overworked, fragmented and burnt out.[14] Interestingly, the employees felt *more* creative under time pressures, which is quite contrary to what their diaries and work output revealed. Why? Time pressure in general lowers creativity because it does not allow the brain to draw new connections between incoming information and data points and hence, fewer new insights or ideas get generated. But, as the researchers offered, when the work is made purposeful and uninterrupted the time pressure acts as a catalyst to creativity. So be careful that you do not stretch your employees to breaking point.

A purposeful stretch is one that leads to genuine creativity. So shares Indra Nooyi, PepsiCo's former chief, 'Every morning you've got to wake up with a healthy fear that the world is changing, and a conviction that, to win, you have to change faster and be more agile than anyone else.'[15] That is what enabled this woman from Chennai to break so many stereotypical expectations as she led PepsiCo to victories across markets.

In the context of inspiring others to move towards design thinking, it all should start with a stretch articulated in the form of a brief.

Get the design brief right

A design brief is the starting point of a productive design-thinking workshop. Tim Brown, of IDEO, qualifies a good brief as, 'A set of mental constraints that gives the project team a framework from which to begin, benchmarks by which they can measure progress, and a set of objectives to be realized.' He further adds, 'A well-constructed brief will allow for serendipity, unpredictability, and the capricious whims of fate, for that is the creative realm from which breakthrough ideas emerge.'[16] A design brief is the most distilled form of desirable results and is typically devoid of the specifics on how exactly the outcome would be achieved.

A brief, as adopted in the advertisement industry, sets the creative-thinking and problem-solving processes into motion. A good session of creative problem-solving starts with a clear brief, also referred to as a *how-might-we* statement. As design thinkers at IDEO would explain, the *how* suggests that an improvement is always possible; the word *might* temporarily lowers the bar for a team to experiment with and indulge in wishful thinking; and *we* establishes ownership of the session at the level of a group, instead of in relation to particular experts. Adopting the right vocabulary and positive framing of a challenge or brief can truly inspire the team to take on the seemingly impossible.

A well-crafted brief is often instrumental in encouraging creativity. Consider, for instance, what Patrick Haggerty, co-founder of Texas Instruments, told Jack Kilby, one of the inventors of the integrated circuit. The idea led to the creation of the world's first handheld calculator. On a plane ride, Haggerty demanded that Kilby build a handheld calculator that 'can do the same tasks as the thousand-dollar clunkers that sit on office desks'. He further specified, 'Make it efficient enough to run on batteries, small enough to put into a shirt pocket, and cheap enough to buy on impulse.'[17] The result was Cal Tech, a prototype calculator that scores of Japanese companies perfected over time.

Here are a few examples of how to formulate a brief: 'To provide the ordinary people with what only the rich can afford' (Big Bazaar); 'Make a watch no thicker than a floppy disk' (Titan Edge); 'Build India's first people's car' (Maruti 800); 'Build India's first indigenous car' (Tata Indica); 'Build a world-class SUV for value-conscious Indians' (XUV500). These cases are discussed in detail in this book.

In 2009, the second edition of the Indian Premier League (IPL) was shifted to South Africa as India was hosting its general election. The story of how Lalit Modi, the former commissioner of IPL, pulled off the cricketing feast in South Africa is remarkably interesting. However, what I am alluding to is another sensation that was born that cricketing season: Vodafone's ZooZoos.

The brief from the Vodafone India team to their ad agency, Ogilvy, was: 'To come up with a new ad for every single day of the tournament.'[18] The tournament would last for over forty days, with two matches being played per day, and the brief was that viewers must not be shown the same ad repeatedly—that there must be fresh content every day. But how do you create so many ads in such a short span of time and that too under a limited budget? The teams from Vodafone, Ogilvy and Nirvana Films, Bangalore, ruled out animation or even the traditional approach of shooting TV commercials. Instead, they came up with the radical idea of featuring in their ads humans wearing white bodysuits, with various expressions pasted on their faces. The rest, as they say, is history. It has been more than a decade since the ads first aired, but ZooZoos are still among the most recognizable characters in Indian advertising.

Another example worth noting concerns the '*Sabse Sasta Din*', or 'Maha Savings Day', campaign launched by Big Bazaar in 2006.

The brief was to 'create a day without a season that truly belongs to us (Big Bazaar) every year'.[19] Typically, the heavy sales months are around festivals or New Year, but what Kishore Biyani, CEO of Future Group (which owns Big Bazaar), wanted was to create a festival-like buying frenzy in an otherwise lull period and capture the market by surprise. The team decided on 26 January as their day and, ever since, has been going after the Republic Day sales.

Initially, the deep discount was for a day, and then it stretched to almost half a week. This set in motion a whole new way of shopping in India, both online and offline. In 2007, the event was made into a three-day shopping extravaganza, where the company saw more than fifty lakh customers visiting the forty-three Big Bazaar stores across India and spending over Rs 15 crore. The Sabse Sasta Din campaign was the harbinger of concepts like Flipkart's Big Billion Days sale and Amazon India's Great Indian Festival. That is how a well-crafted design brief can trigger novel creations.

One of the best examples of getting the brief right and creating an enviable brand around it is India's low-cost airline IndiGo (a part of InterGlobe Aviation). Its more than fifty million annual passengers would no doubt vouch for the company's motto, 'On time, every time.' It is hard to miss out on the constant reminders of 'IndiGo Standard Time', a company shorthand for punctuality, during the flights (it is almost hammered into the customers). It is one company that has once again made time a relevant parameter in the aviation business, in a market where customers are not particularly time-conscious, and, in the bargain, created differentiation for itself. In 2010, IndiGo became the first low-cost Indian carrier to launch a TV commercial, titled 'On time is a wonderful thing', further reinforcing the company's brand promise.[20]

The three guiding principles of the airline are: on time, low fares, and courteous and hassle-free service.[21] Being a late entrant into the highly competitive budget airlines space in India, IndiGo, as of October 2019, had cornered 47.4 per cent of the domestic market, and was the only profitable player in the Indian skies. The company ran over 1,400 daily flights to sixty domestic and twenty-three international destinations, with its young fleet of 248 aircrafts.[22] Operating for ten consecutive years in an industry notorious for its wafer-thin margins is indeed commendable. This requires discipline, as epitomized by the likes of Southwest Airlines and JetBlue. IndiGo's ability to buy Airbus aircrafts in bulk, expand on international destinations and go big on religious tourism in India has further helped in increasing its profitability.

A whole host of ideas, many coming from the trenches of operations, enable the company to achieve remarkable turnaround times for its fleet. Take, for instance, the passenger ramps that the airline introduced a few years back—these have helped cut down the effort and time taken for passengers to board and disembark. The airline was also the first to introduce the practice of getting passengers to dispose of the trash and other waste items with the assistance of the crew, thus cutting down on the efforts required to clean an aircraft and, consequently, minimizing the turnaround time. In most cases, the turnaround time has been cut to as low as twenty minutes, which means that flights can be in the sky for longer durations.

To measure and improve its on-time performance, the company deploys a proprietary Aircraft Communications Addressing and Reporting System (ACARS).[23] The system enables automated communication between the aircraft and ground station. Whenever a flight takes off or lands, the time is recorded in the software in an automated and tamper-proof manner. This enables accurate reporting of flight performance in real time, without any human intervention.

As for convenience, IndiGo's online check-in system is one of the most hassle-free and intuitive anywhere in the world. It has minimal steps and least clutter; the printout of the boarding pass snugly fits into your wallet. IndiGo was the first to introduce check-in kiosks at leading airports, significantly lowering the load on its ground staff and enhancing passenger convenience. The ground staff uses a hand-held device to scan the barcode on passengers' boarding passes, instead of adopting the prevalent approach of tearing the counter leafs and then counting them later. All these steps allow the company to live up to its unofficial moto, 'On time, every time.'

For several such innovative and customer-centric practices, IndiGo was included in *Fast Company* magazine's annual 'World's Most Innovative Companies' list.[24] The citation for IndiGo read, 'For making it feel good to fly cheap.' You may wonder why other airlines in India have not adopted some of the practices IndiGo has—like a ramp for passengers or handheld scanning of boarding passes. It could have a lot to do with the brief, or the lack of it.

Adopt the power of metaphors

Often, good ideas are anchored around compelling metaphors. As Aristotle observed, 'Ordinary words convey only what we know already; it is from metaphor that we can best get hold of something fresh.' The great thinker goes on to claim, 'To be a master of metaphor is the greatest thing by far. It is a sign of genius.' Effective leaders have the ability to coin metaphors and analogies and can unlock the creative potential of their teams. Consider, for instance, the objective Google co-founders Larry Page and Sergey Brin wrote in 2008 to capture the imagination of their engineering teams: 'We should make the web as fast as flipping through a magazine.'[25] The statement epitomized the need for speed in the Internet era and gave an equivalent from everyday life that almost anybody could relate to.

Japanese business leaders have used the power of metaphors and analogies better than most others. For instance, engineers at Honda adopted the metaphors 'man-maximum, machine-minimum' and 'tall boy' to conceptualize Honda City, a car which is short in length but makes up for it in its more-than-average height and is perfectly suited for dense city traffic. The team at Canon drew inspiration from the ease of handling a beer can to design its mini-copier with an aluminium copier drum, radically bringing the cost and size down.

The founders of Sony, Akio Morita and Masaru Ibuka, wanted a 'music player to fit into a shirt pocket' (Walkman), and a video cassette the 'size of a paperback book which could hold an hour of color program' (Betamax)—both unthinkable given the technology and skills at that time. But romanticizing with ideas and possibilities is how the Japanese leaders pushed their troops to innovate.

On how the Japanese strategically adopt metaphors for conceptualizing new product development, Ikujiro Nonaka of the Hitotsubashi University notes, '[Metaphor] is a way for individuals grounded in different contexts and with different experiences to understand something intuitively through the use of imagination and symbols without the need for analysis or generalization. Through metaphors, people put together what they know in new ways and begin to express what they know but cannot yet say.'[26]

Back in India, one successful new product that came out of an intense market research and the adoption of the powerful metaphor 'cheetah', is the Mahindra XUV500. Against the backdrop of Mahindra's hugely successful Scorpio, in 2006, the leaders at the company mooted an idea of 'making a world-class SUV for the value-conscious Indians'. Instead of looking at the customers of today, the team sought the desires of the customers of the future. On the importance of going 'future-back', Anand Mahindra, chairman of the $20 billion Mahindra Group, shared, 'The development of a car is, in a sense, managing the future. You have to get yourself in a time machine and figure out what young people want . . . I believe the world is going to have to give more leeway to designers. There will have to be flights of fancy. Today, what is considered a flight of fancy, I believe will be the convention tomorrow.[27]

After performing a 100-day needs-and-wants survey of over 1,700 customers from across India, Italy, Spain, South Africa and Australia, the team discovered that 'customers want aggressive style and power'.[28] This translated into a design brief: To build a car that offers aggressive styling, muscular looks and a macho stance.

The team adopted the metaphor of cheetah, the world's fastest animal, to connote speed, agility, aggression and muscle. The car's signature monocoque design was inspired by the cheetah, and so were the elements of its bodylines, the muscular wheel arches, the jaw-like front grills and paw-like door handles. Further, to get them to feel the power of a cheetah at first hand, the design team was sent to Masai Mara, Kenya, where they encountered the beast in the wilderness and learnt how its bearing changes over the course of a day. This led them to envision a car that would transform from day to night: from being one you would take to your office during the day to becoming the beast you would take partying at night.

Almost everything was different about this car project. For starters, the car body and interior were designed entirely indigenously by a young team led by a female designer, Ramkripa Ananthan, who identifies herself as an 'out-of-doors type'. She brought empathy into the design, making the car unisex, even though SUVs are traditionally perceived as machines for men.

Sharing her philosophy on design and how the constraints drove her creativity while giving shape to the cheetah metaphor, Ananthan opined, 'Design is a feeling, it is a raw emotion. The design must show your skill sets of balance, proposition and conviction . . . We are this bunch of emotional whackos in an extremely quality and cost conscious delivery environment of engineering . . . The best thing about the Mahindras is that the management allows you to do what you want to do.'[29]

To bring the concept to fruition, the team had to simultaneously design a high-tech R&D facility, the Mahindra Research Valley, in Chennai; a product development programme for the XUV500; and a world-class manufacturing facility in Chakan, Pune. Pawan Goenka, the car's chief architect, called this a daring step, never attempted before in the Indian automobile space.[30]

The initial prototypes and clay models of the car were shown to a group of teenagers, for they would be the ideal customers by the time the car would hit the market. For two years, over 250 prototypes were driven some 2.35 million kilometres across the terrains of New Zealand, Australia, South Korea, Dubai (to check the effectiveness of the air-conditioning in extremely hot conditions), Sweden (for extremely cold conditions), China, South Africa, the US and India.

In September 2011, the XUV500 was launched at a jaw-dropping price of Rs 10 lakh (ex-showroom Delhi). Mahindra also launched a first-in-the-industry loyalty programme, Purple Club, where a car-owner is assigned an exclusive relationship manager. The programme also offers Chakan factory visits and invites for Torque Day, a once-in-a-lifetime experience of driving an XUV500 at the Buddh International Circuit in Greater Noida. A design team's job doesn't end with a well-designed and cleverly-priced product; it goes beyond—to the experience of owning that product.

While the XUV500 bagged several awards and clocked good sales figures, its story is truly of design thinking. The team conducted multi-country, multi-year, deep-dive market research, identified its priorities, went about non-conventional concepts, did rapid prototyping, took the prototypes through rigorous tests and put a well-thought-out price tag to the car. Metaphors, if chosen wisely, can do wonders for employees and customers alike, as demonstrated by the Mahinda XUV500 story.

Widen the aperture

For genuine ideas to flow freely, it is important to broaden the aperture for yourself and your team. It would be naive to enter a design-thinking session with a limited worldview and expect a eureka moment to happen. Having set a stretch goal, you need to broaden the perspective to let in new insights, ideas, temperaments, disagreements and enable some creative abrasion.

Effective innovators follow several ways of broadening perspectives, both at a personal level as well as for their teams and projects. One remarkable Indian leader who has incessantly broadened his thinking and practice is Kishore Biyani, the founder of Future Group. In Biyani's view, 'We need more anthropologists, ethnographers, social scientists and most importantly, more women to be part of every team within the organization.'[31]

As an industry first, in 2011, Biyani appointed the mythologist Devdutt Pattanaik as Future Group's chief belief officer. Pattanaik, who till then had been pursuing mythology as a hobby, said about his new role, 'Nobody is willing to accept the fact that there is an alternative way of doing business than what is being taught in management schools in America and Europe. At the Future Group we are now asking employees to think of new options and not believe that there is one way of doing business . . . This meant looking at the "customised" needs of every individual, rather than settling for the "standardised".'[32]

How many organizations, globally, have identified such roles? How many leaders deliberately surround themselves with such a diverse set of skills? Very few, for this requires foresight and tolerance.

A unique practice that Anand Mahindra follows to broaden the aperture of his leadership team is the Mahindra Universe Programme. It is an annual on-campus event where Anand Mahindra sends his top 35–40 global managers and their spouses for a week-long immersive learning programme to his alma mater, Harvard Business School. Taking senior leaders to top-notch business schools is a well-known phenomenon. But how about letting them bring along their spouses? This is unheard of, at least in the Indian context. But that is how the chairman envisages bringing empathy at the family level, by helping the spouses appreciate the nuances of managing successful businesses.

On the logic of encouraging spouses to attend the learning programme, Anand Mahindra clarified:

> When M&M takes over, say, a French company, the CEO's wife is going to say, 'Are you sure you want to work for an Indian business group? Are they financially sound, are they quality focused, won't they want Indians to run the company?' . . . There are many preconceived notions about Indians . . . To tackle these apprehensions, we organize an annual weeklong executive-development program at Harvard for M&M's senior executives and their spouses.[33]

The explanation helps us make sense of how empathy drives profitability.

Another approach to broaden the perspective is to bring in global talent to address your problems and nudge your employees to think differently. Infosys, one of India's IT behemoths and a pioneer in several good people practices, has a unique programme of bringing external perspective to problem-solving. Through its global internship programme, InStep, Infosys invites undergraduates, graduates and doctoral students from leading global universities to work on real-life, high-impact projects. The select students from leading business and technology schools work on areas like machine learning and robotic process automation, are mapped to mentors, buddies and internship coordinators, and get to present their projects to senior leaders at the organization. The programme has proven a great differentiator for Infosys in establishing itself as a global brand, bringing in diverse perspectives and getting to infuse the thinking of global youth with Indian values.

In the words of Cawley Andrew Bernard-Thompson, an InStep intern from the ESADE Business School:

> Having the opportunity to work in a developing country gives you significant insights into how people live, what motivates them, what frustrates them. These insights are vital to process and product redesign, and you learn how to identify opportunities, mitigate risks, and generally expand operations beyond your conventional perspective. Understanding the how and why of a culture, the basic psychology and motivation behind common processes is an invaluable experience for the future where you have to work in cross-cultural teams.[34]

Since its start in 1999, the year-round training programme has seen the participation of over 2,000 students from across 200 global universities, resulting in sixty-three high-impact cases.[35] The programme offers a win-win for both Infosys and students, who can widen the aperture and develop empathy. Opening up to external talent is a humble way of constantly reminding oneself that you cannot make the best and the brightest work for you; you'd better learn to work with them, in their native context.

Bring on diversity

There is a saying at IDEO: 'All of us are smarter than any of us.' Emerging straight from the imperative of divergent thinking is the necessity for embracing diversity, especially while solving complex, multifaceted problems. Unlike productivity, where variance is detested, creativity embraces variance. It is only through variation, both at the input and the process levels, that thorny problems can be solved elegantly. For this very reason IDEO regularly hires design researchers with social science backgrounds and advanced degrees in fields like cognitive psychology, anthropology and linguistics, to generate nuggets of insights from observations and customer interviews.

Diversity, both at the level of teams and of work environment, has proven to nurture creativity. The most visible form of diversity is gender, but successful firms have gone the distance in nurturing educational, generational, ethnic, regional, religious, PWD (persons with disabilities) and LGBTQ (lesbian, gay, bisexual, transgender and queer) diversity. It is vital to bring in diversity in a design-thinking workshop, and this would be difficult to do if the organization at large is not diverse enough or is not tolerant to divergent viewpoints.

According to the economist Sylvia Hewlett, and her co-researchers Melinda Marshall and Laura Sherbin, there are two types of diversities: *inherent* and *acquired*.[36] Traits like gender, ethnicity and sexual orientation fall under the inherent category, whereas acquired diversity include experiences gained by staying at different countries, selling to disparate customer segments and exposing oneself to diverse conditions. On the basis of a survey of 1,800 professionals and an analysis of forty case studies, the researchers identified that firms that exhibit both forms of diversity, inherent and acquired, are 70 per cent likelier to capture a new market and 45 per cent likelier to grow, as compared to their peers. The researchers claim, 'a team with a member who shares a client's ethnicity is 152 per cent likelier than another team to understand that client.' It suggests that diversity increases compassion, a quintessential aspect of design thinking. Only a diverse team can be right for a creative pursuit.

On why getting the right team is the necessary precursor of creativity, Ed Catmull, Pixar's co-founder, said, 'If you give a good idea to a mediocre team, they will screw it up. If you give a mediocre idea to a brilliant team, they will either fix it or throw it away and come up with something better.'[37]

Robert Iger, the chief of Disney who was instrumental in Disney's acquisition of Pixar, shares his insights on how to manage creative talent. In his memoir, *The Ride of a Lifetime*, Iger notes, 'Managing creative processes starts with the understanding that it's not a science—everything is subjective, there is often no right or wrong. The passion it takes to create something is powerful, and most creators are understandably sensitive when their vision or execution is questioned.' Iger concludes, 'Empathy is a prerequisite to the sound management of creativity, and respect is critical.'[38]

Diversity is to be painstakingly cultivated and tolerated. Twitter's co-founder, Biz Stone, is not a programmer. He is a designer but has contributed immensely to the growth of the company. He even drew the company's logo. Stone believes that being different should be perceived as a source of opportunity. As he once said, 'Everyone else at Twitter was a coder or a computer science graduate. I was not, so I had to create my own opportunities to contribute. I was a designer. My job was to bring humanity to the technology. I focused on the product and made suggestions to improve it. I also helped shape our story for the outside world.'[39]

On encouraging diversity, Stanford's Robert Sutton urges leaders to hire people who make them feel uncomfortable, even those with whom they would dislike working. He encourages leaders to on-board talent they do not need, at least not yet. Though hiring diverse talent would often result in conflict, it is crucial to depersonalize such conflicts, by practising what Andy Grove likes to call *constructive confrontation*—debates where personalities and ranks are taken out from the ideas and notions and they are discussed head-on. As Grove notes, 'From our inception on, we at Intel have worked very hard to break down the walls between those who possess knowledge power and those who possess organization power.'[40] Even towards his retirement, Grove had an eight-by-nine-foot cubicle, much like any other employee in the company. How many CEOs do you know of who work out of cubicles?

When Satya Nadella was transforming the culture at Microsoft, he focused on three core enablers: *customer obsession*; *actively seeking diversity and inclusion*; and being '*One Microsoft*'. In Nadella's view, inclusiveness helps people open up to learning about their biases and changing their behaviour, making it possible to tap into the collective power of everyone around. On the diversity imperative, Nadella says: 'We need not just value differences but also actively seek them out, invite them in. And as a result, our ideas will be better, our products will be better, and our customers will be better served.'[41]

Diversity is especially crucial when your industry lives and dies by creativity. Piyush Pandey, the chief creative officer worldwide of Ogilvy, acknowledges the importance of diversity. As he shares, 'Creating communication requires diverse sets of people

to come together, have conversations, debates and arguments –
all towards the greater cause of creating great work . . . There
is a strange, powerful chemistry between people who seem
completely dissimilar; so, do not reject those who you think
have nothing in common with you. Perhaps, you should build a
relationship because there is nothing in common . . .'[42] Some of
the most remarkable work that Ogilvy India has done under the
leadership of Piyush is the result of the diverse teams that he and
his predecessors have nurtured and the diversity they seek at a very
personal level.

However, the importance of diversity should not be limited
to the creative industries. An Indian company that has done
remarkably well in shaping a truly diverse workforce is Lemon
Tree Hotels. Started in 2002 by Patu Keswani, Lemon Tree is
India's largest hotel chain in the mid-priced sector and operates
seventy-seven hotels across forty-five Indian cities. The company
has a conscious policy of inducting persons with disabilities in
its workforce, and it aims to take their numbers to as high as
12 per cent of the overall employee base. The company employs
wheelchair users, hearing- and speech-impaired kitchen stewards,
bellboys and servers in the food-and-beverage department. They
also hire people with Down's syndrome to staff specific functions.

Lemon Tree's hiring, induction and training programmes
are designed in such a way that each able-bodied employee is
taken through a four-hour introductory sign language training to
communicate with his or her non-hearing colleagues. Staff and
managers are given sensitization and etiquette training on how to
work with persons with disabilities, so that overall productivity
could be kept high and customers could be given a superior
experience. This sizable inclusion of persons with disabilities in
the workforce has shown to improve employees' morale, lower
employee turnover and absenteeism, increase their sensitivity

towards customers and add to a positive social image of the organization.

On the impact of diversity, Aradhana Lal, vice-president of sustainability initiatives at Lemon Tree Hotel, says, '[Our] hearing-impaired staff have been more productive than their hearing colleagues, cleaning an average of 19–20 rooms a day, compared with 15–16 by able-bodied staff. In the restaurant, hearing-impaired employees are often far quicker to notice customers who are trying to attract a waiter's attention. They have higher powers of observation than other people.'[43] Attention to detail and a keen sense of observation are two of the most essential skills required for design thinking, and successful companies go the extra mile in attracting specialists, who might be exceptions to the norm.

But all this diversity cannot happen accidentally. A leader must deliberately nurture and protect this diversity, both through policy measures and by setting examples through personal deeds. The respect and tolerance for diversity must be managed carefully, so that variety does not become an impediment to a team's overall performance. On how diversity can be made functional, IDEO's David Kelley offers a few tips: keep your sense of humour, build on the energy of others, minimize hierarchy, value team camaraderie and trust, and defer judgement—at least temporarily.[44]

'Innovation usually emerges when diverse people collaborate to generate a wide-ranging portfolio of ideas, which they then refine and even evolve into new ideas through give-and-take and often-heated debates,' says Harvard's Linda Hall.[45] She and her co-researchers documented the leadership practices at Volkswagen and Google in fostering an innovation culture, offering the insight that effective leaders draw out slices of genius from each individual and apply them to innovations that represent collective genius. Channelizing diversity to effective ends is a critical function of the leader, especially in a multicultural setting.

Acknowledging that today's teams are more diverse, dispersed, digital and dynamic (4-D), Martine Haas, of the Wharton School at the University of Pennsylvania, and Mark Mortensen, of INSEAD, offer four essentials for managing such 4-D teams.[46] It all starts with the leader setting a compelling direction, which is both challenging and consequential. A great team must have a strong structure, with a balance of skills, temperaments, expertise, educational backgrounds and diversity even on the invisible aspects of working. There should be a supportive context, in terms of rewards, information and education system, which is critical in a geographically distributed team. Finally, the team must hone a shared mindset that would lower the dysfunctional abrasion among team members and avoid the disintegration of the team into sub-groups.

I had the privilege of working with a remarkably diverse team during my time at Wipro. Deputed at the CTO Team located at the Madiwala Office (M-3) in Bengaluru, I was part of a handpicked mix comprising expert individual contributors, brought together by our leader, and Wipro's then chief technology officer, I. Vijaya Kumar. The team had my immediate boss, Vikesh, an empathy expert; Rampi, a technology geek; Raghu, a walking encyclopedia; Malay, a born outlier; Hrishi, a people expert; Pravin, a marketing pro; Hema, an open source evangelist; Ashim, a hands-on engineer; Sudipta, an IP expert; and a few others. Since we were located far away from Wipro's corporate nerve centre (the Sarjapur office) and from the delivery engine (the Electronic City office), we had our own freedom to operate, plant new experiments, commit mistakes, learn from those and share insights—all in a lively manner. It was one of my life's finest professional spells, a period that motivated me to pursue a PhD in innovation management.

Here is another personal experience on diversity, this time from my entrepreneurial career. A few years back I was at Bosch, engaging with the senior management at a three-day innovation and strategy workshop. Bosch, being a true-blue German company, expected almost everyone to attend the event in formals. But at the workshop there was a person donning long hair and wearing kurta pajama. He walked in and sat comfortably among the audience. At first, I thought that he must be in the wrong room, if not the wrong company, but soon I got to know the person.

Meet Rajeev Devasthali, the innovation culturist at Robert Bosch. Rajeev is unlike anybody you would come across at Bosch, or elsewhere in corporate India. My first impression of him was of an artist-cum-college professor who lost his way into the corporate world, but soon I realized the sheer variance he brings to the discussion and to the company culture at Bosch.

A Master of Arts in German studies from Pune University, Devasthali is a proficient tabla player, an international music teacher, well versed in several languages, specialist in German language and culture, author of nine curricular German language-learning books, full-spectrum HR professional and coach, passionate educator, theatre enthusiast and an amazingly good listener.

In his fourteen years at Bosch, Devasthali has always worn his trademark kurta pajama, which speaks as much about his *thick skin* as about Bosch's ability to hone variance. It takes courage on the part of the leadership to attract, retain and draw value from people who are remarkably different from each other. Equally, it was brave of Devasthali not to have given up on his own way of life while contributing to the organization. These are truly divergent thinkers and doers, and we need more of them to nudge our thinking.

Are you missing out on diversity accidentally or, worse still, by design? How would you know if you are short of a critical dimension of diversity?

Tom Kelley, in his book *The Ten Faces of Innovation*, identifies ten personas that make a well-functioning innovation group. Classified under the rubrics of *learning, organizing* and *building* personas, such personalities pride themselves on their uniqueness and appreciate the differences others bring to the table for effective problem-solving.[47] It is highly unlikely that a team has all these ten faces, but it is humbling to understand what it takes to solve problems elegantly. Call it diversity by design, and not accident.

The ten personas are presented below:

The learning personas

- The anthropologist: Brings fresh insights from the field and helps reframe the problems.
- The experimenter: Helps validate insights and ideas through quick and dirty prototypes.
- The cross-pollinator: Draws associations between seemingly disconnected domains.

The organizing personas

- The hurdler: Enables problem-solving in a reliable manner by mobilizing resources.
- The collaborator: Fosters internal and external collaborations effortlessly.
- The director: Maintains the overall big picture and the pace of the project.

The building personas

- The experience architect: Devises genuine and remarkable experiences for all.

- The set designer: Designs an energetic, creative and meaningful working environment.
- The storyteller: Narrates stories to build internal morale and external awareness.
- The caregiver: Offers personalized and empathetic care to all involved.

I would like to think of myself as a cross-pollinator and storyteller. How about you? (You can read more about these personas at www.tenfacesofinnovation.com)

In the next chapter, we look at the importance and means of developing empathy and how to define the problems worth solving.

5

Empathize and Define

'Empathy just doesn't mean that you feel for someone. It means that you can get out of your skin. When you empathize with the other person's point of view, you can hear it and integrate it. Once you can do that then you will inevitably be very curious, you will inevitably be a good listener who wants to get more information from others.'

—Anand Mahindra[1]

Empathy is at the core of design thinking and of a human-centric approach to problem-solving. Be appreciative of the fact that you are solving *somebody's* problem and not just *some* problem. Your great idea would have no meaning if it does not resolve your customer's pain, and the customer will not even tell you about how wrong you are before it gets too late. So you need to learn to anticipate before you react, and this will not be possible without a genuine sense of empathy.

A deep sense of empathy can help you to appreciate why people do what they do and how they would act in the future.

You need to almost live the life of a customer, to get *in* her shoes and not *on* her shoes, to make an effort to understand the pain she feels and then think of possible solutions. One needs to go into the real world and observe real people performing their *acts*: to observe what they *do*, and not what they are *supposed to do*. Rarely would people be able to tell you what exactly they do, let alone why they do it oddly.

IDEO's David Kelley and Tom Kelley share how they develop empathy: 'Our first-person experiences help us form personal connections with the people for whom we are innovating. We have washed other people's clothes by hand in their sinks, stayed as guests in housing projects, stood beside surgeons in operating rooms, and calmed agitated passengers in airport security lines – all to build empathy.'[2] An empathetic approach, note the brothers, 'fuels our process by ensuring we never forget we're designing for real people'.

Empathy converts data into insights, and in this world of big data and data sciences, the premium is on how well you interpret the stream of data and the patterns thrown at you in ways meaningful to humans whose problems you endeavour to solve. We must empathize with the customers and not just scrutinize them on the basis of cold statistics. Every individual interaction can offer a valuable insight, which often gets lost at the aggregate level. For instance, a person with a hearing impairment would engage with a computer very differently from one with a hearing and speech disability or one with a visual disability coupled with a low level of English literacy. Such an approach is deeper and more ethnographic than it is quantitative and statistical. The idea is to convert a need into a demand and then into a desire.

Microsoft's CEO, Satya Nadella, identifies himself as someone who is 'excited by ideas but grounded by empathy'. On how a deep sense of empathy translates into customer obsession and innovation, Nadella explains, 'At the core of our business must be the curiosity and desire to meet a customer's unarticulated and unmet needs with great technology. There is no way to do that unless we absorb with deeper insight and empathy what they need.' Nadella further adds, 'When we talk to customers, we need to listen. It's not an idle exercise. It is about being able to predict things that customers will love. That's growth mindset. We learn about our customers and their businesses with a beginner's mind and then bring them solutions that meet their needs.'[3]

A good example of how a deep sense of empathy and customer centricity helped transform Microsoft's culture is the way Azure embraced Linux and other open-source efforts, to the utter surprise of the tech world. Similarly, Microsoft's efforts to strengthen its relations with arch-rivals Apple, Samsung, Google and Amazon speak volumes about how the company has put its customers ahead of its industry structure and past equations.

Empathy is not just a leadership trait but is required by anybody attempting to generate new insights and bring an idea to fruition. Unless empathy is embedded in a company's work culture, a widespread adoption of design thinking would be elusive.

We will now discuss why empathy must be the starting point of problem-solving and why the traditional approaches of getting to the problem often prove inadequate.

The traditional market research is broken

The nineteenth edition of IBM's 'Global C-suite Study' identifies personalization as one of the key CXO priorities. The report reads, 'Leading organizations are modeling a new path to insight; they are design thinkers. They use data to interrogate their environments, create context and reveal what's deeply human about their customers. To achieve the elegant and irresistible design of the customer experience, they don't start with solutions; instead, they seek to ask the next best question.'[4]

When it comes to the limitations of market research in genuinely innovative efforts, Sony's co-founder Akio Morita has an important insight to offer. As the creator of the Walkman, one of the world's first global consumer products, Morita contends, 'I do not believe that any amount of market research could have told us that the Sony Walkman would be successful, not to say a sensational hit that would spawn many imitators. And yet this small item has literally changed the music-listening habits of millions of people all around the world.'[5] The statement has an uncanny resemblance to the one made by Steve Jobs about market research.

Christian Madsbjerg and Mikkel Rasmussen, from the strategy consultancy ReD Associates, note that most people in business associate the human sciences—anthropology, sociology, political science and philosophy—with academia, and for good reason.[6] On how awfully short traditional methods of generating market intelligence are, the consultants note, 'In the rush to reduce consumers to strings of ones and zeros, marketers and strategists are losing sight of the human element. Consumers are people, after all. They're often irrational, and they're sometimes driven by motives that are opaque even to themselves.'

The interviewing techniques, focus group discussions, customer surveys, conjoint analyses, agency researches, online polls, etc., are time-tested ways to confirm your biases and not to challenge them. These methods offer us information, often at second or third hand, which does not spring up new surprises. As the ad guru Piyush Pandey notes, 'Research captures what's on the surface. It does not capture what's inside. It doesn't capture what drives consumers, what motivates them, what captures their imagination, what they want to hear, and so on . . . Research of the real kind destroys presumptions and teaches us things that the tourist or superficial research never can . . . Understanding what people eat, where they live, how they live, what pleases them, displeases them . . . that's research.'[7]

Does the customer deliberately misguide us in terms of what her real problems are and what she needs? Or does it happen unknowingly? According to Malcolm Gladwell, customers make their product choices based on unconscious reasoning, whereas market research insists on finding a *why* for those decisions and actions and would like to reduce the explanation to a beautiful story, which may be an oversimplification of hard facts and nuanced insights. In his book *Blink*, Gladwell notes, 'While people are very willing and very good at volunteering information explaining their actions, those explanations, particularly when it comes to the kinds of spontaneous opinions and decisions that arise out of the unconscious, aren't necessarily correct.' Gladwell further observes, 'We like market research because it provides certainty – a score, a prediction . . . But the truth is that for the most important decisions, there can be no certainty.'[8]

The best marketers and advertisers know the hazards of traditional market research. They relentlessly strive for gaining first-hand insights, by being one with the customers. Instead of outsourcing market research and relying on stale information, they choose to go out in the open, be an anthropologist and get some counter-intuitive insights. They examine the real cause of customer behaviours—the complex interplay between customers' lives and their social, cultural and physical worlds. One does not have to be trained as a social scientist or an ethnographer to do so. It just necessitates embracing diversity and practising empathy, while being curious and non-judgemental on the field. It also takes humility to realize that behaviours are never right or wrong but always meaningful.

India's largest FMCG company, Hindustan Unilever (HUL), offers us some insights on this subject. For a long time now, the company has been practising a 'Rural Stint' programme, where every trainee goes through a 4–6-week apprenticeship at a remote part of India, interacting with consumers, staying with them, selling to the local kirana stores, going to the local markets and seeing the world through the customers' eyes.

On how these compulsory rural stints for trainees help bring about customer centricity in a genuine way, Leena Nair, chief HR officer at HUL, says, '. . . [W]e send people on a rural stint to get a real understanding of rural India which forms a bulk of our consumers; equally they go on an international stint to get exposure to working across cultures and geographies . . . I still remember the best moments in this company when I was a management trainee, living in a village, understanding what it takes to influence and change, even if it is some 500 people in a little village in India with no roads to reach there. These are life transforming experiences as a leader.'[9]

The combination of global exposure and local insights often lead to breakthrough innovations, as demonstrated by HUL's Pureit, the world's largest-selling water purifier brand. The core insight as to whether there was a need for a non-electricity-based, highly affordable and reliable water purifier emerged from the development team's engagements with the villages of India where potable drinking water remains a major concern. Their initial research revealed that the usual practice of boiling water to make it safe from germs is cumbersome, time-consuming and expensive, and that it alters and spoils the taste of water. The alternatives were largely unaffordable, difficult to use and required electricity and pressurized tap water. To add to this, the transportation and storage of water also remain major concerns in most Indian villages. 'To get sustained use from consumers, we had to pull the aspiration trigger,' says Yuri Jain, vice-president of HUL's water team and head of the Pureit project.[10]

To address the opportunity, HUL formed a cross-functional team while tapping into open-source technologies and leveraging external partnerships, including one with the London School of Hygiene & Tropical Medicine. It was an imperative to overcome the limitations of pressurized tap water and the absence of electricity, while creating a purifying technology that meets the standards set by the United States Environmental Protection Agency. Apart from the challenge of achieving extreme affordability, the development team also had to achieve extreme reliability of the product, while killing all bacteria, viruses and parasites in the water and making the device fail-safe, of the kind that dispenses no water if the purification process stops. On product design, HUL had to meet the standards of ergonomics, aesthetics, the taste and look of the water, and the consumer aspirations associated with a consumer durable.

It took the team over 200 prototypes before the aesthetic, affordability, durability, reliability and manufacturability requirements were met.[11] Pureit was soft-launched in 2004 in south India and was made available pan-India in 2008. The product was priced at Rs 1,800, with the recurring cost of Rs 300 for the GermKill battery kit to be replaced after about 1,500 litres.[12] At that economics, a litre of safe drinking water costs just thirty Indian paise. The brand also claims that it saves three cylinders of LPG gas per year if one were to use Pureit instead of boiling the water—another instance of a deep insight on how to make the cost relatable to consumers.

Pureit being a new category by itself, HUL had to create new channels for educating and reaching out to the customers.

The company extensively built direct-to-home channels and developed awareness among doctors through its 'Protecting Lives' programme. The team deployed 10,000 demonstrators as 'water experts', who would educate consumers and give them a direct, one-on-one proof of purity. With scale, HUL pushed the traditional retail channels and leveraged its Project Shakti network of rural women entrepreneurs. Today, the product is available in thirteen countries, has touched over 80 million lives and has provided 106 billion litres of safe drinking water since 2005.[13]

The case of HUL's Pureit shows that in order to get genuine insights, it is vital to challenge the convention. Undue reliance on consultants, market research agencies, the existing opinions of customers or focus group discussions mostly lead to the same old information. Such discussions always start with asking what people want, as if people always know what they want and that they have the right means of communicating their wants, let alone their desires. It is almost impossible to get to the latent needs of the consumers with such passive techniques. As a result, you can only expect a modest, incremental change from this approach, and not something radical.

Create new channels to listen to customers

Now that we understand that conventional means of gathering market intelligence, like excessive reliance on experts, are not good for gaining genuine insights, it is vital to devise new means to listen to your customers. Some of the most novel ideas come from the fringes of the markets, and unless there are mechanisms to listen to such voices, the organization risks becoming insular. That is one reason why some of the most remarkable insights come from extreme users, who would be far out of your standard bell curves of market intelligence. It is important to remember that where you *learn* from need not be the same as where you *earn* from. One of the maxims at IDEO is, *Familiarity breeds honesty.* And it is critical to get yourself familiar with the context as early as possible.

One of the most popular techniques adopted for understanding customers is the focus group, where a bunch of present or prospective customers of a product are brought together to decipher their perceptions and usage patterns. But focus groups are not without their flaws. Google Venture's Jake Knapp notes that focus groups are generally limited by poor group dynamics: shy people not talking, loudmouths talking too much, sales pitches and a group-formed opinion that does not reflect anyone's honest feelings.[14] If you have sat through any such session or have conducted one, you would know the truth in Knapp's observations.

An approach to overcoming group biases is to study an *Unfocus Group.* It is a group comprising different users of the product or service in question, and they bring to the table quite different, sometimes contrasting, viewpoints. Instead of calling in the 'experts', the idea is to invite active, new, old, passive and even disgruntled users who bring in surprising perspectives. These are problem exploration-cum-solution validation exercises, providing an opportunity to lead users and even non-users to co-design the product or experience along with the experts. If no two individuals in a group are similar in any way, it is the ideal composition of an Unfocus Group.

On the virtue of adopting Unfocus Groups in the innovation process, Tom Kelley notes, 'We invite extreme people passionate about the product or services we're trying to develop. Unfocus Groups offer inspiration on innovative design themes and concepts. They provide human grounding for designers and project leaders. They also demonstrate in a physical, tangible way what truly excites and drives people.' As Kelley concludes, Unfocus Groups, 'add another human level to the process of innovation.' [15]

Another approach of taking a deep dive into the customer's milieu is *sense-making*, a concept derived from phenomenology, which is the study of how people experience life. Christian Madsbjerg and Mikkel Rasmussen from ReD Associates state that a sense-making-based anthropological approach to understanding the customer and her context is particularly useful in answering the *big unknowns*.[16] They propose a five-stage approach to get from raw facts to actionable insights, all by adopting nonconventional approaches. First up, think of the customer's problem as a phenomenon, with emotional valence, from the customer's perspective and not from the company's. Next, identify broad themes, go to the field and gather raw data, without any hypotheses or prejudices. This thematic data-gathering involves unbiased observations and posing open-ended questions, as well as adopting videos, diaries, photographs, field notes, customer journals and other design artefacts.

The third step is to draw broad patterns from the qualitative data that you have collected. You get to the root causes and connect those to get to a coherent explanation. Along the way, some of the themes get refined and yet others emerge organically. The fourth stage involves drawing broad insights from the explanations of the phenomena you have observed, describing *why* the customer does what she does. Finally, you create a business-impact case, where your *sense* of the issue takes shape into potential leads. Several companies have started hiring non-conventional profiles to get into the lives of the people they serve.

Samsung employs scores of designers, engineers, marketers, ethnographers, musicians and even writers to look for the unmet and unstated needs of their future customers, and to distil key cultural, technological and economic trends.[17] In 1996, the leadership at Samsung ushered in a *design revolution*, vowing to have design competencies in-house, instead of relying on external consultants or design agencies. This initiated a large-scale transition from an efficiency-focused culture to a customer-focused one. Samsung brought in faculty members from well-known arts colleges and had its employees trained for extended periods of time, away from their work milieu.

Another promising way to listen to emerging customers and engage with the larger ecosystem is through start-ups. By virtue of most start-ups working on the interstices of what large companies often miss out on, such engagements can often yield surprising insights.

Satya Nadella nudged his leadership team to become more customer-centric by changing the way they went about their annual retreats. Once a year, Microsoft's top 150 leaders come together for an offsite where they conduct product demos, share product plans and reconnect with each other. Nadella brought two remarkable changes to this age-old leadership retreat. First, he would invite founders of the companies Microsoft had acquired in recent years to bring in a fresh, outside-in perspective. Second, he would schedule customer visits during the retreat. Cross-functional teams comprising senior researchers, engineers as well as sales, marketing, finance, HR and operations executives would set out to visit Microsoft customers, including schools, universities, large enterprises, non-profits, start-ups, hospitals, and small businesses. The leaders get a first-hand understanding of the power of diverse cross-functional teams in solving customers' problems.[18] This was a new channel of understanding customers that Nadella opened, and it has since become a way of life for the leaders at Microsoft.

It is important to learn in the *line of action*. About the imperative of listening to the people on the margins and on the frontlines, Andy Grove reminds us, 'People in the trenches are usually in touch with impending changes early . . . Factoring in the news from the periphery is an important contribution to the process of sorting out signal from noise.'[19]

Take, for instance, the 'Shadow Board' at Mahindra. With the intent of 'hearing the voice of the young', in 2003, Mahindra institutionalized Shadow Boards, comprising a dozen promising managers, all under the age of thirty-five. The platform offers young managers a voice at the highest levels of decision-making.

On the impact of Shadow Boards in bringing new perspectives to the table, Anand Mahindra notes, '[They] provide a fresh source of ideas from the "front line" of the businesses, they foster a feeling of participation in important decision-making, and they provide top management with a periscope into the fresh and young talent in the group.'[20]

One of the direct outcomes of Shadow Boards was the 2010 launch of the Navistar trucks, which emerged from the insight that since many of the company's utility customers are buying commercial vehicles, it would be a good idea to upsell them a better product.[21] Today, Shadow Boards have become an integral part of the innovation management programme at the company and a constant source of fresh ideas and talent.

As for Anand Mahindra himself, he maintains a constant connect with the youth and with the global consumer market trends through Twitter. At 7.5 million followers, he is one of the most-watched business leaders in India, and one should read his tweets to appreciate the witty side of the leader. This allows him to be the customer that his company aims to serve.

Be the customer you wish to serve

Mahatma Gandhi used to say, 'Be the change you wish to see.' In the realm of design thinking, a useful maxim is, 'Be the customer you wish to serve.' The world's very first wildly successful consumer product, the Sony Walkman, epitomizes this maxim. In the words of Sony's co-founder Akio Morita, 'Our plan is to lead the public with new products rather than ask them what kind of products they want. The public does not know what is possible, but we do.' On being the customer that Sony wished to serve, Morita affirms, 'So instead of doing a lot of market research, we refine our thinking on a product and its use and try to create a market for it by educating and communicating with the public.'[22]

When Steve Jobs famously quipped, 'Our job is to figure out what they're going to want before they do . . . People do not know what they want until you show it to them,' many perceived him as arrogant. The general sentiment was, only Jobs can get away with dismissing customers. But if you study Jobs's life and work, you will realize that he was arguably the most discerning consumer of his own products.

Ken Kocienda, who worked with Jobs on the iPhone and iPad projects, offers some perspective on how Jobs was the perfect customer for his innovations: 'Even though he was a high-tech CEO, Steve could put himself in the shoes of customers, people who cared nothing for the ins and outs of the software industry. He never wanted Apple software to overload people, especially when they might already be stretched by the bustle of their everyday lives.'[23]

Kocienda defines empathy as, 'Trying to see the world from other people's perspectives and creating work that fits into their lives and adapts to their needs.' And by this definition, Jobs was a deeply empathetic person (at least towards the customers, if not so much towards his employees, as some may argue). With his empathy and deep sense of design, Jobs transformed no less than seven industries: personal computers, animated movies, music, phones, tablet computing, digital publishing and retail stores.[24]

Before becoming the CEO of PayPal, Daniel Schulman worked with Virgin Mobile. As the CEO of Virgin Mobile, he once spent twenty-four hours on the streets of New York City, without any money or mobile phone or even a place to stay. This was a time when Virgin was supporting a charity for homeless youth and the company decided that the best way to empathize with the homeless was to live like them, at least for a day. Of his experience, Schulman recollects, 'We panhandled, and I was not particularly good at it—it took me six hours to solicit enough money to buy a little food. Most people looked right past me, as if I were invisible. We spent a lot of time trying to find a safe place to sleep—we kept getting kicked out of places, and eventually we ended up in a skateboard park.'

On how this experience shaped his thinking, Schulman reflects, 'I lived like that for only 24 hours, which of course is nothing—and it was during the summer, so the weather was not terrible—but it was enough to give me a large dose of empathy for people who have to live on the street.'[25] How many CEOs do you know of who have slept on the streets to understand their customers better?

I know of one—Siddhartha Lal, CEO of Royal Enfield, who loves to ride in the Himalayas. A mechanical engineer from Cranfield University, Siddhartha (Sid) scripted a remarkable turnaround at Royal Enfield in a matter of years. At the age of twenty-six, Sid was made the CEO of Royal Enfield, which was one of the dozen businesses under Eicher Motors. By focusing on a few core businesses and investing in quality improvement, cost-cutting, capacity enhancement and new product development, Sid gave Enfield a royal leap. Between 2000 and 2017, the stocks of Eicher Motors grew by 64,146 per cent, much backed by the resurgence of Royal Enfield.[26] How did Sid do it? By being the very customer he wishes to serve.

Every bike that the company launches, Sid takes it for a test ride on the most extreme terrain and under the most demanding conditions. As the CEO writes, 'My first long ride in the Himalayas was in 2010 when I was riding with my friends, and we got stuck in a small village for many days due to the flash floods that wrecked the Leh region. While we could not complete the trip, our single biggest insight was that the best motorcycle for the Himalayas is not one that tries to dominate its landscape, but one that is able to go with its flow.'[27] That is a first-hand customer insight that no market research can offer. Royal Enfield's internationally successful Interceptor 650 and Continental GT 650 are a testament to the fact that the company's CEO understands domestic customers as well as global ones—and that is because he is willing to sleep on the roads.

A leader's personality and her educational background and relevant (as well as non-relevant) work experience play a significant role in how much of a customer she can be. Xerxes Desai, former managing director of Titan, was one of the architects of innovation culture at the company. Desai studied history at the Elphinstone College, Mumbai, and majored in philosophy, politics and economics at Oxford University. Before becoming the first chief of Titan, this Tata veteran used to design properties for Taj Hotels. Did his insights on history and philosophy, coupled with his expertise in designing customer experiences, have something to do with the remarkable success of Titan? Yes, it surely did. Desai had developed an intricate understanding of the customers—what appeals to them, functionally, aesthetically and cerebrally—and that is what led him to launch Tanishq, initially against the wish of the leadership team at the Tata Group.

One of the most remarkable examples of the convergence of art and science that Xerxes brought to Titan was the adoption of Mozart's Twenty-fifth Symphony for Titan's signature tune. Aired in the late 1980s, the tune remains popular even today and is recognized by vast swathes of Indians, across age groups and economic strata. Reflecting on the catchiness of this three-decade-old tune, Piyush Pandey comments, 'Customers have changed, the product has changed, the country has changed, but the music has endured.'[28]

Another example of a leader whose passion for his products can only be matched by his insights about the market is Anand Mahindra. He finished his graduation from the Sir J.J. College of Architecture in Mumbai, before leaving for Harvard University to study filmmaking at the Department of Visual and Environmental Studies. After graduating magna cum laude from Harvard, Anand went on to do an MBA from Harvard Business School. An architect, a filmmaker, a businessperson or an automobile aficionado—how would you describe Anand? He is everything and more. And that is what he brought to the designing of the ambitious and wildly successful Mahindra XUV500, a vehicle that he proudly drives himself, in order to never be away from the pains and aspirations of the customers he aims to serve.

One more businessman who epitomizes insight-driven innovations and takes pride in his own passion for understanding customers is Kishore Biyani. The very creation of Big Bazaar emerged from a deep understanding of Indian consumers. Biyani learnt, very early in his entrepreneurial journey, that a middle- or lower-middle-class Indian finds the clean and shiny setting of a modern retail outlet intimidating and concludes, 'This is not for me.' Those who belong to this segment, comprising a good 50 per cent of the population, find comfort in crowds and decide on the basis of collectivism. They need to see a lot of people buying the stuff before they do, and this gem of an insight helped Biyani design the narrow lanes and lower ceilings of the conspicuously crowded Big Bazaars, transforming the shopping environment in India for good.

The idea was to offer the look, feel and touch of the local mandi while providing the quality, range and convenience of supermarket shopping, without any frills. Biyani knew that if the shops were neat and empty, the masses would never turn up. The company ensured that their salespeople don't intimidate the customers by their looks or behaviour. Which B-school or management programme teaches you these things? You need to know the customer and your market like the back of your hand.

On his passion for studying the market and getting to know his rapidly changing customers, Biyani notes: 'Till date, most of my Sundays are spent outside shopping malls watching human behaviour . . . My job is to transform these observations into actionable ideas.'[29]

Ideas like stocking grains in open sacks and putting a weighing scale alongside as well as a *chakki* (flour mill) right at the store, do not come from any market research but only through keen observations and an understanding of culture. Being the very customer and spending time with your existing and would-be customers are sure-fire ways of challenging your long-held assumptions, gaining new insights and avoiding complacency. And while you are at it, do not shy away from putting technology to use to further your reach and augment your understanding of your markets.

Leverage technology to glean actionable insights

Though nothing beats first-hand observations or ethnographic techniques, some of these methods have limitations on larger scales and under time constraints. That is where the adoption of technological tools, such as analytics, machine learning and deep learning are useful, and if deployed in suitable contexts they can throw up insights which might complement human observations. The strides in computing offer more processing power than we can meaningfully use, and it must be leveraged to get insights from raw data. Such information can be highly valuable, if not a game changer. The combination of computer-driven information and human-inspired insight, which addresses the *what* and the *why* respectively, is often referred to as *hybrid insights*. In other words, a combination of mind and matter can pave the way for gaining useful insights.

Real-time experience tracking (RET) is a particularly effective technique for understanding the unmet and unstated needs of the customers. Pioneered by Emma Macdonald and Hugh Wilson of the Cranfield School of Management, RET adopts the power of mobility and analytics to gain an understanding of the rich perceptual and emotional worlds of humans.[30] It uses rapid, SMS-based micro surveys to gauge a customer's emotional and functional involvement with a product or service, at a particular moment. Instead of relying on ethnography or customer diaries, such short and frequent inquiries help capture the frustrations and joys that customers experience while engaging with a brand. With pervasive mobile telephony and affordable data-crunching applications, qualitative observations can well be supplemented with quantitative information. Further, tools such as video ethnography, audio and video journal exercises, and computer interaction analysis can enhance the accuracy and lower the cost of observations in large-scale settings.

Netflix has been particularly adept at using sophisticated technologies to generate actionable market insights. From its early days, the company has prided itself on being a tech start-up in the entertainment business. Its key strategies—the significant move from DVD rentals to a subscription model, building on user reviews and ratings to strengthen its movie-recommendations engine, and investing in creating original content for specific audiences and genres—were all informed by analytics.

Talking of the customer analytics competencies Netflix had in 1998, Marc Randolph, Netflix's co-founder and first CEO, notes, 'Every customer. Every order. Every shipment of a DVD. Our data warehouse knows where every customer lives, how and when they joined, how many times they've rented from us, and how long, on average, they kept their discs. It knows exactly what time someone visited the site, where they came from, and what they did once they got there. It knows which movies they looked at and which ones they chose to put in their cart. It knows whether they completed checkout—and if they didn't, it knows where they gave up. It knows who was visiting us for the first time and who is a repeat customer.'[31]

The tech company gathers data from its over 150 million subscribers, implements rigorous analytics to discover customer behaviour and buying patterns and then recommends movies and TV shows based on viewers' preferences. On the adoption of analytics, Xavier Amatriain, Netflix's former engineering director shares, 'We know what you played, searched for, or rated, as well as the time, date, and device. We even track user interactions such as browsing or scrolling behavior. All that data is fed into several algorithms, each optimized for a different purpose . . . We can use the behavior of similar users to infer your preferences.'[32] As early as 2013, about 75 per cent of viewer activity on Netflix was driven by recommendations that came from the company's fine-grained analysis of user data.

Another case in point is the grocery delivery company Bigbasket, which, in just about half a decade, has established itself as a formidable player in the hypercompetitive, hyper-local market of grocery delivery services. The customer-centricity ethos of the company is backed by the significant investment it has made in customer analytics. Bigbasket's leadership believes that any investment in analytics should yield *Definitive Actionable Insights (DIAs)*—insights that can be readily executed and offer immediate results and possibilities of course-correction.

Bigbasket is built as a retail company powered by technology, and not as a technology company doing retail. This mindset of the founders enabled them to focus on key customers and supply-chain-related matrices, and to use technology to run businesses while never becoming a slave of technology. To appreciate how business drives technology, look at the four elements of the company's culture: a maniacal focus on customers; speed and sense of urgency in everything they do; ownership even if everything is not in your control; and freedom, but with a sense of personal responsibility for doing the right thing.[33] These are not only fresh, simple and meaningful statements but are all knitted together by actionable insights. You cannot be customer-focused without knowing what to do about an agnostic customer; and without the right understanding, speed and control would remain out of reach.

Standing in the customer's shoes (Bigbasket's way of demonstrating customer-centricity) offered them valuable, but difficult to meet, market-related pointers. Through market analysis, the company gained three core insights: 1) Customers need the full basket and not just groceries or fruits or vegetables or poultry items; 2) Only a fill rate of above 99 per cent would create customer delight; and 3) Customers would be disappointed with unscheduled deliveries. Bigbasket understood that most grocery purchases happen at the beginning of the month, though there might be unplanned top-ups a couple of times a month and fruits and vegetables can be bought several times. They also found that just about 10 per cent of the total monthly purchases comprised new items. Equipped with this data and enabled by technology, the company introduced a no-questions-asked return policy from day one, a 10 per cent refund on orders missing the scheduled delivery slot and several sophisticated routing and tracking algorithms, apart from homegrown analytics tools to achieve near 100 per cent fill rates for fruits, vegetables and even frozen products.[34] Machine learning and data analytics help the company ferry its 3,000-plus delivery vans and bikes at 5,000 routes across Indian cities, guided by real-time traffic maps. The company understands that every basic improvement in route optimization results in customer delight.

The holy grail of analytics at Bigbasket is to deliver a superlative customer experience, while driving rapid growth at a manageable cost and being able to address the 'segment of one' in terms of a customer's unique preferences based on the purchase history. The company adopted an open-source analytics tool, heavily customized it and, with several proprietary and constantly updating algorithms, achieved a significant flexibility, lowering the total cost of ownership as the operations scaled. In the words of M.S. Subramanian, the head of analytics at Bigbasket, 'The hypothesis driven problem-solving approach with the focus to deliver definitive, actionable insights has helped Bigbasket use Analytics as a strategic differentiator.'[35] Taking the game up a few notches, Bigbasket adopts IoT (Internet of things) to assess the state of packaging, whether the product is frozen, cold or hot, and maintain different temperatures for individual products across their journey from the warehouse to the customer's doorstep.[36] That is how you tie technology to customer experience.

Bigbasket is an example of how technology can be leveraged to understand customers better, shape products and services quicker, train and retain frontline employees frugally, and deliver a superior customer experience. The often neglected element in the theory of customer-centricity is the idea that other human beings can be central to a company's value chain. The key is to embrace human-centricity and empathy holistically and not just on the frontlines.

Get to the customer's 'jobs to be done'

There is a serious limitation with adopting quantitative market research techniques, which may, at best, show that a customer who is of a certain profile is more likely to purchase online as opposed to somebody else. But this kind of market research does not establish causality, as to *why* the customer does what she does. In the era of big data, we have more information but perhaps few insights, especially when it comes to new product development. Creativity calls for, says Akio Morita, 'something more than the processing of existing information. It requires human thought, spontaneous intuition, and a lot of courage.'[37]

How do you get to the real insights? Harvard's Clayton Christensen, a pioneer in research on innovation who gave us the concept of *disruptive innovation*, proposes that we must start from the customer's *job to be done*. A job to be done is an understanding of what the customer, in each circumstance, wants to accomplish and what she is *hiring* your product or service for. If your offering helps her achieve the desired outcome, and more, she will continue to hire you; and if the offering falls short of her expectations, she will *fire* you. This paradigm shift, from being a company providing goods or services to becoming one hired by a customer as a means to an end, gets us to a more nuanced understanding of the customer.

Clayton Christensen and his co-researchers, Taddy Hall, Karen Dillon and David Duncan, offer a set of principles that can help us understand the *job to be done* concept.[38] Firstly, job is shorthand for what an individual really seeks to accomplish in a given circumstance, in a way that it is always more than a task. Secondly, circumstances are more important than customer characteristics, product attributes, new technologies or trends. Finally, and most importantly, jobs are never simply about function—they have powerful social and emotional dimensions. The researchers suggest, 'A deep understanding of a job allows you to innovate without guessing what trade-offs your customers are willing to make. It is a kind of job spec.'

Take, for instance, the two-wheeler market in India. There are three strategy groups: one, the 100–150 cc bikes, dominated by the likes of Hero Splendor; two, the unisex scooters, such as Honda Activa; and three, the 350-plus cc category, led by Royal Enfield. The value propositions for the three categories are mileage, convenience and machismo, respectively. Which of them is more successful? Difficult to say, for each has identified a unique 'job to be done' for its customer segment. Both on functional and emotional dimensions, the jobs are reasonably well-defined, and the companies have largely been disciplined about addressing those jobs.

Since its launch in 1994, the Hero Splendor (previously Splendor) has been consistently topping the economy-segment market in India. The bike was launched as a follow-up to the phenomenally successful CD 100, the debut product of the Hero Honda joint venture, inked in 1984. Since 2001, the company has been the world's largest maker of two-wheelers (by volume), and has sold over 90 million bikes, most of them Splendors. The job to be done for Splendor was noticeably clear. On the functional dimension: mileage; and on the emotional dimension: styling.

Here is what Hero's one-time partner and now arch-rival Honda has to say about the Splendor's dominance in the rural market. Honda's Noriaki Abe concedes, '. . . [I]n rural areas, Hero is very, very strong. We never give up, but it is very difficult to penetrate in rural areas . . . We are trying to launch many models in the motorcycle field. But in 110 cc segment, we could not find one very strong scooter to compete with Splendor.'[39]

The only vehicle which has managed to challenge the dominance of the Splendor is the Honda Activa. Though a late entrant in India, Honda has taken the pulse of the changing Indian demographics and offered them a compelling product. The job to be done in the case of the Activa—on the functional dimension: convenience; and on the emotional dimension: a hassle-free ride.

The product has managed to break several stereotypes associated with scooters in India, clearing the misconception that scooters are meant only for working women, for low-income group families; and, most importantly, that scooters cannot be stylish. Between 2001 and 2019, Honda sold over 15 million Activas—a record for scooters in the Indian market. [40] You only have to look at the Indian streets to see how scooters are swiftly replacing bikes in rural and urban settings alike.

The third, almost unrivalled two-wheeler category in India, is the 350-plus cc segment, which is dominated by Royal Enfield. Established in 1901, Royal Enfield is the world's oldest motorcycle brand still in production. There is no reason for an old, bulky, fuel-inefficient, high-maintenance bike like the Bullet to still excite the value-for-money-conscious, utilitarian Indian consumers, but the bike has grown from strength to strength. While doing very little in the way of clever market (re)positioning, the company has stuck to its 'vintage value', resulting in a delivery waiting period of well over six months, which is unheard of in the global bike market.[41] The job to be done in the case of Royal Enfield Bullet— on the functional dimension: ruggedness; and on the emotional dimension: machismo.

The sales of Royal Enfield bikes went from a humble 50,000 units annually in 2005 to over 8,00,000 units by 2019, at a time when the market was replete with options, ranging from low-cost entry-level and mid-range bikes to low-cost cars and scooters. That is the virtue of discipline. You painstakingly know your customers' jobs to be done, deliver a compelling performance and stick to the fundamentals.

Do not limit empathy to customers

One of the common misunderstandings about design thinking is that it is all about customer-centricity. Though the customer is a very vital element in business, a narrow focus on the customer may take the attention away from other people involved in the overall experience management, especially the customer-facing employees. Design thinking urges you to adopt a human-centric view and not just focus on the customer or the end user.

As Howard Schultz, the long-time CEO of Starbucks, states, 'Starbucks has three primary constituencies: partners, customers, and shareholders, in that order, which is not to say that investors are third in order of importance. But to achieve long-term value for shareholders, a company must, in my view, first create value for its employees as well its customers.' Starbucks is one of the very few companies globally that offer full healthcare benefits and equity in the form of stock options to every employee, including part-time workers who work for at least twenty hours a week. A proof of the company's employee-centricity.

An organization that has made empathy very much a part of its hiring criteria is Google. Apart from a candidate's cognitive ability, role-related knowledge and leadership experience, the company looks for 'Googleyness'—a unique combination of the following qualities: thrives in ambiguity, values feedback, challenges the status quo, puts the user first, does the right thing and cares about the team. 'Emotional intelligence for us is closely correlated to

Googleyness and how we evaluate Googleyness,' says Lindsey Stewart, a recruitment manager at Google.[42] Google, which selects a mere 0.2 per cent of the total applications it receives annually, insists on getting the right skill sets and mindsets through the door, and only then do the toolsets begin to matter.

The most enduring way to achieve customer-centricity is through employee- and partner-centricity. When you take care of your employees, they take care of your customers, and for generations to come. To appreciate this relationship, you ought to go no further than the 26/11 terrorist attack at the Taj Mahal Palace hotel in Mumbai, where fifteen Taj employees died while helping as many as 1,500 guests to safety.

Here is a first-hand account from Raymond Bikson, CEO of the Taj Group, narrating the bravery of Karambir Singh Kang, the hotel's general manager:

> Karambir found out he'd lost his wife, Neeti, and both their sons, Uday and Samar, 14 and 5. They were trapped by fire in a suite where they were staying, while Karambir worked tirelessly to save other guests . . . His bravery is typical of almost all the hotel's associates on duty that night and of the others who came in when they heard what was happening.[43]

Can you cite a better example of customer-centricity stemming from employee-centricity than this one? I doubt it.

Rohit Deshpande and Anjali Raina, of the Harvard Business School, interviewed scores of hotel staff, management and guests at the Taj hotel to get an understanding of the source of this acute level of customer-centricity.[44]

On the basis of their investigation, the authors identified three people-practices at Taj that stand out and could explain what happened during the 26/11 siege. Firstly, the company primarily hires from tier-2 and tier-3 towns in India, where people still care about human values, such as respect for elders and teachers, humility, discipline and honesty—core values for the company as well as for the hospitality industry. Secondly, at Taj, new joinees are supposed to spend almost eighteen months in training, much more than the twelve-month industry norm. As they often stay on the hotel premises and interact with the guests a lot longer in unsupervised settings, the new employees are encouraged to behave as customers and not as the company's ambassadors. This allows the employees to experience 'moments of truth' at first hand and develop a deep sense of customer-centricity. The employees are expected to create unscripted experiences because they are not only empowered but also empathetic. They are taught to anticipate customer desires by observing the unstated and unarticulated needs of the guests.

Thirdly, the hotel has an innovative rewards, recognition and gratitude system called STARS (Special Thanks and Recognition System), under which employees are rewarded by their immediate supervisors and higher-ups on the basis of compliments they have received from their guests and peers. Many believe that STARS is one of the key drivers of employee- and customer-centricity at the Taj.

Pampering employees is certainly a well-regarded practice, but how about vendor-centricity? What does it take to be empathetic to the scores of, often nameless and faceless, vendors and suppliers with whom an arm's-length transaction seems more than sufficient?

To answer this we must turn to the Indian jewellery industry. While we often get amazed by the glitter or the price tags of jewellery displayed at well-lit showrooms, few of us realize that the places where these ornamental pieces are made are essentially sweatshops. At these manufacturing units, swarms of *karigars*, artisans, are packed into a small room without adequate lighting or ventilation and are exposed to toxic fumes for over sixteen hours a day. These 'cottage' setups take a heavy toll on the workmen who are rendered incapable of any work by the time they turn forty-five. The glamour of the jewellery industry often does not let you face up to this ugly truth.

India's largest jewellery maker, Tanishq, has taken up the charge of improving the lives and skills of the karigars it works with. Since 2001, Tanishq has set up fourteen Karigar Parks, where over 1,400 karigars work. The company provides these workmen with equipment, material, training and, most importantly, a safe working environment. The artisans typically come from places like Jaipur, Kolkata, Hyderabad, Thrissur and Coimbatore, where they have traditionally worked under suboptimal conditions. Tanishq also offers boarding, lodging, recreation and gymnasium facilities to the karigars.[45] To further improve the working conditions of the karigars, and to increase their productivity and strengthen their work ethics, Tanishq initiated a 'Mr Perfect' programme in 2010, with a view to providing a clean and modern workspace for the craftsmen and enhancing their skills.

On how Karigar Parks and the Mr Perfect programme have helped the workmen, C.K. Venkatraman, Titan's managing director, notes, '[The programme] injects respectability, prestige and glamour into the manufacturing of jewellery. From dingy workshops, we have created well-ventilated, clean environments that are comparable with modern offices. This will encourage artisans to happily remain in this profession for generations to come.'[46]

The two examples from Tata Group are testament to the importance of empathy and human-centricity at this 150-year-old enterprise. In the words of R. Gopalakrishnan, executive director of Tata Sons, 'We are hard-nosed business guys who like to earn an extra buck as much as the next guy, because we know that extra buck will go back to wipe away a tear somewhere.'[47]

But the question remains: Is empathy just an art form or could it be engineered? The next section offers some perspectives on cultivating empathy in a systematic manner.

Empathy can be engineered

The objective of empathy is to go from the obvious to the counter-intuitive, from the explicit to the latent, and from data to deep insights. This will not be possible if the design thinker lacks an emotional connect with the problem and with the person facing the problem. A high level of emotional intelligence is the starting point.

According to Daniel Goleman, a leading authority on emotional intelligence, empathy is the ability to understand the emotional makeup of other people and is the skill of treating people according to their emotional reactions.[48]

An earnest sense of emotional intelligence comes with the development of key mental faculties. It starts with cultivating *self-awareness*, which is the act of knowing one's emotions and recognizing a true feeling *as it happens*. Next is *managing emotions*, which is to gain control over one's emotional state. The third level is *motivating oneself*, which enables one to direct emotions towards a desired outcome, such as by delaying gratification. Only when one learns how to recognize, manage and harness feelings can one develop empathy—an ability to understand and influence others people's emotional states. Goleman calls this a fundamental *people skill*.

Being empathetic is deeply linked to being compassionate and mindful. As Goleman puts it, 'Empathy builds on self-awareness; the more open we are to our own emotions, the more skilled we will be in reading feelings . . . The key to intuiting other's feelings is in the ability to read nonverbal channels: tone of voice, gesture, facial expression, and the like.'[49] Building a case for mindfulness,

Goleman further proposes, 'Empathy requires enough calm and receptivity so that the subtle signals of feelings from another person can be received and mimicked by one's own emotions.'[50]

As the spiritual leader Thich Nhat Hanh explains, mindfulness is essentially about 'keeping one's consciousness alive to the present reality.'[51] The opposite of mindfulness, notes this Vietnamese monk, is 'machine thinking'.

Ed Catmull, arguably one of the most creative persons in the movie-making industry, identifies mindfulness as crucial to creativity. Catmull says, 'If you are mindful, you are able to focus on the problem at hand without getting caught up in plans or processes. Mindfulness helps us accept the fleeting and subjective nature of our thoughts, to make peace with what we cannot control. Most important, it allows us to remain open to new ideas and to deal with our problems squarely.'[52]

A master on mindfulness, His Holiness the Dalai Lama identifies compassion as the founding virtue of empathy. He says, 'Compassion is the truth of the human being, and it comes about by developing an altruistic attitude on the individual level . . . In fact, genuine compassion can be experienced only when clinging to the self is eliminated . . . The deliberate practice of compassion can bring about a radical change in an individual's outlook, leading to a greater empathy for others.'[53] At a spiritual level, interdependence between all living beings is the rationale for practising empathy, and the feeling becomes inescapable when the world is hit by a major catastrophe, such as global warming or a pandemic.

Let us now direct our attention to the application of empathy in the realm of business.

In his book *Hit Refresh*, Satya Nadella narrates an incident that took place during his interview at Microsoft, when he was asked the question, 'Imagine you see a baby lying in the street, and the baby is crying. What would you do?' Nadella, who was in his twenties at the time, had said, 'You call 911.' Years later, when he reflects on his callous response, he wonders how apathetic he was and how his life's experiences—especially the birth of his son, Zain, who suffers from cerebral palsy—changed his worldview and made him a highly empathetic person.[54] Nadella does not claim to have had any innate sense of empathy. He says that his life taught him how to be more empathetic, and that his aim is to cultivate a growing sense of empathy for people around him.[55]

The importance of empathy needs to be emphasized, especially because our traditional approaches of understanding the markets and customers have not taken us to new planes. Empathy is a skill, and like any other skill it can be learnt, practised and improved upon. And yet empathy at the workplace has the negative connotations of weakness and indecisiveness.

Some of the practices that could help you develop empathy include listening with intent, observing with purpose and deferring your judgement. These are discussed in detail in Chapter 10, 'How to Be a Design Thinker'. The section below offers a few useful methods for engineering empathy. Let us take the example of a first-time car buyer. Your car seller would like to empathize with you being a first-time customer and devise means to lower your anxiety. The following tools and techniques —design artefacts— could be the appropriate means of doing so.

Problem exploration using mind mapping

Mind mapping is an immensely powerful tool to quickly get to a holistic and collaborative understanding of the problem space. It not only helps capture the problem but also directs you to explore the non-obvious, leading you to new insights about the issue at hand.

Mind mapping is best done in a group and right at the outset of your problem-solving expedition. According to Tony Buzan, who popularized the concept of mind mapping, 'Normal linear note-taking, and writing will put you into a semi-hypnotic trance, while mind mapping will greatly enhance your left and right brain cognitive skills.'[56] Mind mapping allows you to take into account disparate domains, so that you can connect the dots and draw new patterns that would have been invisible had you relied on a linear way of thinking and writing.

For our case of the first-time car buyer, a simple mind map would look something like Figure 8. Certainly, many more details, in terms of the categories and the specifics of each category, could be added to it. But the idea here is to get to a quick start by getting to understand the problem in its entirety before picking on the aspects to focus on.

Figure 8: Problem exploration using mind mapping

Stakeholder map

Since innovation or creative problem-solving involves various stakeholders, it is important to identify the key constituencies and map their motivations and concerns. The exercise not only helps in understanding the problem from different stakeholder perspectives but also assists in implementing the solutions. It is critical to study the intents of various stakeholders and ensure that the objectives of all participants are aligned.

The ethos of human-centricity in design thinking means that you cannot just be looking at the paying customer narrowly and ignore the human ecosystem around the customer, in terms of buyers, users, opinion leaders, influencers, family and friends. Ignoring anyone's interest might jeopardize the project, and it is advisable to understand the intents of various key stakeholders early enough.

On the importance of understanding the stakeholders, Roger Martin, from the University of Toronto, and Tony Golsby-Smith, from Accenture, have this to say: 'Although listening to and empathizing with stakeholders might not seem as rigorous or systematic as analyzing data from a formal survey, it is in fact a tried-and-true method of gleaning insights, familiar to anthropologists, ethnographers, sociologists, psychologists, and other social scientists.'[57]

Figure 9 represents a simple stakeholder map for the first-time customer of a car. Once again, we use the elegant technique of mind mapping as it allows for holistic thinking and representation.

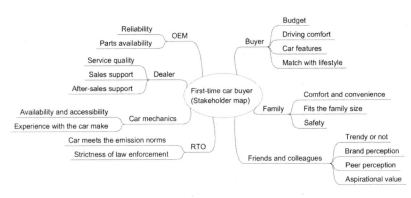

Figure 9: Stakeholder map

Some of the points mentioned in Figures 8 and 9 would overlap, and that is natural. The idea is to look at the same problem from multiple perspectives: focusing first on the problem and then on the people associated with the problem.

Customer journey map

An approach to exploring the problem terrain further is to take a temporal view and look at the journey a customer takes as well as the stages where she faces challenges. The customer journey maps, or day-in-the-life scenarios, are powerful means of visualizing a situation where an existing process or product is not working well and is leading to a suboptimal customer experience.

A good journey map can depict the emotional state of the customer across time and offers possible points of intervention where the customer experience could potentially go bad. It offers a view that is often lost if we rely only on problem exploration or stakeholder maps, because these approaches don't take into account the dimension of time, and time is of great relevance in shaping an experience. Think of how crucial timing is if you have ordered a birthday gift for a loved one on Amazon.

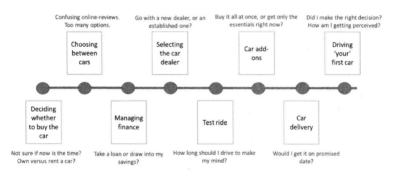

Figure 10: Customer journey map

In the customer-journey map depicted in Figure 10, each major milestone in the purchase journey is identified, along with key customer concerns. To sellers, this map offers insights into the purchasing process and possible avenues to ease customer anxiety.

Empathy map

Experts say that more than 80 per cent of communication is non-verbal, and the same applies to the context in which you ask your customers to share what they need or how frustrated they feel with the existing ways of doing things. It is not just sufficient to capture what the customer *says*, or even what she *does*, but also to decipher what she *feels* and *thinks*. Of course, inferring somebody's feelings and thinking is not easy, as it calls for remarkably high levels of emotional intelligence and an ability to defer your judgement while being good at identifying patterns. Anthropologists and ethnographers are trained to gauge such non-verbal cues that can throw up surprising insights (surprising even to the subject).

One way of making sense of the *whole customer* is through the empathy map. This visual tool helps capture what the customer says, does, feels and thinks about an issue or an existing solution. Figure 11 presents an empathy map in the context of the first-time car buyer.

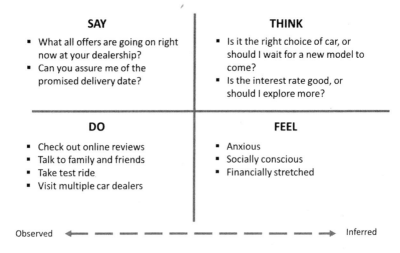

Figure 11: Empathy map

By observing non-verbal or non-visual cues, like thinking and feeling, the seller can come up with complementary service offerings or partner with others to help the customer make a more informed and favourable decision.

There are several other methods—such as Pain/Gain Analysis, Buyer Personas and Scenarios, among others—that can be adopted by sellers to develop a more comprehensive appreciation of customers. A more detailed view is available on the IDEO U website and in the resources section of the Stanford d.school website.

As Jon Kolko, founder of Austin Center for Design, says, 'Those models—primarily diagrams and sketches—supplement and in some cases replace the spreadsheets, specifications, and other documents that have come to define the traditional organizational environment. They add a fluid dimension to the exploration of complexity, allowing for nonlinear thought when tackling nonlinear problems.'[58]

Innovative companies embed these artefacts in their routines, much like how Japanese firms have made quality management a part of their business philosophy.

In the next section, we will explore the means of narrowing down our focus to the most significant insights to work on and problems to address.

Picking the problem worth solving

The hallmark of effective problem-solving is focus. You need to discern the vital few from the trivial many. Germans, arguably some of the best problem-solvers around, have a phrase that fits here: *Weniger aber besser*, which translates to 'less but better'. Design thinking is about focusing on a very few problems which, if solved, would have maximum impact. These problems would stem from a deep dive into the customer's mindset and milieu, and would, along the journey, get validated by the customer. No marks for solving a problem which is not important, however genius your solutions may be. This is where you move from deliberate divergence to intense convergence.

The problem with empathy is that it soon gets overwhelming. Adam Waytz, from the Kellogg School of Management, highlights some of the side effects of too much empathy.[59] Citing empirical studies, Waytz builds a case as to why, in certain health and human services professions, employees often feel cognitively exhausted and demotivated through *compassion fatigue*. He indicates how empathy may be a zero-sum game, where often empathizing with one's inner circle might lead to apathy with others. For example, an employee whose job requires her to listen to customer complaints and pacify disgruntled colleagues might feel exhausted by the time she reaches home, and her immediate family might see a quite different her. A more alarming fallout of empathy is dishonesty, in a way that you might be more willing to lie or cheat if the act involves helping somebody. The resolution, suggests Waytz, is to focus on specific stakeholders and on certain problems that are worth solving.

In an empirical research involving 480 experienced marketing managers, Imperial College's Johannes Hattula, and his co-researchers Christian Schmitz, Martin Schmidt, Sven Reinecke, showed how the more empathetic managers used their personal preferences to predict what customers would want and ignored the market research.[60] The researchers argue that empathy activates experienced managers' own consumer identities and heightens their personal consumption preferences, making them, paradoxically, more insensitive to their customers.

Not all stakeholders are of the same importance. For instance, Amazon must consider the sellers, the logistics partners, the development community, investors and, of course, the buyers, among other stakeholders. Which of them is the *most* important? For Jeff Bezos, it is the buyer. In the case of Google, the key stakeholder is the user, and customer-centricity reflects in the following statement that Larry Page and Sergey Brin made at Google's IPO, 'Serving our end users is at the heart of what we do and remains our number one priority.'[61] They chose user-centricity over returns for employees, investors or partners.

According to Harvard University's Robert Simons, 'Your most important customers are not those that generate the most revenue but those that can unlock the most value in your business.'[62] When Paytm started, their highest priority was to get the small merchants on the platform, because they unlock the real value of mobile payments. Imagine if a merchant refuses to accept Paytm, however much a customer desires to use Paytm or however many cashbacks Paytm is willing to offer. So trying to make incremental improvements on multiple fronts would distract you from making substantive progress in one key dimension that matters the most to your key stakeholder.

So much for *who* to focus on. Now let us look at *what* to focus on.

A conversation with a disgruntled customer, or a field observation, might lead you to a plethora of problems and opportunities that you may find difficult to manage. All problems might look equally compelling and urgent. Picking the vital few from the trivial many is not only important for doing justice to your efforts but to set the correct expectations with your customers. Picking the critical problems or opportunities require discipline and an ability to say *no*.

The three rules useful in prioritizing problems are as follows: 1) not every problem is worth solving; 2) not every problem is solvable; and 3) a problem fully understood is half-solved. Going after a problem where you can make the greatest impact is as useful in design thinking as in life. Let us understand each maxim in detail.

Not every problem is worth solving

The Italian economist Vilfredo Pareto instructed us long ago that 80 per cent results come from 20 per cent efforts and time. Some of the most adept problem-solvers, from the consultants at McKinsey to the residents at hospital emergency units, intuitively resort to the 80/20 principle. They develop effective means to get to the most severe problems and then spend the rest of their time solving the selected problems systematically. In fact, the critical question asked at McKinsey during any engagement is, 'So what?'—which translates to, 'How does this new data point or information help us deliver a significant value addition to our clients? If it does not make the cut, just ignore it.'

This 80/20 rule manifests itself in one of the most used acronyms in the consulting industry: MECE (mutually exclusive and collectively exhaustive). If you cannot break a problem down into three or five mutually exclusive but collectively exhaustive, components, you have not sufficiently thought through the problem. Design thinking calls for a similar level of certainty. When picking the problem worth addressing, you must raise your expectations and pick only the issues that make the maximum impact on the customer. If you pick a problem which, even if solved brilliantly, does not make the customer's life significantly better, your efforts would be futile. Successful design thinkers know the importance of putting more wood behind fewer arrows.

Not every problem is solvable

Equally important is to acknowledge that not every problem is solvable. Even if you think that one problem, if solved, can yield disproportionate benefits, you need to appreciate the limits of your capabilities and resources, so that you can reframe or re-scope your problem. There are some problems which just cannot be solved. But does that mean you cannot do anything about the impact of those problems on your life or on the lives of your customers? Certainly not. With applied creativity, you can lower the adverse impact of a problem which, for the time being, does not look solvable.

Here is an example. I have a friend who drives a Hyundai Santro in the rather unforgiving traffic of Bangalore. If you are a working executive who drives a Santro, and you get promoted at your job, what would be your next step? Most people would tread up to a sedan. But our man preferred not to. Instead, with this extra money, he got himself a chauffeur (for his Santro), bought a Kindle and began reading e-books. He now finishes a book every week, sitting on the rear seat of his car, and cannot be more thankful for the same Bangalore traffic. By the way, he is also generating employment. Did he do anything about the traffic problem? No, he did not, as his car is still on the road. But did he reduce the impact of the problem on his life? Affirmative.

A problem fully understood is half-solved

The many problems that might confuse you at first might be manifestations of the same root cause, and if you don't make an effort to get to the real issues, you would always be lost in the noise of symptoms. One way of picking the vital few from the trivial many is to go back to the drawing board and perform critical thinking. You might realize that the real problem lies deep under, and you would be better off going narrower and deeper. The very process of understanding the problem, preferably along with the customer, can yield more clarity on the real issues and also help generate some preliminary solutions.

To pick the most important problems, you need to forego your own assumptions. The problems you *think* are worth solving don't matter; what's important are the problems your customer *feels*. You will have to abandon your pet projects, your best plans, and do what Stephen King reminds us of in the context of writing, 'Kill your darlings, kill your darlings, even when it breaks your egocentric little scribbler's heart, kill your darlings.'[63]

Now that you're equipped with these three insights—not every problem is worth solving; not every problem is solvable; and a problem fully understood is half-solved—it is time to define the constrains and objectives to go after.

Getting to the legitimate constraints

A good problem definition has some well-defined, legitimate boundaries. The key is to arrive at the non-negotiables early in the process, much like the shopping cart design team at IDEO that identified safety, convenience and affordability as the legitimate constraints of their project.

One of the guiding philosophies of innovation at Apple, especially during the Steve Jobs era, was to make products as intuitive and straightforward as possible. When the team was working on the Safari Internet browser, their objective above all was *speed*. The entire team rallied around speed, and as a result, when the browser was launched in 2003, Steve Jobs famously declared it to be three times faster than Microsoft's Internet Explorer.[64]

Similarly, when the iPhone was being created, the imperative was to get the touchpad intuitive, because both Apple and its customers were taking a leap of faith, and they needed guidance all the way. For Bigbasket, the legitimate constraints are: deliver a fill rate of 99.5 per cent, on-time delivery of 99 per cent and out-of-stock experience of less than 1 per cent; and do this day after day in all the cities where Bigbasket is present.

Here is an example of how legitimate, and not hypothetical, constraints can motivate a team to break new grounds in design and creativity. In 1995, when Tata Motors was mooting the idea of designing and developing an entirely indigenous car, Ratan Tata offered them a stringent guidepost. As the former chairman of Tata Group reflects: 'We started out to design an Indian car from scratch. Ambassador, much as it is maligned, is the ideal size for the traveling Indian public. So, we decided to design a car with the internal volume of an Ambassador, the size of a Maruti Zen, and ease of entering and exiting, particularly for the rear seats. We thought of pricing it close to the Maruti 800, which is a very successful car, and adding the economy of diesel. Finally, we package this into a contemporary design.'[65]

Nearly 98 per cent of the parts used in Tata Indica were made in India, and in the process the company created an ecosystem of component suppliers and ancillary capability providers. When the car was launched with the slogan 'More Car Per Car', it immediately caught people's attention and later went on to create history for Tata Motors. It remains on Indian roads even after two decades. Sadly, the negative publicity received by Tata Nano has dwarfed the pioneering effort by Tata Motors in creating the Indica, and the importance of offering legitimate constraints during the project-definition stage.

A few boundary conditions can yield remarkable levels of creativity, provided the constraints are genuine. Before getting into problem-solving, one still needs to frame the problem with all its conditions and aspirations, so that it can be relayed across teams.

Framing the problem sharply

Framing a problem is an art, and it can be learnt and improved with practice. Consider the following two problem statements: (A) 'How might we lower the employee attrition rate by 5 per cent?'; (B) 'How might we lower the employee attrition rate by 5 per cent, without increasing the cost of operations by more than 2 per cent?' Which of the two problem statements would yield better ideas? Probably, statement B. Why? The second framing has a constraint in it, which makes the problem more real, and, hence, would result in high-yield ideas, as compared to the first framing.

Once again, read the following two problem statements: (A) 'How might we lower the employee attrition rate by 5 per cent, without increasing the cost of operations by more than 2 per cent?'; (B) 'How might we change our incentive system to lower the employee attrition rate by 5 per cent, without increasing the cost of operations by more than 2 per cent?' Which one now? I guess this time it would be statement A. Why? What's the issue with the second problem statement? The issue is that it has an answer embedded within the problem statement—'change our incentive system'. This answer would narrow down the possible ideas, because now the problem solvers would think very much along the lines of incentive system and would possibly miss out on other, more elegant, ways of addressing the issue of employee turnover.

A good selection and framing criteria must be both brief and explicit, so that you do not suffer from either type-1 (failed idea) or type-2 (missed idea) errors.

There are three criteria for a robust problem framing: 1) impact, 2) eqifinality and 3) constraint, as shown in Figure 12.

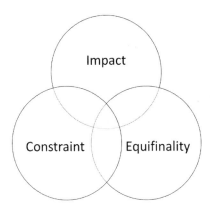

Figure 12: Conditions for a robust problem framing

A good problem is one that excites people and leads to an ultimate impact, not just for the customer but also for the team involved. Framing a problem is a great opportunity to lift the morale of your team, and it must offer a genuine stretch. For instance, which of the two statements inspire more: A) 'How might we eradicate polio from the length and breadth of India?'; or B) 'How might we provide polio vaccines to every healthcare facility in India?' Perhaps statement A is more inspirational, because it talks about the ultimate impact.

Equifinality is a construct borrowed from *systems thinking*, where an end-state could potentially be reached with any number of means. To put it in simpler terms, equifinality allows you to potentially address a problem with a multitude of solutions. One way of ensuring equifinality for a problem statement is to not put the answer or the approach right into the problem statement. For instance, of the two statements, which one would yield more ideas: A) 'How might we eradicate polio from the length and breadth of India?'; or B) 'How might we train a large number of healthcare workers to help eradicate polio from the length and breadth of India?' Here, option A would offer more ideas. The second framing limits possible solutions to the most obvious ones. It is like short-circuiting the entire creativity process.

A good problem statement must have legitimate constraints. These constraints come from deep empathy and discovery of needs, pains and desires, and also from what is technically feasible and makes business sense for the organization. If the brief hasn't got sharper even after all the efforts put into the problem-discovery phase, and with genuine constraints highlighted, then it means that the problem has not been understood well. Finally, which of the two statements would yield better results: A) 'How might we eradicate polio from the length and breadth of India?'; and B) 'How might we eradicate polio from the length and breadth of India without letting it ever relapse again?' This time, it is B.

A good problem statement must be tight enough (by having legitimate constraints), but not too narrowly defined (with equifinality ensured). The solutions are only as good as the problem statement. If adequate attention is paid to defining a problem neatly, the ensuing ideas would be of high quality.

Innovating in the absence of the customer

So far we have discussed the importance of attending to market trends and customer behaviours. But what if there is no apparent customer need? Do you still risk an innovation? In the absence of paying customers and markets, there is hardly any reliable data. But that should not preclude you from having insights about the possibilities. You can still ask some intelligent questions pertaining to what can and cannot happen.

As researchers Roger Martin and Tony Golsby-Smith propose: 'A truly rigorous thinker considers not only what the data suggests but also what within the bounds of possibility could happen. And that requires the exercise of imagination—a vastly different process from analysis.[66] It calls for reframing the questions and challenging the status quo.

It is not only difficult to understand the desires of existing customers, but it could often turn out to be hazardous. Sometimes the current customer base could come in the way of innovating for future customers. Listening too intently to your existing customers can blindside you. Harvard University's Joseph Bower and Clayton Christensen note that if we adopt the rational, analytical investment processes that most well-managed companies have developed, it becomes nearly impossible for us to build a cogent case for diverting resources from known customer needs in established markets to markets and customers that seem insignificant or do not yet exist.[67] Companies usually become successful when they remain too intimate with their well-paying and happy customers, but they have little inkling of what is coming.

Especially when it comes to new, unproven technologies, incumbents typically choose to play safe and stick to their well-proven value networks. A disruptive technology, propose Bower and Christensen, offers a different package of attributes from the one mainstream customers have historically valued, but the performance trajectory of such a technology is so steep that it can soon begin to cater to the mainstream market. As it happened with cloud computing and mobile wallets, both pioneered by non-incumbents, the well-entrenched enterprises would not find it compelling to listen to non-customers unless they are dislodged from their positions. It is because disruptive technologies and the niche markets that they serve seem financially unattractive to established companies.

So what is the antidote? Listen to the internal stakeholders who are working at the cutting edge of technology and to the customers who are the lead users of emerging technologies, seeking new performance attributes. Our classic market research methods would be counterproductive when it comes to identifying the next wave of disruption. You would have to learn to *ignore* your most valuable customers to introduce something disruptive.

But how do you innovate in the absence of a paying customer? How do you adopt a technology in which your current market shows no interest? Do you persist with your idea when the industry leaders have pronounced it impossible and declared you insane?

That is precisely what Titan did with Edge, the world's slimmest watch. The standard watch calibers, or movements, made by Titan in the early 1990s were 2.6 mm to 3.5 mm thick. The R&D and design teams at the company wanted to further reduce the thickness to 1.15 mm—a technical impossibility. It meant reducing their size by more than half without compromising on functionality, robustness, water resistance and, of course, the looks. The Swiss had dismissed and ridiculed the idea of such a watch, deeming it fit only for a museum.

In the absence of customers asking for such a slim watch and with industry leaders declaring Titan insane, Xerxes Desai rallied his team towards the impossible. About the audacious project, code-named 9092, Xerxes had said, 'What's the purpose of creating such a movement? Is it just to create history? We should create a movement and a watch that will be of high quality and reliability, and not just something for a museum. It should also be affordable.'[68] That is legitimate constraints and strategic stretch rolled into one statement.

The team had the herculean task of designing the watch's stepper motor, acquiring thin and long-lasting batteries, manufacturing the case, grounding the sapphire crystal, making the movement work and testing the watch in the harshest conditions. On the design and engineering challenges, Michael Foley, chief designer of the 9092 project, reflects, 'The challenge was to design the watch and then to make sure that there was a manufacturing space to build a viable watch, capable of production. It was an iterative process—you design a product and then you "engineer it out".'[69] The statement summarizes the spirit of design thinking.

In May 2002, after four years and twenty prototypes, Titan launched the Edge, a watch just 3.5 mm thick, with a movement as thin as a credit card and the whole watch slimmer than a floppy disk. The product won the prestigious Red Dot Design Award, first in 2002 and again in 2014, for the Titanium Edge, the lightest watch yet.[70]

The story of Titan Edge offers us invaluable insights on how to design and innovate in the absence of the customer. Firstly, set yourself an aspiration, which is not just about delighting a customer but also about demonstrating your technical and business capabilities. Secondly, put your best people on the project, because the success of the project can mean a lot for your organization. Thirdly, once the project succeeds, look at creating new markets to realize the returns on your investments. Even when there is no apparent customer to start with, design thinking can lead the way.

Let us now understand the means of generating high quality ideas to address the most critical problems.

6

Ideate

'The tendency to welcome new ideas in principle then reject them in practice is a feature, not a bug. Every species has its niche, and every niche has its risk and reward. The human race's niche is the niche of new. Our reward is rapid adaptation: we can change our tools faster than evolution can change our bodies . . . Creating something new may kill us; creating nothing new certainly will.'

—Kevin Ashton[1]

So far, we have understood how to develop deep consumer insights and frame problems that are worth solving. We now delve into the fun stage of design thinking, where the team has the liberty to go wild and think of as many ideas as possible to tackle the problems.

If I say that the first idea that you get for any problem is the most non-creative one, would you agree with me? Perhaps not. But that is what seems to be the case with ideation. Think of the source of your first few ideas. They would mostly spring from past experiences, gut feeling or sheer common sense, and none of these is directly linked to creativity. High-quality ideas come after the first few, except that most people do not persevere that far. Most would rather settle for the first wave of mediocre ideas than wait for the better ones. Staying with the problem is vital, but so is the need to persistently seek more ideas. 'The best ideas rarely come on a mountaintop in a flash of lightening,' says Marc Randolph, co-founder of Netflix. Randolph further notes, '[Ideas] make themselves apparent more slowly, gradually, over weeks and months. And in fact, when you finally have one, you might not realize it for a long time.'[2] So the key to powerful ideas is perseverance.

In a series of experiments involving students, adults and professional comedians, Brian Lucas and Loran Nordgren of Northwestern University showed that both the quantity and quality of ideas went up for those participants who persisted with their problem-solving tasks.[3] The researchers revealed that the disfluent nature of creative thought led some of the participants to underestimate the importance of persistence as they soon became judgemental. If only these subjects had persevered with the task, they would have had more and different kinds of solutions. Across the rest of the group, the ideas became better with time, regardless of the domain knowledge or expertise level of the problem-solvers.

Tanishq is one such story where they went wrong initially but later, through a series of improvisations and ingenious ideas, carved out an enviable position for themselves in the highly fragmented Indian jewellery market. The first Tanishq store opened in July 1996 at Cathedral Road in Chennai. The company retailed diamond and gemstone-studded jewellery in 18 carats, and introduced an international design and shopping experience to India. The store was more of an art gallery, with mood windows and enough open space for customers to move around and browse—a far cry from how jewellery was displayed in most traditional stores across India. And the result was a total disaster.

For one thing, Indian customers were used to buying 22-carat jewellery, and even the most upmarket consumers thought that such a store was not for them. Bhaskar Bhat, Titan's former managing director, admits that introducing 18-carat European-style jewellery in this market was a disaster.

It took the company months of introspection, a spring of fresh ideas and some creative repositioning to revive the fortunes of Tanishq. The first major idea was to have the price tag carry the full details of the gold and gems used in a piece of jewellery, to attack the rampant under-caratage and lack of transparency in the industry. The second breakthrough was the introduction of 'Karatmeter', an X-ray based spectroscope that performs non-destructive testing of gold purity. The device was introduced with a national campaign that had the tagline, 'There's a thief in the family,' aimed at encouraging people to get their jewellery tested for free at Tanishq stores and making them realize that they were being duped by their local jewellers. The campaign was sensational and drew massive traffic at Tanishq stores across the country.

Another idea that led to a boost in the sale of Tanishq jewellery was the 'Impure to Pure' scheme. Launched in 2002, the scheme encouraged customers to exchange their 19-plus-carat jewellery with a 22-carat Tanishq piece after paying only the manufacturing charges. The company was happy to bear the cost of gold. This led to a huge jump in brand popularity, and several stores clocked over Rs 1 crore of sales in a day, owing to the scheme.[4]

Yet another breakthrough for Tanishq was the launch of the Golden Harvest scheme, under which a customer pays equated sums for eleven months, whereafter Tanishq contributes a month's deposit and the customer can buy gold for twelve months' worth of deposits. For several years now the scheme remains one of the most significant means of new customer acquisition for the company.

More recently, the idea that has picked up pace with company's new and existing customers is the Gold Exchange scheme. Under this scheme, a customer comes to exchange gold, Tanishq melts the gold and arrives at a value and deducts 2 per cent as commission. The customer either gets the cash or gets to buy a new piece of jewellery for the money.

To further strengthen its bond of trust with consumers, the company invites hundreds of women customers and their spouses to visit the Tanishq factory in Hosur, Tamil Nadu, where they can see the manufacturing process and touch kilograms of pure gold. That was again a first in the industry.

Tanishq also made massive strides in designing jewellery for period Bollywood movies, such as *Paheli*, *Jodha Akbar* and *Padmaavat*, which further helped boost the company's image and appeal across a wide array of customers. As for addressing niche customer segments, Tanishq created two brands: Mia, dealing in 14-carat gold for the entry segment and primarily focused on working women; and Zoya, selling premium jewellery with precious stones to the ultra-high end of the market.

The case study of Tanishq demonstrates how no one idea is enough for success and why it is critical to pivot from your failed entries as early as possible. You take a hypothesis to the market, learn fast, change your tactics and keep introducing new experiments. Some would fail, such as Tanishq's 18-carat jewellery experiment, and some would succeed wildly, like its Gold Exchange and Golden Harvest schemes. But what should remain constant is your will to experiment.

Ideas are like Lego blocks

One of the biggest misconceptions about creativity is that it takes a brilliant idea to solve a complex problem. While this may be true in pure sciences, in most commercial contexts, or even in day-to-day living, it is never that one silver bullet that does the magic. It is, in fact, a series of seemingly simple ideas that counts. The key is to have enough ideas that solve specific segments of the overall problem, and then the thorny task looks very much tenable. Since creativity comes from combining concepts in an unusual fashion, and since it is exceedingly difficult to trace the origins of ideas, you are better off generating as many ideas as possible with the hope that some of them would click. That is what great scientists and artists do. As the author Walter Isaacson notes, 'The sparks come from ideas rubbing against each other rather than as bolts out of the blue.'[5]

In a way, ideas are like Lego blocks—the more components you have, the greater the potential outcomes you could develop. Think of it: What could you possibly do with a single Lego block? Not much, I reckon, except to think of how many different uses you can put it to, which could be a great way to exhibit your divergent thinking skills or test somebody else's. With ten Lego blocks, you could create a far greater variety of combinations, and that would only grow with 100 Lego blocks. With an even higher number of base elements, you could create newer combinations—some may work and others would not. The same is true with ideas. It is the combination of seemingly simple ideas that makes the remarkable ones. Consider, for instance, how the commonplace paper along with some not-so-strong glue gave us the Post-it Note, the quintessential element of every serious brainstorming session.

The analogy of Lego blocks also conveys the notion of playfulness. Idea generation is an act of *disciplined play*, especially when it involves your hands. (Thinking with your hands is crucial, as we discussed in Chapter 3.) Dr Stuart Brown, a researcher in this area and founder of the National Institute for Play in the United States, explains how play links the hands with the minds. In his

TED Talk, Dr Brown notes, 'The human hand, in manipulation of objects, is the hand in search of a brain; the brain is in search of a hand; and play is the medium by which those two are linked in the best way.'[6]

Pure play is characterized by a lack of purpose—the act is more important than the outcome. The same can be said about creativity. The act of creating is often more important than the ensuing ideas, and that is why a higher quantity of ideas is needed to come up with ideas of superior quality. On the creative benefits of play, Dr Brown proposes, 'Nothing lights up the brain like play. Three-dimensional play fires up the cerebellum, puts a lot of impulses into the frontal lobe, the executive portion, [and] helps contextual memory [to] be developed.'[7] Exploring the basis of play, Dr Brown, along with David Kelley, designed a Stanford d.school course titled 'From Play to Innovation'. Through this course, they attempt to break the work-play differential and bring the elements of play right into the act of problem-solving. One of the greatest thinkers of the past century, Albert Einstein defined creativity as *combinatorial play*. Could there be a better definition of Lego blocks?

Most start-ups challenge the status quo, in part, because of the playfulness of their founders who are able and willing to build, test and move on from hypothesis to hypothesis. Flipkart's example, from the early days of e-commerce in India, shows us how a series of simple ideas can enable a brand to succeed even in the highly competitive e-commerce market.

In 2008, as Flipkart started selling books and CDs, its founders realized that, owing to scant credit-card penetration in India, their sales were relatively flat. Even as of 2010, just about 10 million Indians had a credit card, and fewer still would use one. To overcome this limitation, Flipkart launched its cash-on-delivery (COD) feature in April 2010 and saw an instant jump in orders, especially from tier-2 and tier-3 parts of India. Though companies like Indiaplaza and Rediff had cash-on-delivery options before Flipkart, the scale and popularity of Flipkart's offer turned the tide in its favour.

But with the COD feature came other problems, such as a spike in the number of order returns, leakage in cash collection and dipping customer satisfaction. As a response, in late 2010, Flipkart created its own logistics arm, Ekart. The unit offered much-needed predictability and robustness to the company's inventory-based delivery model. Within months, there was a steep hike in customer satisfaction levels, and this helped Flipkart expand into selling music, movies, games, electronics, mobiles, large appliances, personal-care products and stationery.

On how Ekart came to be the game changer for the company, Flipkart's co-founder Binny Bansal reflects, 'After struggling with third-party couriers, we decided that we should do a pilot of our own . . . Once the (Ekart) pilot was successful, it was clear that this would be a core part of our business. Within a couple of months, we figured out that the NPS [net promoter score] of our own deliveries was 50 per cent higher than that of other courier partners. Then we threw more resources into it. And soon we expanded to 20–30 cities.'[8] This is how an experiment-led concept scaling takes place.

To sweeten the deal for online shoppers further, in mid-2011 Flipkart launched an ultra-flexible '30-Day Replacement Policy' that lowered the adoption barrier for new customers and, resultantly, many more Indians joined the online purchase feast. To supplement this, Flipkart, in partnership with Bajaj Finserv, launched a 'No Cost EMI' scheme in May 2016—a monthly instalment-based payment programme, with no down payment, no processing fee and no interest.[9] As another push towards penetrating the smartphone resale market, the company introduced its 'Buyback Guarantee' scheme for phone replacement in 2017. The trick here was the assurance of a pre-fixed price at which the company would buy back an old phone. This way Flipkart could retain customers for a longer time.

Flipkart is a telling case of how a series of simple ideas that emerged from responding to latent needs of the market can usher new growth opportunities for businesses. Each problem solved led to another, and while solving a series of problems elegantly the company grew from strength to strength. Some of the tactics from Flipkart were eventually adopted by Amazon India to find its footing, especially in the mobile phone segment, one of the top categories in e-commerce.

To grow amid uncertainty you often need to embrace and invite errors. It is important to not fear anomalies or errors, because, as the philosopher and historian Thomas Kuhn reminded us years ago, 'Truth emerges more readily from error than from confusion.'[10] You are better off making errors than freezing with indecisiveness and confusion. Unless you are comfortable with mistakes, radical new insights would elude you, and this requires having low latent inhibitions (more on this later).

Adopt hybrid brainstorming

One of the most widely adopted techniques of ideation is brainstorming. It is a structured way of breaking away from the structure. Alex Osborn, an American marketing executive, introduced the concept of brainstorming in the 1930s. Since then, almost all organizations worldwide have come up with their own approaches to idea generation using brainstorming and have experienced different levels of success. On the power of brainstorming in setting an innovation culture, IDEO's Tom Kelly notes, 'Regular brainstorming is as critical to an organization as regular exercise is to your health.' The rules of brainstorming make the exercise productive, or else it is chaos. Some of the effective brainstorming rules adopted by IDEO are listed below:[11]

1. Sharpen the focus: Start with a problem statement that is broad enough but not fuzzy.
2. Mind the playground rules: Build on the ideas of others; stay focused on the topic; defer judgement; encourage wild ideas; have one conversation at a time; be visual; and go for quantity (and not quality).
3. Number your ideas: It helps keep pace and motivates the team to reach certain milestones.
4. Jump and build: When ideation reaches a plateau, take a small deviation, or go back to a previous idea to infuse new thoughts.
5. Remember to use the space: Share your ideas in a visual medium that everyone can see and contribute towards.
6. Stretch your mental muscles: Do a little warm-up or give participants some pre-work before they turn up for the session.
7. Get physical: Frequently convert ideas into prototypes, preferably in three dimensions.

Most teams would agree to be following such practices, but the truth remains that the popularity of brainstorming is only matched by its ineffectiveness. Most brainstorming sessions are far from reliable in coming up with non-obvious ideas, let alone encourage wide-scale participation. Research also suggests that group brainstorming sessions are not as effective as they are perceived to be, and in numerous cases individuals were observed to have outperformed groups both in terms of the quantity and quality of ideas. These are the four prominent explanations of why group brainstorming sessions are often wasteful: *idea block, evaluation apprehension, groupthink* and *free-riding behaviour*.[12]

Idea block happens when you find it difficult to think of an idea while being compelled to listen to somebody else's. Since effective brainstorming almost pushes you into building on other people's ideas, you tend to block your own, original ones in the process. This problem gets further exacerbated by your fear of being evaluated by others, making you kill all the wild ideas right in your head. A high power-distance, collectivism and a consensus-driven culture, typical of an Indian context, only worsens that 'evaluation apprehension'.

The dual assault of idea block and evaluation apprehension quickly results in groupthink, where the entire group, however diverse, starts to think like one mind, and the discussion soon withers down to the lowest common denominator. When groupthink starts to kick in, individuals have no incentive to speak up; they prefer to go with the flow, and this raises the free-riding or social-loafing tendencies among participants. If a brainstorming session is not managed well, a team of seven is no better than a team of five or three. So what is the solution?

Over the years, I have been practising an approach of ideation which is a blend of solo thinking and thinking in teams, a combination of writing or drawing and speaking, and this has turned out to be more effective in terms of not only idea productivity but also team camaraderie. Participants are first allowed to think individually about a specific problem, write down or sketch out their solutions, preferably anonymously, and then they open up for further discussion and develop their ideas. Now that all the participants have *made their point*, there is a lower tendency of idea block or evaluation apprehension, and since all have written down their ideas individually, the tendencies of groupthink and free-riding are also minimized. This blend of solo and group ideation is what I call *hybrid brainstorming*. What also helps is to put a number target for how many ideas everyone must generate before opening up the discussion, as it brings discipline and reduces free-riding.

Another useful brainstorming practice comes from Pixar. The animation company adopts a technique called *plussing*, where an individual can criticize an idea only by offering a better idea or by adding to the existing idea. Here, the 'yes, but', gets replaced by 'yes, and', and enables the discussion to move forward. It means that participants would be more open to soliciting candid feedback, for now they know that their ideas will not be shot down; some of them would even build a sense of ownership, because now their ideas have the desired attention.

Paul Paulus and Huei-Chuan Yang, of the University of Texas at Arlington, have shown that in an idea-generation session, participants who write their ideas down and build on others people's written ideas outperform groups that rely solely on a non-written exchange of ideas.[13] The cognitive capacities of participants are freed up when they write down their own ideas and read those of the others, since nobody has to *memorize* anyone's ideas anymore and everyone can focus on generating better ideas, faster. The researchers offer that 'brain writing' can potentially lower the chances of idea blocks, evaluation apprehension and social loafing, typically associated with conventional oral brainstorming. An electronic brainstorming session, like IBM's 'Innovation Jam', could further help participants contribute more meaningfully to large-scale ideation exercises.

As Jake Knapp of Google Ventures, who has for years handled design-thinking programmes for Chrome, Google Search, Gmail and other projects, observes, 'The ideas that went on to launch and become successful were *not* generated in the shout-out-loud brainstorms.' Advocating an approach where individuals work on their ideas and sketching those out before soliciting feedback from colleagues, Knapp adds, 'When each person sketches alone, he or she will have time for deep thought. When the whole team works in parallel, they'll generate competing ideas, without the groupthink of a group brainstorming. You might call this method "work alone together".'[14]

Even with the documented and anecdotally known limitations of brainstorming sessions, most organizations continue to rely on this approach. Why? Are organizations immune to research and blind to their own less-than-satisfactory experiences of brainstorming exercises? Or does brainstorming serve other purposes than merely generating ideas?

Robert Sutton and Andrew Hargadon of Stanford University seem to have an explanation for this apparently counter-intuitive practice. They suggest that brainstorming sessions, especially in the context of product design, serve the objectives of: 1) supporting the *organizational memory* for designing solutions; 2) providing skill variety for designers; 3) encouraging an *attitude of wisdom* (acting with knowledge while doubting that one knows); and 4) creating a *status auction* (a competition for status, based on technical skills).[15] Hence brainstorming lives on. But can the practice be improved with some mindfulness? Absolutely, and a hybrid-brainstorming approach could just be the answer.

But another question remains: How big should a brainstorming group be? The unit of creative problem-solving is a small group and not an individual or a big team. Right from the legendary 'skunkworks' at Lockheed Martin to the 'smart creatives' of Google, there are always these *two-pizza teams* that do the magic. At Apple, innovation mostly happens in small groups focused on shared objectives and working in complete secrecy.

When it comes to ideation, the most appropriate team size is two. I have seen that a pair can outperform an individual as well as any group larger than two individuals. A solo ranger gets exhausted very soon and the ideas tend to plateau, whereas a group of three or more people often leads to the issues of idea block, fear of evaluation and free-riding tendencies. The pair, however, may be changed over time, much like speed dating, to keep the vitality intact.

One of the central themes in Walter Isaacson's book *The Innovators* is collaboration, often between people with remarkably different skills and personalities. At the very beginning of the age of computers, it was the duo of Ada Lovelace and Charles Babbage who together gave shape to the mechanical general-purpose computer, the Analytical Engine. The technical competencies of Presper Eckert coupled with the people skills of John Mauchly gave the world the first digital computer, ENIAC. The technological acumen of William Hewlett met with the management discipline of David Packard to bring about Hewlett-Packard, and eventually gave rise to the Silicon Valley. And then, the strategic orientation of Robert Noyce gelled with the technological genius of Gordon Moore to give birth to one of Silicon Valley's most admired companies, Intel.

The 'idea man', Paul Allen found in Bill Gates an ideal collaborator. As Allen concedes, 'Our collaboration had a natural tension, but mostly it worked productively and well.'[16] Almost around the same time, the chemistry between the introvert geek Steve Wozniak and the minimalist marketer Steve Jobs led to the creation of one of the most iconic brands ever, Apple. As Wozniak recollects, 'Every time I'd design something great, Steve would find a way to make money for us.'[17] More recently, it was the pair of Larry Page and Sergey Brin at Stanford University that revolutionized the way we access the web and look for information; the personalities of Page and Brin couldn't be any different from each other, but what drove them both was 'a healthy disregard for the impossible'.[18]

On the power of small teams, John Doerr, one of the earliest investors at Google, reflects, 'As we've seen repeatedly—in Search, in Chrome, in Android—a team composed of a few percent of the company's workforce, acting in concert towards an ambitious common goal, can change an entire mature industry in less than two years.'[19] So the next time you run an ideation session, divide the group into smaller teams to multiply their output.

Explore the intersection of disciplines

Ideas are born when disparate knowledge domains collide, and the more mutually remote such disciplines, the better the quality of resulting ideas, at least in terms of novelty. It is not so much by delving into one domain that you get to a counter-intuitive insight, but by looking broad for inspiration. At such intersections the likelihood of serendipity is highest, and history informs us that some of the most influential scientific discoveries and inventions were born of sheer serendipity—except that serendipity always favours the prepared mind, the mind that intentionally exposes itself to that intersection, waiting for a new connection to form. Protecting your ideas fiercely, remaining steadfast to your discipline and investing excessively in furthering a narrow expertise are sure-fire ways of reducing the odds of hitting upon a genuine insight or coming up with a breakthrough idea.

Creative individuals and innovative organizations almost always engineer interdisciplinary intersections at their office spaces and work environments, in their task-allocation and problem-solving routines, hiring exercises and workflow designs. They deliberately expose themselves to the uncertain, the unpredictable, so that they always return to base with a remarkably different level of knowledge.

Take, for instance, Bell Labs, whose inventions include transistors, solar cells, laser, Unix operating system and

C programming language among several other important enablers of today's digital age. 'Abstract theories intersected with practical problems there, and in the corridors and cafeterias eccentric theorists mingled with hands-on engineers, gnarly mechanics, and businesslike problem-solvers, encouraging the cross-fertilization of theory with engineering,' writes Walter Isaacson. 'In its long corridors in suburban New Jersey, there were theoretical physicists, experimentalists, material scientists, engineers, a few businessmen, and even some telephone-pole climbers with grease under their fingernails.'[20] If Bell Labs was proficient at innovation, it was not out of serendipity but by design.

Frans Johansson, in his book *The Medici Effect*, talks about two types of ideas—*directional* and *intersectional*. Directional ideas emerge from combinations of concepts in a certain domain and evolve incrementally along predictable directions, whereas intersectional ideas spring from the combination of two or more diverse disciplines, generating concepts that lead in different, often unpredictable directions. Intersectional ideas are undoubtedly risky but hold the promise of pushing the frontiers of problem-solving further and frequently offer a much more radical solution. Consider how engineers at British Telecom designed their network operations in the way ants discover the shortest trails; or how the architect Mick Pearce reverse-engineered the termite's way of keeping its habitat cool to design the award-winning Eastgate Centre in Harare, Zimbabwe.[21] These are examples of intersectional ideas.

Few companies have explored and exploited the intersection the way Apple has, especially in the Steve Jobs era. In the words of the late genius: 'The reason that Apple is able to create products like the iPad is because we've always tried to be at the intersection of technology and liberal arts.'[22] About Apple's innovation philosophy, Jobs once famously noted, 'It's in Apple's DNA that technology alone is not enough—that it's technology married with liberal arts, married with the humanities, that yields us the result that makes our heart sing.'[23]

It is the convergence of science, art and craft that allows the innovators to think, feel and experience their creations before their customers do. Good designs adopt both heuristics and algorithms—the former often builds on liberal arts, while the latter stems from the scientific realm. However, most organizations rely extensively on data-backed algorithms, ignoring, to their own peril, the importance of non-measurables and the intuitive. That is why design thinking stresses on developing deep empathy and adopting non-conventional means of engaging with customers.

An organization that literally lives at the intersection of disciplines is Marvel Studios, creator of films like *Avengers*, *Iron Man*, *Captain America* and *Thor* among other hits. The franchise, now owned by Disney, has raked in over $17 billion from its last twenty-two movies—the highest for any franchise ever. What is the recipe? According to Kevin Feige, Marvel Studio's president, the key is 'expanding the definition of what a Marvel Studios movie could be. We try to keep audiences coming back in greater numbers by doing the unexpected and not simply following a pattern or a mold or a formula.'[24]

Spencer Harrison from INSEAD, and Arne Carlsen and Miha Škerlavaj from the BI Norwegian Business School in Oslo, offer an understanding of how Marvel Studios breaks the pattern, systematically and predictably. Based on a deep dive of twenty Marvel Cinematic Universe (MCU) movies released through the end of 2018, and an analysis of more than 300 interviews with producers, directors and writers, and 140 reviews by leading critics, the researchers offer the following principles for Marvel's success: 1) select for 'experienced inexperience'; 2) leverage a stable core; 3) keep challenging the formula; and 4) cultivate customers' curiosity.[25]

Firstly, for its movies, Marvel Studios looks for directors and actors from different and unrelated genres, such as horror, espionage, comedy, etc., and not necessarily for those with experience in superhero films. It allows incoming directors and actors freedom to experiment with a bigger budget and on a grander, tech-intensive canvas. Secondly, MCU balances the novelty of ideas, styles and voices with a constant core that moves from movie to movie and offers predictability; this stable core acts as gravitational pull for new talent. Thirdly, the franchise keeps experimenting with its success formula in terms of dramatic, visual and narrative elements. Their movies can range from ones that appeal just to the youth to ones that are very realistic and offer an intense social commentary. Finally, MCU has a knack for cultivating customer curiosity through its plots, sub-plots and characters. For example, their famous post-credit scenes offer a preview of what is coming next.

Exposing oneself to the intersection and learning from it are both deliberate acts. When asked about the inspiration that led him to start Aravind Eye Hospitals, Dr Venkatappa Govindaswamy (Dr V) did not name an eye hospital or even a healthcare organization. Instead, he responded with, 'McDonald's.' The idea behind his thinking was: if McDonald's can deliver the same product and the same quality of service regardless of who is behind the counter, why can't that level of process standardization be achieved in a cataract surgery? Dr V thought so, and the rest is history. It was the perfect marriage of Dr V's empathy for the plight of the poor and his intimate understanding of efficiency and scale made possible by the application of technology and engineering.

Another fascinating case of the intersection of disciplines is the architecture of IIM Bangalore. The Pritzker Prize-winning architect Balkrishna Doshi shares: 'The architecture of Fatehpur Sikri and the courtyards of the Madurai temples majorly influenced me when designing this campus.'[26] The generation of intersectional ideas require lower *associative barriers*, and this, in turn, calls for lower latent inhibition. We will discuss this aspect in Chapter 10, 'How to Be a Design Thinker'.

Imitate with grace

One of the most overlooked facts about innovation is that all innovations start with imitation. There are no original ideas; there are only original *configurations* of existing ideas. When you create something, you are not an author as much as an *editor*, much along the lines of how the American organizational theorist Karl Weick defines originality: 'Putting old things in new combination and new things in old combination.' And yet, the myth about originality persists, perhaps because we all want to give creativity a special status in an otherwise routine life.

   In defence of imitation, Sony co-founder Akio Morita notes, 'We all learn by imitating, as children, as students, as novices in the world of business. And then we grow up and learn to blend our innate abilities with the rules or principles we have learned.'[27] He further notes, 'The original meaning of the Japanese word *manabu* (to learn) is *manebu* (to imitate).' And guess where Japanese learnt their quality systems from? The 'Zero Defects' programme of NASA. Toyota revolutionized automobile manufacturing by picking up the just-in-time philosophy of an American grocery store, Piggly Wiggly. Howard Schultz, former CEO of Starbucks, discovered coffee's magic on a business trip to Italy. Reflecting on the insights that he had gathered from visiting coffee houses in Milan and elsewhere, Schultz said, 'I am a sponge, always soaking up store design, layout, and salespeople's behaviors, and over the years I've been intrigued by many types of stores that have nothing to do with coffee.'[28] Interestingly, when you are at the top of an industry, you must look elsewhere for inspiration and imitate without inhibitions.

To learn is to imitate; and yet, we often are so dismissive of imitation.

Human beings have always been creative, but only recently have we started giving creativity an elevated status. Kevin Ashton, in his book *How to Fly a Horse*, takes the originality myth of creativity head on. He defines creative thinking as, 'Thinking in general but with a creative result.'[29] Creating something can be explained without resorting to the concept of genius or making great leaps of the imagination. In other words, creating is an ordinary act and creation is its extraordinary outcome.

Citing the example of the Wright brothers, Ashton shows how the duo was led to their first flight through a series of steps and not the proverbial leap. They built on the ideas of several others before them, including the work of Karl Wilhelm Otto Lilienthal, dubbed the 'flying man'. History is replete with cases of how the latecomers, laggards, imitators ended up outperforming the first movers, because they did not hold the assumption that originality was sacrosanct. Yet we like the stories of epiphanies, maybe because, as Netflix co-founder Marc Randolph notes, 'they align with a romantic idea about inspiration and genius'.[30]

Let us talk about a few such examples from India.

It is common knowledge that India's Ola Cabs imitated Uber. But look at what happened next. Since its start in 2010, Ola has moved ahead by adding layers of sophistication on top of imitation. It offers you more options, from hatchbacks, sedans, luxury cars and autos to shared rides, outstation bookings and, more recently, self-drive. Ola introduced the OTP-based customer confirmation system, launched features like OlaMoney, Ola Select, Share Pass,

OlaMoney Postpaid and travel insurance. Within a decade since its launch, the alleged imitator and late entrant differentiated itself so much that today it will not be out of place to say that while Ola has copied Uber, Uber cannot copy Ola anymore.

Many would be mistaken into thinking that the idea of Big Bazaar was down to the genius of Kishore Biyani. That is only partly true. As he writes in his book *It Happened in India*, the concept of Big Bazaar came from the Chennai-based Saravana Stores. The low-margin, high-turnover stores down south offered Kishore and his team a perfect platform to learn from.

On how embracing imitation gave his retail venture a flying start, Biyani says, 'We dissected every aspect of Saravana to develop our own hypermarket model. Saravana disproved many of the accepted norms of modern retail. Unlike the hypermarkets seen abroad, Sarvana showed that a store could operate on multiple floors. Also it proved my belief that hypermarkets in India have to be situated within the city, rather than in the suburbs as it is abroad. It also has to be near a transportation hub because most Indians don't own cars . . . Saravana also confirmed, much against the belief of many sceptics that utensils, jewellery and fashionable garments could be sold under the same roof.' Biyani clarifies, 'People may say we were inspired by the Wal-Marts of the world, but it was at Saravana that Big Bazaar was born.'[31]

The key to getting a lot of useful ideas is to look at the existing good practices of your own and other industries, and then imitate, before you improve.

Break the pattern, systematically

David Ogilvy once said, 'The majority of businessmen are incapable of original thinking because they are unable to escape from the tyranny of reason.'[32] The observation is as acute today as it was a few decades ago. Creativity, especially in a corporate setting, does not come effortlessly.

The link between intelligence and creativity is little understood. It is often assumed that the more intelligent one is, the higher one's creativity; and then there are others who believe that the two are inversely related. Neither of these views is entirely true, as intelligence and creativity are linked through a host of other factors, a critical one being *latent inhibition* (more on this later).

Prominent psychologists Jacob Getzels and Philip Jackson showed that most creative students tend to have lower IQs than the least creative ones.[33] Teachers often do not like their students demonstrating creative talent, as these are the students who rock the boat and ask difficult questions in class. Hence, teachers tend to give preferential treatment to the less creative students who perform as expected. Sounds familiar?

Suffice to say that if intelligence is about identifying, replicating and predicting a pattern, creativity is about breaking that pattern, which is anything but easy, for our mind loves patterns. Yet all creations are pattern-destroying in nature. While intelligence builds on convergent thinking, creativity calls for divergent thinking. And as you would have experienced, generating options is often more difficult than choosing between options. 'The test of a first-rate intelligence,' notes the American writer F. Scott Fitzgerald, 'is the ability to hold two opposed ideas in the mind at the same time and still retain the ability to function.'[34] Creativity is that first-rate intelligence, and it comes with practice. However, a higher IQ doesn't necessarily mean higher creative achievement, something that we will be discussing in detail in Chapter 10.

Here is an example of cutting the clutter in an otherwise heavily competitive market. In the 2013 Maha Kumbh Mela in Allahabad, Hindustan Unilever (HUL) came up with a very clever campaign called 'Lifebuoy Roti Reminder'. The idea was to print 'Lifebuoy *se haath dhoye kya*? [Did you wash your hands with Lifebuoy?]' on over 2.5 million rotis cooked at 100 kitchens over the duration of the mela. Since roti is eaten with hands, the reminder of washing hands right at mealtime worked. The team also distributed free soaps to patrons.

About the brilliant campaign and its execution, Sudhir Sitapati, general manager, Skin Cleansing, HUL, remembers, 'The idea came from the insight that handwashing with soap before eating can prevent transmission of many disease-causing germs, but people often ignore or forget to do this simple act. A reminder at the right time can go a long way to ensure this habit is followed. This was the starting thought from which we developed a unique intervention – the Roti Reminder.'[35]

How do you practise pattern-breaking? Could there be some patterns for pattern-breaking?

Mohanbir Sawhney and Sanjay Khosla from Kellogg School of Management have identified seven patterns of idea generation. 1) *Anomalies*: the way Chai Point designed a tea-vending machine noticing that avid tea drinkers often settle for coffee because their favourite tea is not available on demand; 2) *Confluence*: how Ola became possible with the confluence of Google Maps, GPS, payment wallets, smartphone penetration and low data rates in India; 3) *Frustrations*: Phanindra Sama founded redBus after he discovered, to his frustration, that no aggregator existed for booking bus tickets; 4) *Orthodoxies*: P.C. Mustafa and his cousins challenged orthodoxies in founding the idli/dosa batter brand iD Fresh Food; 5) *Extremities*: Mirchi & Mime restaurant in Mumbai, where guests are served exclusively by speech- and hearing-impaired service staff; 6) *Voyages*: Salesforce CEO Marc Benioff credits his spiritual voyage to Kerala as the inspiration behind his philanthropic vision; and 7) *Analogies*: Dr Devi Shetty designed Narayana Health while drawing on the principles of efficiency that apply to the assembly line.[36] These methods are simple, effective and scalable.

The following section presents methods that would help you in generating a high quantity and quality of ideas in a systematic manner. To demonstrate the efficacy of these techniques, we continue with the case of the first-time car buyer.

Challenge assumptions

The quickest way to break the pattern is to question the practices that have been taken for granted. Every industry has a set of unwritten, unsaid rules that shape the thinking of its insiders and even of outsiders. Real breakthroughs start with someone contesting some very core assumptions. The British inventor James Dyson challenged the assumption that a 'fan must have blades', to design the Dyson Air Multiplier; and so did Michelin, in challenging that a 'tyre must have air', to design the revolutionary Tweel.

Hal Gregersen from the MIT Leadership Center refers to the method of challenging assumptions by the term *question burst*.[37] Here, instead of jumping at solving the problem, the participants are encouraged to pose relevant questions around the problem. Such questions are aimed at challenging the assumptions and are typically framed in an open-ended manner. After about one or two rounds of such four-minute question bursts, the team is then encouraged to reframe the problem statement before getting into generating solutions.

On the power of challenging assumptions, Roberto Verganti, a professor at the Stockholm School of Economics, notes, 'In order to find and exploit the opportunities made possible by big changes in technology or society, we need to explicitly question existing assumptions about what is good or valuable and what is not—and then, through reflection, come up with a new lens to examine innovation ideas.'[38] He offers that criticism could be a valuable starting point to unearth novel insights and generate non-incremental ideas. Verganti suggests that a brainstorming session could start with individuals reflecting on the problem statement and identifying and contesting assumptions; this should be followed by having them work in teams and then inviting outsiders to further critically examine their assumptions, which would help them break away from *functional fixedness*—the tendency to look at an object or a situation in the traditional manner.

Figure 13 presents some of the core assumptions and possible ideas in the case of our first-time car buyer.

Core assumptions	Possible ideas
The car would be driven by the owner	• Tie-up with companies that provide drivers on rent • Create a pool of drivers serving your premium customers
The owner is interested in buying a brand-new car	• Start a subsidiary that sells pre-owned cars • Nudge the customer into buying a new car by comparing it with a pre-owned car
Owner would be particular about the model and the car	• Offer discounts to push slow-moving models or colours if the customer doesn't seem to be very particular
Owner would have sufficient parking space for the car	• Tie-up with companies that may offer multi-level parking mechanisms

Figure 13: Challenge assumptions

Contesting these assumptions could open a new line of exciting ideas—some useful and others not so much. But we need to have many ideas to get to some promising ones.

Look across the value chain

An especially useful starting point for addressing customer pain points or anxiety is the *buyer utility map*, a technique introduced in *Blue Ocean Strategy*.[39] Here, you look at the entire buyer journey and identify possible value additions at its specific stages. We already have a journey map from our empathizing exercise (Figure 10), and now it is time to identify the objectives you would like to achieve for your customers.

Some of the maximizers could be value for money, comfort and peace of mind. By applying a specific objective to a stage, you can think of novel means of adding value to your products or services, or alleviating customer pains.

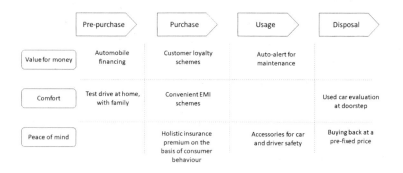

	Pre-purchase	Purchase	Usage	Disposal
Value for money	Automobile financing	Customer loyalty schemes	Auto-alert for maintenance	
Comfort	Test drive at home, with family	Convenient EMI schemes		Used car evaluation at doorstep
Peace of mind		Holistic insurance premium on the basis of consumer behaviour	Accessories for car and driver safety	Buying back at a pre-fixed price

Figure 14: Across the value chain (adopted from Blue Ocean Strategy)

Figure 14 indicates some of the ideas you may think of, but the method greatly helps in uncovering potential avenues of differentiation and revealing the blind spots in your approach of customer engagement.

Look beyond current users

Another useful technique that comes from *Blue Ocean Strategy* is the 'Three Tiers of Non-customers' framework, which would help you pay attention to the relatively large pool of your non-users. Except for Google or Facebook, there is hardly any company in the world that can claim to have more users than non-users in the overall population, and yet a disproportionate amount of management attention often goes into pleasing the known users.

The technique of looking beyond your current users pushes you to think of the issues with the *dissatisfied users* (they are unhappy and would soon leave you), the *refusing users* (they just do not want to do business with you), and the *unexplored users* (those whom you never saw as your potential users). You then ask who they are, why they are not your users and how to entice them. Figure 15 depicts this adapted framework, along with a few pointers on customer acquisition.

	Dissatisfied users	Refusing users	Unexplored users
Who are they?	Want to upgrade to a high-end car	Don't find it convenient to drive in traffic.	Foreign tourists
Why are they this way?	They are unaware of your product range	Find it difficult to get well trained drivers	Don't have a valid DL; not aware of such car facilities
How to entice them?	Incentivize upsell with better exchange deals	Offer a pool of drivers for your premium customers	Create a rental model for your car

Figure 15: Look beyond the current users (adopted from Blue Ocean Strategy*)*

In this approach, users can be replaced with employees or partners, and the same analysis could be adopted to address issues around employee morale or vendor loyalty.

Design for the extreme

Another approach of breaking out of a fixed mindset is to take your thinking to an extreme and then devise possible responses to the challenges you would face. Building on the philosophy of *lead-user research*, the method of designing for the extreme helps you in considering ideas on the margins, which never get much attention in the usual circumstances. For instance, the introduction of subtitles in movies, a solution initially aimed at viewers with hearing disabilities, has led to an overall increase in viewership of films in foreign languages. Similarly, tactile feedback on mobile phones, which was originally meant for visually-impaired users, has become immensely useful for all.

Thinking of extreme conditions for a user, product or problem could help you in arriving at unique ideas while also increasing your competitive differentiator. Imagine, for instance, that your first-time car buyer is a diabetic and must commute long distances for business. How would you like to look at your car design or services as a seller? Figure 16 offers you some insights in this regard.

Extreme conditions	Possible ideas
A diabetes patient driving the car for a long duration	• Auto alert for taking medicines • Storage of water and medicines near the dashboard
Foot sores from long-duration driving	• Automated reminders for taking a break and exercising • Means of exercising within the car
A female driver stranded in the middle of the night	• SOS feature in the car to relay the location to nearest police station or car service centre

Figure 16: Design for the extreme

Some of the extreme conditions that you design for could directly touch upon human constraints, whereas others could be related to the extremes of nature, such as total loss of connectivity during a storm or torrential rain.

One of the questions that I have received while advocating this technique is, 'Is it not advisable to ignore such extreme cases and focus on the mainstream customers, and does it not increase the overall cost of the solution?' No, it does not, provided such ideas are not a retrofit to your existing solutions. Today's extreme customer might be tomorrow's mainstream customer, and by anticipating some of the fringe challenges you only make the overall solution more robust.

Analogous design

A lot more ideas emerge when you explore the intersections of disciplines. Some of the problems that you deem insurmountable in your context might be solved routinely in another context, in another industry. It is easy to get overwhelmed by one's situation, but if you only take a pause, look around yourself, the answer might well be within your reach.

Look at how air traffic controllers talk to pilots, or how military personnel on the field communicate with each other—with minimal words and minimal chances of error. Or, how training on emotional intelligence could help improve communication under stressful situations.

Analogous design pushes you to look truly beyond your domain to seek fresh inspiration for solving your apparently tricky problems. Returning to the case of the automobile dealer, think of what all you can learn from the best hotels, airline companies, star-rated restaurants or even hospitals and apply that to serving the first-time car buyer. Figure 17 offers some insight into this.

To be adept at this method, one ought to have enough breadth of perspective and an understanding of other industries and domains. Too much expertise in your niche domain would

	Airlines	Hotels	Restaurants
Value for money	Dynamic or tiered pricing basis the supply-demand gap		Offering discount during off-peak hours
Comfort	Technology-enabled car delivery status check	Loyalty programs across car services or new purchase	
Peace of mind		Product cancellation window without penalty	Star ratings for services, basis a recognized body

Figure 17: Analogous design

limit your associative abilities. That is why it is always advisable to work with a diverse team.

Ideation triggers

Finally, let us invoke the time-tested lateral-thinking triggers to address the problem. Lateral thinking, if used in a disciplined manner, can help break patterns in surprising ways. Edward de Bono, in his book *Lateral Thinking*, offers a host of methods for creative problem-solving.[40] *Inside the Box,* a book by Drew Boyd and Jacob Goldenberg, is another useful guide for problem-solving in newer, simpler ways.[41]

Building on these two books, here is a simple method comprising four ideation triggers: *Eliminate, Divide, Combine* and *Automate.* Figure 18 presents the application of these ideation triggers.

I encourage you to add ideas to the blank sections, such as the type of automation solutions you can come up with to add to the convenience of purchasing or driving the car. As you can

	Eliminate	Divide	Combine	Automate
Value for money	No down payment for the car		Sales of accessories with the car, at a bundled price	Calculate car price on the basis of customer relation
Comfort		Split car ownership into owning and renting the same car	Club car servicing with re-purchase offers	
Peace of mind	Complex formalities during insurance pay-out processing	Limit the owner's risk in advent of a damage		Calculate insurance premium on the basis of car vitals

Figure 18: Ideation triggers

see, the tool can also be combined with the Across Value Chain method to generate even more granular ideas.

There is no suggested sequence in which these methods must be adopted. Depending on the problems, the time availability and the skill sets of the team, any number of methods can be used and in any sequence. These are reasonably independent approaches.

Another powerful and emergent technique for generating ideas is to involve the crowd. With democratization of knowledge, capital, ideas and talent, it is naive to assume that the best solutions would exist within your team or your organization. There is a considerable need to open up to the outside world to seek ideas for your pressing problems. These outsiders could be customers, partners, former employees, experts, academics, hobbyists, veterans or almost anybody. Linux, Wikipedia, Topcoder, InnoCentive, NineSigma and many such knowledge and problem-solving platforms demonstrate the power of crowdsourcing.

Kevin Boudreau, of Northeastern University, and Karim Lakhani, of Harvard Business School, have identified four forms of crowdsourcing engagements—*crowd contest, collaborative community, complementor* and *labour market*—each suited for specific problem-solving objectives.[42] Crowd contests are suitable for solving complex or novel problems that involve discovery through experimentation, and they lead to multiple solutions. Examples include HackerRank, Tongal, Kaggle and Project Euler. Collaborative communities enable aggregation of diverse talent, ideas and knowledge of multiple solvers to build something more enduring and larger than usual, such as the open-source community, Wikipedia or the OpenIDEO platform. Crowd complementor models help in the creation of platforms, which complement the core products and services, the way the Google Play Store community complements Android mobile phones, or the way Tesla is creating the ecosystem for electric vehicles.

Finally, crowd labour markets are technology-enabled platforms matching seekers with solvers, much like a spot market for talent, except that these are focused on innovation and discovery and there are well-identified financial rewards. The low transaction costs of such arrangements make these models favourable for one-off problem-solving endeavours, as with the crowdsourcing marketplace Amazon Mechanical Turk. The adoption of crowdsourcing as a means of problem-solving depends on the management's ability to divide labour, govern arrangement between the seekers and solvers, and design suitable commercial constructs.

With these ideas in place, it is time to pick the most powerful ones and scale those systemically. In the next chapter we delve into the various methods of evaluating ideas and getting to the most promising ones.

7

Prototype and Test

'We should bear in mind that not all innovative ideas are successful, and we should not jump to the conclusion that a failure means that this is not the way to go.'

—Ratan Tata[1]

Design thinking is a series of divergent and convergent stages. You apply divergent thinking while empathizing and convergent thinking while defining the problem; and once again divergent thinking when ideating and convergent thinking to pick the most promising ideas.

According to the American psychologist Adam Grant, the biggest barrier to originality is not idea generation but idea selection.[2] He offers the cases of Segway (a false positive that was forecasted as a hit but turned out to be a flop) and the sitcom *Seinfeld* (a false negative that was expected to fail but turned out to be a hit). Often, the fear of the unknown kills a new idea. The only way, it seems, to pick the best ideas is to perform validation, and prototyping teaches you just that.

There is a saying at IDEO: 'If a picture is worth a thousand words, a prototype is worth a thousand meetings.' If the openness to experimentation is the lifeblood of any creative organization, then prototyping, which is the willingness to go ahead and try something by building it, is the best evidence of experimentation.

Prototyping is about engaging with customers in advance and reaching out to them with a very low-resolution solution to get an early feedback. Such an approach of *iterative rapid-cycle prototyping* helps in securing funding, organizational commitment and customer trust, and in building the team's morale and making them believe they are headed in roughly the right direction. The thumb rule in prototyping is, *minimum planning and maximum action.*

One of the masters of the prototyping mindset was Thomas Edison, who famously quipped, 'None of my inventions came by accident. I see a worthwhile need to be met and I make trial after trial until it comes. What it boils down to is one percent inspiration and ninety-nine percent perspiration.'³

In the design thinking context, a good and early prototype serves three core functions. Firstly, it takes ideas from the abstract to the concrete, giving them the much-needed body and soul. Instead of merely contemplating the worth of your ideas, you now have something visible to critique and improve upon. Secondly, a prototype helps get the buy-in from your team members, senior managers and customers, as at least one of the possible outcomes. Of course, there would be iterations along the way, but as the saying goes: 'Perfect is the enemy of good.' So it is vital to get started. Thirdly, prototyping makes it possible to seek feedback and avenues of improvement more objectively and readily.

You are more likely to offer your critical views on a scenario than on an idea. Even better than a scenario in this respect is a compelling story; and better than a story is an improvised role play. The more concrete and real an abstract idea becomes, the easier it gets to understand it and seek feedback, and that is how a project moves forward, albeit slowly, but mostly in the right direction. By lowering the threshold of success, prototypes allow you to keep multiple concepts alive for longer, help you to recycle a lot more ideas and offer you the courage to discard unviable ideas with an informed confidence. This could also lower the guilt of having missed out on something exciting, or prematurely abandoning something promising, because you gave every idea its due chance.

Karl Duncker, the famous Gestalt psychologist, performed more experiments aimed at assessing the causes of creativity than most researchers of his time. Through a series of studies, Duncker arrived at this remarkable conclusion, as summarized by the author Kevin Ashton: '. . . [A]ll creation, whether painting, plane, or phone, has the same foundation: gradual steps where a problem leads to a solution that leads to a problem. Creating is the result of thinking like walking. Left foot, problem. Right foot, solution. Repeat until you arrive. It is not the size of your strides that determines your success but how many you take.'[4] What Duncker showed us long ago is that creativity is a highly iterative process and not the proverbial leap of faith.

The iterative nature of design-thinking-led innovation is best captured by the following statement by Ken Kocienda of Apple: 'We always started small, with some inspiration. We made demos. We mixed in feedback. We listened to guidance from smart colleagues. We blended in variations. We honed our vision. We followed the initial demo with another and then another. We improved our demos in incremental steps. We evolved our work by slowly converging on better versions of the vision. Round after round of creative selection moved us step by step from the spark to an idea to a finished product.'[5]

Before we delve deeper into the techniques of prototyping, it might be useful to know what happens in the absence of a prototyping mentality.

The high cost of 'just doing it'

A bad advice often given to entrepreneurs and businesspeople is, 'Just do it.' Many companies have fallen by the wayside 'just doing it' than is commonly acknowledged, and that is where a prototyping mentality plays a critical role. In the fast-paced world of business, just a few mistakes are enough to tarnish a painstakingly built reputation and can even lead businesses to shut shop. The MIT Media Lab formalizes this in its motto, 'Demo or die.'

The very Flipkart that had won the hearts of online shoppers in India, with several firsts like cash on delivery, Ekart, and thirty-day replacement policy, ended up hurting itself at the launch of its first Big Billion Day sale. Without any prototype or pilot in place, the company went about the sale, offering deep discounts on most products. Launched on 6 October 2014, India's biggest online sale clocked a gross merchandizing value of $100 million within just ten hours, but what happened next was a disaster.[6]

The online traffic that the Flipkart site drew in an hour dwarfed the number of hits recorded on the Indian Railways website over several days. As a result, less than 10 per cent of the customers who came to the Flipkart site could make a purchase. A massive surge in demand rendered the website dysfunctional— customers were unable to place orders, payments could not go through and several other technical and human glitches ground the shopping portal to a halt. The excitement around clocking record sales soon turned into a doomsday scenario, with the co-founders eventually issuing a public apology.[7] Hundreds of customers took to social media to vent their anger, and a nascent brand was at risk of suddenly becoming irrelevant, crushed under the weight of its own ambitions.

Another episode that almost cost the co-founder Sachin Bansal his job was the idea of Flipkart going 'app only'. Somewhere in 2014, Bansal began pushing the notion of shutting down the Flipkart website and having the customers access their shopping portal exclusively through a mobile app. Citing reasons like growing traffic on mobile phones, superior customer interface, ease of customization and collecting customer usage data, Bansal vowed to remove the 'crutch of the desktop' while taking Flipkart towards its 3.0 avatar.

What followed was a massive wave of confusion and distrust among employees, who questioned why Flipkart must shut down its website in order to improve its app. Couldn't they coexist? But Bansal was not of that opinion, as Myntra, a Flipkart company, had already been running app-only operations for a few months. Incidentally, Myntra had to forego more than 30 per cent of its orders by closing its website.

It took some beating from the customers and internal leaders to bring Flipkart executives back to their senses. They aborted their app-only stance by the end of 2015.[8] Acknowledging the mistake, Peeyush Ranjan, former engineering head at Flipkart, admitted, 'Websites push users to install app. But only 4 percent of the people actually install the app.'[9] Flipkart's leaders should have had this insight beforehand. But how could they? They never went for a prototyping approach to validate their hunch.

As Google's Eric Schmidt and Jonathan Rosenberg note, since the key factors of production—information, connectivity and computing—have become cheaper and ubiquitous, the cost of experimentation and failure has dropped significantly.[10] And innovative companies are good at exploiting this fact.

Prototype to seek clarity

A prototype is a facade and not the real product, and it should be treated so. It should help you get closer to something that would really click with customers and be different from what was offered to them before, or even be better than what others have produced. These are like *minimum viable products* or *minimum viable processes* that help the team move forward. You could have a prototype that *looks* like the desired outcome, and another one that *works* like it. A sense of directional clarity and speed of correction are more important than accuracy.

Once you have answered the question that you had set out with at the start of the prototyping journey, go no further. The purpose is served, and you must pause. On the virtue of pivoting and moving on gracefully from successful or not-so-successful prototypes, Jonathan Ive, former chief design officer of Apple, notes, 'We should not be afraid to fail—if we are not failing, we are not pushing. 80 percent of the stuff in the studio is not going to work. If something is not good enough, stop doing it.'[11]

Demos are at the heart of product development and innovation at Apple. As Ken Kocienda reflects: 'Demos were fundamental to our work at Apple. We used them to highlight the potential, explore the concepts, show the progress, prompt the discussion, and drive the decisions for making our products . . . [S]oftware demos need to be convincing enough to explore an idea, to communicate a step toward making a product, even though the demo is not the product itself . . . Demos served as the primary means to turn ideas into software.'[12]

Prototypes are not just meant for products and services but also for new process models and business models. Here is an example of a prototype for a new process. Tanishq is one of India's largest jewellery manufacturers and as a part of their jewellery-making process they melt large amounts of gold in crucibles. After a few months of use, a typical crucible would be rendered ineffective. However, the company had a problem of recovering gold from the used silicon carbide crucibles lying in its Hosur factory. The management had no means of extracting gold from these crucibles. Globally, there were no techniques available for scrapping precious trapped gold from such crucibles, and, as a result, the gold had to be written off. But not for Rajsekhar, one of the operators at the factory.

Being close to the problem and away from stares of the senior leadership, Rajsekhar came up with a radical idea of a prototype: 'Why not crush these crucibles?' Instead of proposing steep investments in crushing facilities, which may or may not work, Rajsekhar decided to have a go at crushing the crucibles himself. He brought his friend's road roller to the factory and, to everyone's surprise, demonstrated that crushing actually helps recover gold. Through this rusty prototype, four-and-a-half kilos of gold were recovered, worth lakhs of rupees. Cost of prototyping? Almost zero. Lesson learnt? Significant. The story also demonstrates one of the maxims of innovation: *better to ask for forgiveness than seek permission.*

That is the power of prototypes. They not only help you get clarity but also serve to correct others who doubted your intent. The key is to keep the cost of failure, both monetary and socially, minimal.

Innovative organizations encourage their creative teams to take up prototyping early on instead of working in the dark for too long. Further, making it culturally acceptable to show off your low-fidelity work-in-progress is the hallmark of successful start-ups. As the co-founder of Paypal Peter Thiel reminds us, 'Jeff Bezos's founding vision was to dominate all of online retail, but he very deliberately started with books.'[13] A standard product, such as books, is a low-fidelity prototype that could prove if online shopping really works and if it could be scaled across markets.

One of the practical lessons on prototyping can be borrowed from Kishore Biyani. In every major format, whether it was Pantaloons or Big Bazaar, he always opened the first store in Kolkata. He chose the city because it is away from the scrutiny of investors, competitors and the media. It allowed the team to experiment, offering them crucial time to examine and correct the course of expansion, and pivot, if required.

On the importance of prototyping, Biyani observes, 'Prototyping has played an extremely crucial role in everything we have attempted . . . Every initiative, every concept or format we launched, always went through a prototype phase. We built it on a small scale and opened it to a customer interface. We then watched and learnt from how customers reacted to it, before we scaled it up.'[14]

That is the prototyping mentality in action in a context which is far removed from new product development. While prototyping takes time and might seem to delay the launch, the learning is invaluable and does lead to a faster scaling of the concept, because now you are much more confident on what works and, more importantly, why.

Designers at IDEO believe that good prototypes do not just communicate—they persuade. What counts is expressing the idea quickly and cheaply.

Be quick and dirty

A popular maxim at innovative organizations is, *fail often to succeed sooner*. The trick is to answer most of the *difficult* questions as early and as cheaply as possible, so that there are fewer surprises later. The faster your ideas are made tangible, the sooner you can evaluate and refine them and reach the best solution. The failure must be contained in a manner that many experiments could be packed within a given budget and time frame. These must be quick and dirty prototypes, or, as IDEO likes to call them, *paper-thin prototypes.*

The rule that design thinkers live by is that early prototypes should be fast, rough and cheap. The greater the investment in an idea, the more committed one becomes to it. The goal of prototyping is not to create a working model; it is to give form to an idea to learn about its strengths and weaknesses, and to identify new directions for the next generation of more detailed, more refined prototypes. Don't let your inner perfectionist slow you down.

For instance, if you must choose between two user interfaces for a mobile app, instead of coding and creating the actual interface, you may use sticky notes to visualize various layouts. These are simple hacks to get to the go/no-go answers without necessarily going through the whole design process. A team's odds of success depend a lot on how quickly they get their first prototype to test and move on to next, more sophisticated ones. Being 'quick and dirty' helps, especially if there's high uncertainty around.

Talking of experimentation, one person who has lived by the virtues of being quick and dirty is Sir Richard Branson. The founder of Virgin Group has started over 300 different companies. Not all have been successful, but a lot of them have managed to disrupt industries, and, interestingly, none of his 300-plus companies has ever gone bankrupt. The billionaire entrepreneur knows how to keep his experiments well in check, draw insights from failures and move on to the next experiment. As Branson likes to put it, 'I never get into a venture with an idea of making a profit. If you can create the best in its field, you will eventually be able to pay your bills and make a profit.'[15]

Take the case of Booking.com, the world's largest online accommodation platform. One of their management tenets is: *Anyone at the company can test anything without the management's permission.* The company runs about 1,000 rigorous tests simultaneously, amounting to well over 25,000 tests annually. Not all these experiments are visible to the users, because just about 10 per cent of the experiments generate a positive result. The company has an experimentation platform which has been adopted by over 75 per cent of its 1,800 technology and product employees. By packing in an exceptionally large volume of experiments, the company has, paradoxically, lowered the costs and the risk associated with experimentation.

This demonstrates how the online world has embraced experimentation and failure, and how leaders must lead with an experimental mindset. Experiments take away the guesswork from the innovation equation. As David Vismans, chief product officer at Booking.com, notes, 'If I have any advice for CEOs, it's this: Large-scale testing is not a technical thing; it's a cultural thing that you need to fully embrace. You need to ask yourself two big questions: How willing are you to be confronted every day by how wrong you are? And how much autonomy are you willing to give to the people who work for you? And if the answer is that you do not like to be proven wrong and do not want employees to decide the future of your products, it is not going to work.'[16]

Here is what Jeff Bezos says about experiments: 'If you know in advance that it's going to work, it's not an experiment.'[17]

Another example of quick and dirty prototyping comes from Asian Paints, India's largest paint-maker and a household name. In one of the workshops I conducted with the research and technology team of the company in Mumbai, a bunch of technologists tried figuring out an elegant way of taking off old paint from a wall before it gets repainted. If you have ever tried removing old paint or distemper from a wall using a sand paper and the like, you would understand the pain it involves. Alas, most of the work is done by painters or contractors and not necessarily the buyers or customers. However, in the true spirit of human-centricity, an elegant solution would be desirable.

While contemplating on the best way to scrape off wall paint, one of the engineers at that Asian Paints workshop came up with a quick prototype to demonstrate an idea. The prototype involved a whiteboard duster tied to a scotch tape role. The rectangular surface would go on the wall and the circular one would be held by hand, and there would be a container for the dust while the painter conveniently scrapes off unwanted paint from a wall and smoothens it. While the final idea was far from elegant, at least the rudimentary prototype set the discussion rolling. I wish I had taken a photograph of that model to share with you in this book, but you would see the final product in the market in the not too distant future.

One of the useful models when prototyping is the *Goldilocks quality* test. Proposed by Google Venture's Daniel Burka, Goldilocks quality is the sweet spot where the prototype is neither too low in quality (with people refusing to believe in it) nor too high (which would take you days, without the prototype attaining a final shape).[18] It must be good enough to elicit an honest feedback from your customers and team members, but not too complex or costly to build.

The strategy is to divide a larger creation into a series of smaller prototypes, where each could be tested at a lower cost and preferably in isolation, and without severely jeopardizing the overall concept.

Break prototypes into manageable hypotheses

What do you do when you have a large idea to be put to test? You break it down into smaller, manageable hypotheses, where each could be tested independently. This would also help you prioritize which one to test first and decide when to stop validating your ideas before rejecting those entirely or going back to the drawing board.

To paraphrase Thomas Edison, one of the greatest design thinkers of all time: the real measure of success is the number of experiments that can be crowded into twenty-four hours. Edison packed his day, and that of his small team, with experiments—essentially ways of proving or disproving his hypotheses—and pushed them towards achieving 'a minor invention every ten days and a big thing every six months or so'.[19] Instead of getting intimidated by the size of the problem, you must break it down into manageable experiments, where each failed or successful test takes you closer to the result, while offering you greater clarity.

When the iPhone team was deciding on the size of the home screen icon, instead of performing endless A/B tests or resorting to pure algorithms, the team devised a simple mechanism to *size up* the problem. Scott Herz, one of the members of the iPhone project (then called 'Project Purple'), came up with a simple game comprising a series of icons of different sizes placed at different locations on the screen, and as the user touches those images the device detects the optimal size for the icon. Just after a few games played by the team members (the entire project was carried out in secret), the software team could decide on the right size as fifty-seven pixels square.[20] This was an application of gamification to solve a complex question involving heuristics. And remember, the team had no historical data to fall back on, nor a swarm of lead users to run tests with.

That might not be the most scientific approach or the most elegant one, but considering the strict timelines that Project Purple was under and the demanding boss that it had, the hack worked just about fine, and the team moved on to the next problem. On how hard data complements intuition, Apple's Ken Kocienda notes, 'We used algorithms and heuristics like they were the left and right sides of our collective product development brain. Employing each involved an interplay of craft and taste, and we always tried to strike the correct balance.'[21]

Stefan Thomke, of the Harvard Business School, and Jim Manzi, from Applied Predictive Technologies, state that although the process of experimentation seems straightforward, it is surprisingly hard in practice, owing to myriad organizational and technical challenges.[22] They offer a set of questions that managers must answer before running experiments: Does the experiment have a clear purpose? Have stakeholders made a commitment to abide by the results? Is the experiment doable? How can we ensure reliable results? Have we got the most value out of the experiment? It is important to be rigorous and scientific, else managerial biases often creep into decision-making.

When the leadership at Google had to answer a fundamental question—'Do managers matter?'—they resorted to a hypothesis-based, data-driven approach. Named 'Project Oxygen', this multi-year programme helped Google to *sell management to engineers*. Adopting double-blind qualitative interviews and data analytics, the people operations team got to the key insight that engineers hate being micromanaged on the technical side but love being closely managed on the career side. On how data complements intuition, Prasad Shetty, the leader of people analytics group at Google, notes, 'Organizations can get bogged down in all that data. Instead, I wanted us to be hypothesis-driven and help solve company problems and questions with data . . . It's really about observations—staying with people and studying their interactions. We're not going to have the capacity to follow tons of people, but what we'll lose in terms of numbers, we'll gain in a deeper understanding of what managers and their teams experience'[23] That is empathy in action.

Today, Google has a greater harmony between managers and engineers. The company has remained true to its data-driven approach to problem-solving but has learnt the power of empathy along the way. As Google CEO, Sundar Pichai, puts it: 'To do well and innovate, you need to have a construct by which people can work together, not build on individual people who are superstars.'[24] And that is for a company that prides itself on hiring A-grade talent.

Do the last experiment first

What to prototype and what *all* to prototype? While anything can be prototyped, not everything needs to be. As David Kelley says, you only need to prototype the most unbelievable part of the solution, the leap of faith, and not the entire solution. There are some components that are routine and believable, and then you have the real risky ones that could make or break the deal in the context of your project. You just need to work on the latter.

To ensure that you are not overdoing the prototype, spending too much time and resources on it, and checking the obvious, it is advisable to perform the *last experiment first*. If the most critical final frontier does not work, there is no point in reaching there and later wondering why. It could lead to escalation of commitment. A clarity on the end-state and the ability to test it out could well mean the difference between a false start and an early finish.

Many start-ups are based on the core assumption that once there is a compelling product, customers would queue up and investors would shower their money on the founders. The small team gets immersed in creating their 'dream product', only to find that it is not exactly what the customers need and are willing to pay for. Instead, would it not have served the company well to tease out the pricing question early in the game? If a finished product would fetch you $10, will a half-baked one get you at least $2? That's a question worth answering.

When Netflix co-founders Marc Randolph and Reed Hastings were mooting the idea of selling DVDs-by-mail they performed a very crude, cheap prototype. They would mail a CD in an ordinary envelop over the normal post and see what happens next. As Randolph recollects sharing with his team, 'If it breaks, it breaks, and we know that this idea would never work. If it gets there, you got something to listen to on Tuesday night.'[25] They did the last experiment first, before spending countless hours and money on building the website, warehouses, raising capital, and hiring talent. What they shipped was a CD and not a DVD, but the intent was to see if an optical disc can survive an inter-state shipment. And it did.

From a different context, here's a question I often get asked: 'Should I do a PhD programme?' Scores of working executives and students have quizzed me on my PhD experience, wondering whether doing a PhD would be a wise move in furthering their careers. The short answer is always, 'No', for the returns on investment in your PhD programme, regardless of the institution or the supervisor, take a long while to accrue; and even if you do get good returns, the opportunity cost remains difficult to justify. Regardless, if the person persists in their inquiry, I just ask one question, 'What after the PhD programme?'

On an average, a third of them say that they have an interest in teaching, a third in moving up the ladder of their careers, and the final third admit that they are indecisive. To those who wish to teach, I pose, 'Have you taught before?' Surprisingly, many say they haven't, and yet they somehow believe that doing a PhD programme would make them a *better* teacher. The only suggestion I offer to them is, 'Start teaching today and see if you love teaching. Gauge if you really need a PhD to better your teaching skills or to bring in more credibility.' That is what's meant by 'doing the last experiment first'. If your final objective is to be a great teacher, start teaching today, and then work backwards to see if you need a PhD or just more self-discipline. No need to overinvest and then seek avenues to realize returns. Invest in proportion to the anticipated returns, whether it is life, career or relationships.

One of the compelling exemplars of doing the last experiment first is Paytm. Several people attribute the success of Paytm to India's demonetization move in 2016. I have only one question for them, 'Why only Paytm?' If demonetization was a great opportunity for digital wallets and mobile-based payments systems, how did Paytm leverage the disruption better than any other player? There were scores of contenders: MobiKwik (started in 2009), Freecharge (2010), Airtel Money (2012), PhonePe (2015) and Zeta (2015). The business models of these companies were not radically different from Paytm's; the difference was in their approach towards market penetration.

One97 Communications launched Paytm (short for Pay Through Mobile) in August 2010 as a prepaid mobile and DTH recharge platform. By early 2012, Paytm enabled payments for data cards, post-paid mobile and landline bills, as well as for utilities such as electricity and gas bills, toll tax, bus and train tickets and online purchases. It soon became India's largest mobile wallet. In 2013, the company started offering 'cashbacks' to users, and this one move led to a surge in new and repeat users at the platform. By August 2015, the RBI-approved Paytm wallet had over 100 million users.[26] The number has steadily grown since then. But why?

The secret of Paytm's success is that it did the last experiment first. The last experiment, or the most crucial hypothesis to be proven, was, 'Will the millions of vendors across India accept mobile wallets to receive payment?' Their key concern was not whether buyers or customers would adopt Paytm; rather, it had to do with the adoption level for sellers, especially those who work on cash.

At least two years before the demonetization tsunami hit the Indian economy, the team at Paytm was busy reaching out to the hinterland of the country, educating millions of shopkeepers about the benefits of mobile wallets and especially about the ease of managing exact change. The value proposition for the merchants was hassle-free management of loose change and no risk of theft or loss of cash. Further, with zero setup fee, zero annual fee and no hardware involved, there was a minimal adoption barrier. As a merchant, all you needed was a mobile phone, and not even a bank account.

The enrolment of offline merchants started in September 2015. By 2016, the company launched its 'Paytm Force' programme, as a part of which over 3,000 trained and certified e-commerce specialists helped merchants with services like catalogue creation, order fulfilment, complete account management, and query resolution for embracing mobile payments.[27] Over the month of demonetization—November 2016—the team hired 10,000 agents to expand their offline merchant network and accelerate onboarding, while most of the other players were still waking up to the opportunity. By the end of November 2016, Paytm already had over 1 million offline merchants enrolled, and was well-placed to take on the demonetization challenge.[28] With the mobile app supporting ten regional languages, the traction was especially high in small towns and villages, where vegetable and fruit vendors, and owners of kirana stores, food stalls and pharmacies welcomed this convenient way of receiving money over mobiles.

With over 12 million active merchants, and 250 million KYC-verified customers, the company's early investments in sensitization, education and incentivization have paid off handsomely. To sweeten the deal further, in November 2018 Paytm introduced instant bank settlement for its merchants. By May 2019, the company clocked over 400 million monthly transactions, five times its nearest competitor.[29]

When the government launched the UPI-based transaction app BHIM, all Paytm did was introduce another feature on its already trusted and heavily used app, seamlessly enabling UPI transactions. Ditto for FASTags. When the National Payments Corporation of India, under the guidelines of National Highways Authority of India and Indian Highways Management, mandated the use of electronic tags for payment of toll tax across India, Paytm stepped right up with its reusable, rechargeable RFID tags.[30] Interestingly, Paytm introduced FASTag as early as September 2016 and was fully prepared for the December 2019 deadline.[31] Once again, a case of fortune favouring the prepared mind.

The insight we can draw from the Paytm case is that if you take care of the most critical of your hypotheses, the rest will fall in place. Since all experiments call for money and time is always at a premium, you may be better off picking the most crucial experiments first and then going to the more moderate ones. If the most unbelievable part of the equation is not resolved, it could be a death knell for your business.

We now look at some of the contemporary means of concept validation, especially in contexts involving intangibles.

Visualize through storyboarding and scenarios

Prototyping of physical objects is relatively straightforward because there is a lot more tangibility to an idea that can be touched, seen and improved. How do you prototype a service or an experience? Services have far fewer tangible components, and there is a lot more involvement of the dimension of time, so you must think in terms of sequence of activities, emotional engagements and 'moments of truth'.

Incidentally, the movie-making industry regularly prototypes emotions and experiences through techniques like storyboarding and scenarios. Storyboards use visual means to map out the entire script of what a movie would look like, so that the director and the team don't miss out on vital elements. Before hard commitments are made, such storyboards can offer flexibility on how the exact experience would be rendered. In a creativity workshop, storyboards could be comic-book-like frames showing actions and dialogues, and with stick figures and sticky notes you can really play around with multiple flows without much of a cost. An effective storyboard is both functionally relevant and emotionally resonant with the solver and the seeker.

Another powerful technique of validating an insight or an idea is to conjure up possible scenarios and take the audience through those to elicit their honest response. One could test out multiple future scenarios to tease out customer reactions and validate ideas. Scenarios can also help in anticipating unforeseen challenges and thinking up remedial measures, and these are best done with the customer by the side. Meaningful scenarios keep the audience focused on the core of the idea, without getting lost in its mechanics or aesthetics. Scenarios allow you to visualize how your solution interacts with users over time.

If the design team is willing to defer judgement, high-fidelity scenarios could be portrayed, and with the help of augmented reality and virtual reality, a lot more realism can be brought into the prototypes. These could be handy means to prototype solutions involving complex human engagements, such as counselling a patient in a hospital or engaging with an agitated customer at an airport lounge.

The scenarios can also be demonstrated through role plays and skits. These are not just fun ways of communicating and getting an idea validated but are also participatory. Customers can be a part of the skit and can almost live the desired experience, while making real-time course-correction possible. A short video-based scenario presentation can be an effective approach to share and validate an idea, and with the omnipresent smartphone, the cost of such prototypes has come down radically.

Storyboards, improvisations through role plays and skits, and scenarios are all experiential approaches to prototyping that allow the team to render design in not just space but also time, making the intended customer experience lifelike. Remember, an experience must be delivered with the same care as that with which it is conceived, and prototyping can help weed out the dampers from the intended delight.

Take, for instance, Walt Disney World, dubbed as 'the happiest place on earth'. Disney has identified that during a visit to a theme park there are as many as seventy-four moments of truth between the guest (a visitor) and the cast member (an employee). Each of these contact points, called 'the stage', offers the cast member avenues to create a memorable experience for the guest.[32] By mapping out various scenarios and possible outcomes, the company has covered almost everything that could potentially go wrong during somebody's visit to any of Disney's theme parks. In fact, Disney cast members are never ever allowed to say these three words: 'I don't know.' As one of the cast members says, 'If a guest asks you a question, you always have to have an answer, no exceptions. If you don't know it, find out, but don't say you don't know. If it's a silly question, make up a silly answer.'[33] That's how Disney manages the several million moments of truth on a daily basis and keeps improving customer experience.

Engage through stories

The American poet and political activist Muriel Rukeyser famously observed, 'The Universe is made of stories, not of atoms.' Great stories outlive writers, narrators, aeons and contexts, and if you can create one for your concept, it goes a long way in changing customers' perceptions and habits. As for validating ideas, one of the most effective and reliable means of testing your concept is to put it across in the form of a narrative. On the power of stories, author Daniel Goleman observes, 'The emotional brain is highly attuned to symbolic meanings and to the mode Freud called the "primary process": the messages of metaphors, stories, myths, the arts.'[34]

A design thinker must be a master storyteller. She must be able to craft and narrate stories which are compelling, consistent, emotional and believable for people to open their deepest feelings and take a leap of faith in a new direction. A well-accomplished storyteller himself, Tom Kelley, maintains that stories persuade in a way that facts, reports and market trends seldom do, because stories make an emotional connect—they make heroes out of real people.

Chip Heath, from Stanford University, and his brother Dan Heath, from Duke University, offer a succinct checklist of what makes a message stick. In their book *Made to Stick*, the Heath brothers offer the 'SUCCESs principle' of effective storytelling.[35] The first element is *Simplicity*, with which you talk about the core of your idea. The second is *Unexpectedness*, by which you violate people's expectations. The third attribute is *Concreteness*, which involves providing your audience with sensory information. The fourth is *Credibility*, so that people find it difficult to refute your idea. The fifth is *Emotions*, whereby you get your audience to feel for you and your idea. And finally, *Stories* is how you engage them. That is the SUCCESs principle of narrating a 'Simple, Unexpected, Concrete, Credentialed, Emotional Story'.

An often-overlooked feature of a good story is unexpectedness. As Chip Heath puts it, 'The most basic way to get to someone's attention is this: Break a pattern.' However, the story must always be authentic. It should help your audience validate the idea at face value without getting intimidated or second-guessing your intentions. Think of what makes Malcolm Gladwell such a good writer. In every book of his, he almost always starts a chapter with a real story. The names of key characters, the facts and contexts are presented with such a high level of detail that these stories stick—like the one about the crime scene in New York that Gladwell recounts in *Tipping Point*, or the police shootout case in Bronx that he refers to in *Blink*. His stories make his concepts memorable. In his own words, 'There is a simple way to package information that, under the right circumstances, can make it irresistible.'[36]

So, the next time you are putting your favourite idea across to a stony buyer, do not start by asking, 'How do you feel about this new product or feature?' Instead, start with, 'Tell me an instance when you felt frustrated with this product and wished something in it must change.' Such engagements help start conversations. By making your customer talk and engaging with her, you get an access to her psyche, and that is where your idea must reach to make a lasting impact.

However, storytelling as an art is not particularly appreciated in the corporate world, especially in India. R. Gopalakrishnan, executive director of Tata Sons, has said: 'In the world of business, storytelling is not a skill that is particularly envied—the expression has pejorative undertones and suggests tall tales and fiction rather than fact.'[37]

Ameen Haque, an expert storyteller and the founder of Storywallahs, laments that most business leaders aren't aware of the power of stories and do not use the tool adequately, often leading to uninspired employees and indifferent customers. He offers the following tips of business storytelling: 1) speak to people's emotions, 2) build common ground, 3) build contrast, 4) have truth well told, and 5) do not state the obvious. On this basis, a good construct for a sticky story is, 'Imagine a world where . . .'[38]

Since a powerful story goes a long way in talking to the subconscious of the customer, as a design thinker you must learn to be particularly good at narrating compelling, authentic stories. They often allow you to seek feedback early, impersonally and in an unbiased manner.

Are you dogfooding enough?

The learnings about what works and what does not work in the prototypes has to be eventually linked back to the real context. It is easy to get lost in new idea streams and move away from bringing the current project to a logical closure. A prototyping mentality comes in handy here, to realize that testing is just one step to make the prototype better and not the final step towards product launch.

There might be situations where a paying customer may not exist, or it might not be feasible to take a novel concept to the market for the risk of failure. It typically happens in the hi-tech space when a company tries to introduce an unproven technology.

A useful approach would be to conduct the tests within the organizational realm, with the internal lead users. Most high-tech companies are expert adopters of their own technologies. The practice is called *dogfooding*. The idea is to be the harshest critic of your own products and services, so that you can gain valuable insights about the innovation before it is made public.

For instance, years before Amazon Web Services (AWS) was launched, it went through rounds of internal adoption and improvement. Since 2000, scores of internal teams have used AWS's elastic cloud storage and computing services for their projects, giving their leadership teams confidence to go ahead with the launch.

On how AWS took shape within the organization, AWS CEO, Andy Jassy, notes:

> It began way back in the 2000 timeframe when the company wanted to launch an e-commerce service called Merchant.com to help third-party merchants like Target or Marks & Spencer build online shopping sites on top of Amazon's e-commerce engine . . . We expected all the teams internally from that point on to build in a decoupled, API-access fashion, and then all of the internal teams inside of Amazon expected to be able to consume their peer internal development team services in that way. So very quietly around 2000, we became a services company with really no fanfare.[39]

After years of serving internal customers, Amazon launched AWS in 2006 and ushered in an era of cloud computing.

That is what Wipro did for its home-grown AI platform, Holmes. The platform was initially trained to address internal tech services issues and queries, before being deployed on the client environments. Ramprasad K.R. (fondly called Rampi), one of the chief architects of Wipro Holmes, offers how early prototypes performed with Wipro's workforce and tech partners enabled the product to take shape:

> In the year 2014, we started developing bots for our IT helpdesk using a corpus of historical information and applying machine learning and natural language processing techniques. By September of the same year, we had deployed 10 bots working in the area of help desk, processing more than 10,000 help desk tickets per day. They continue to function taking up responsibilities of categorizing issues, assisting in task assignment and will eventually move to automating resolutions. They learn continuously and are always on 24x7.[40]

The internal adoption of Holmes freed up Wipro's precious people resources while helping the machine learn. By the end of 2015, over 12,000 employees were redeployed internally into high value adding activities, thanks to such internal rollouts. As for external deployment, by 2017 there were over 2,000 instances of Holmes bots running with 175 customers.[41] That is how dogfooding helps to not only prototype and validate the concepts but also to foresee avenues of improvement before your ideas are subjected to customer scrutiny.

The message is: *if you do not have a ready customer, be one.*

Solicit feedback, non-judgementally

One of the key principles of design thinking is to seek timely and honest feedback from the people who matter. A delayed or skewed feedback does not help the progress of your problem-solving or innovation sprint and, resultantly, the mistakes become far too costly to correct. Seeking unbiased feedback necessitates having a few rules and structures in place, so that people can reach out without the fear of being reprimanded for a crazy idea.

To solicit feedback in a non-judgemental manner and to bring a sense of candour in the organization, Pixar has created Braintrust, a team comprising writers, directors, heads of story and other functions who are entrusted with the responsibility of giving critical feedback without killing genuinely divergent thinking. Braintrust started with the production of *Toy Story*, in 1993, when five men of unbounded enthusiasm and pragmatism—John Lasseter, Andrew Stanton, Pete Doctor, Lee Unkrich and Joe Ranft—came together. Braintrust remains Pixar's primary means of seeking honest feedback on projects.

On the importance of Braintrust in fostering a culture of honest feedback, Pixar's co-founder Ed Catmull notes:

> The Braintrust, which meets every few months or so to assess each movie we're making, is our primary delivery system for straight talk. Its premise is simple: Put smart, passionate people in a room together, charge them with identifying and solving problems, and encourage them to be candid with one another. People who would feel obligated to be honest somehow feel freer when asked for their candor; they have a choice about whether to give it, and thus, when they do give it, it tends to be genuine.[42]

Over the years, the team has become well-defined and a part of Pixar's way of working. To further develop empathy in the team, animators are made to take acting lessons and most employees are exposed to domains outside their core areas of expertise. That is difficult but essential in a creative industry, which must surprise its audience and yet must keep the endeavour within the framework of a given time and budget.

Even the most creative professionals draw from timely and candid feedback, and it makes a huge difference between a great idea (in your head) and a winning innovation in the market.

When demonstrating your prototype, bear in mind that the intent is to solicit valuable feedback and not sell the concept. This is a very tricky balance to achieve, especially if you are working under a tight schedule without easy access to your intended customers.

In his book *Sprint*, Jake Knapp offers an entire chapter on how to conduct customer interviews for validating ideas and making progress on a project.[43] According to him, just about five customer interactions are sufficient to understand what works and what doesn't in a well-done prototype. The trick, however, is to get the right audience in the room and incentivize them to offer honest feedback and even useful ideas to further your project. These could be the lead users of your desired product or service, or they could offer you a perspective on the problem, if not a clue for a possible solution.

The key matrix along which to evaluate your ideas would be: desirability, technical feasibility and business viability (as discussed in Chapter 3). An idea need not necessarily score high on each of these parameters, for the weightage of the parameters depends on the team's priorities and the stage a given project is in. For instance, if you are a well-funded start-up you might still pursue an idea if it scores extremely high on desirability and not so much on business viability. However, it would be foolhardy to completely miss out on any of the parameters, because for a sustainable outcome all three dimensions matter. But what happens when an idea does not make the cut in the first go? Should you abandon it?

Inventory your (failed) prototypes

What if you made a prototype painstakingly and it does not get through? What do you do with that prototype? You should not junk it at least. Rather, keep it and, better still, display it for others to draw inspiration from and for you to resort to it when you stumble on your next problem.

IDEO has a place for such experimental products, failed prototypes and weird artefacts: the Tech Box. Conceived by Dennis Boyle, one of IDEO's oldest employees, the Tech Box has come to represent the company's library of innovation elements and serves as a starting point to look for ideas for unsolved and even unidentified problems. These are part tools and part toys. As Boyle likes to put it, 'This is more about serendipity. Making a lateral connection between slightly odd things that might give us a different perspective.'[44]

Call this cross-pollination, or, in the words of the legendary Steve Jobs, 'connecting the dots'. But you need to be planting enough dots before you could connect them, and that's why inventorying your (failed) mock-ups is a good practice. So, the next time your ideas do not work, don't just chuck them away. On the importance of experimenting and prototyping, the psychologist Adam Grant has said, 'On average, groups that make decisions based on experiments will outperform those guided by debate between experts.'[45] And yet how many of your decisions go through experimentation? So for your next problem-solving event, adopt a 'validation through try-outs' and not a 'validation through decibels' approach.

In the next chapter, we look at how select ideas can make a real-world impact through the process of scaling.

8

Scale

'Google's objective is to be the systematic innovator at scale. Innovator means new stuff. And scale means big, systematic ways of looking at things done in a way that's reproducible.'

—Eric Schmidt, former CEO of Google[1]

How good is an idea that does not scale? As the author Walter Isaacson shares, 'Innovation requires having at least three things: a great idea, the engineering talent to execute it, and the business savvy (plus deal-making moxie) to turn it into a successful product.'[2] It would not be wrong to say that scale is the real proof of innovation, for that's how the idea realizes an impact. In this chapter, we talk about how to turn validated ideas into the ultimate impact.

On the scale imperative, Peter Thiel opines, 'You should focus relentlessly on something you're good at doing, but before that you must think hard about whether it will be valuable in the future.' For future-proofing your ideas, Thiel offers the following checklist: 1) Can you create breakthrough technology instead of incremental improvements?; 2) Is now the right time to start your particular business?; 3) Are you starting with a big share of a small market?; 4) Do you have the right team?; 5) Do you have a way to not just create but deliver your product?; 6) Will your market position be defensible ten and twenty years into the future?; and 7) Have you identified a unique opportunity that others don't see?

Speaking of scale, the company that comes to mind is Reliance. In the words of Reliance chairman Mukesh Ambani, 'Our fundamental belief is that for us growth is a way of life and we have to grow at all times.'[3] Ambani has thought through Thiel's checklist and the outcome is for the market to see. Reliance Jio is a stellar example of scale. The story of Jio has all the elements of design thinking. The idea emerged from first-hand insights about how consumers at the 'bottom of the pyramid' use mobile phones. They like to talk more than ever, seek entertainment and information on their phones, like to carry out business transactions and yet want unlimited features at almost zero cost. That is what Jio offered when it was launched in September 2016, disrupting the Indian telecom market, irreversibly.

The service was first introduced in December 2015 for the employees and partners of Reliance, so that the tech team could get hands-on feedback. That's dogfooding in practice. By late 2019, Jio became India's largest mobile network operator and the third largest in the world.[4] Think of the lowest rates of 4G connectivity globally, free voice calls from Jio to Jio and Jio to landline, a smartphone (LYF) at just under Rs 3,000 and a host of freebies, and yet the business stands to become EBITA positive by September 2017.[5] The initial investment? A whopping Rs 1,50,000 crore. Is that not scale at speed?

The following statement by Mukesh Ambani offers a peek into his mind and tells us what scale means to his enterprise. The billionaire says:

Jio is not just a telecom network, it is an entire ecosystem that allows Indians to live the digital life to the fullest. This ecosystem consists of devices, broadband, powerful applications and services distributed to every doorstep in India. Jio's media offerings will include the most comprehensive library of programming of live and recorded music, sports, live and catch up television, movies and events . . . Jio is about unleashing creativity and connected intelligence through the smartphone.[6]

Through the levers of coverage, quality, data and affordability, Jio has indeed transformed the telecom landscape in India and, according to the insiders, this is just the beginning. Reliance Jio is a case of true scaling, an example of what Eric Schmidt calls one of Google's core insights: optimize for scale, not for revenue, and let great products grow the market for everyone.[7]

As a testimony to the scaling potential of Jio, in April 2020 Facebook announced $5.7 billion investment in the platform, making Facebook the largest minority shareholder of Jio Platforms Limited. On the synergy, David Fischer, Facebook's chief revenue officer, and Ajit Mohan, VP and managing director, Facebook India, write, 'One focus of our collaboration with Jio will be creating new ways for people and businesses to operate more effectively in the growing digital economy. For instance, by bringing together JioMart, Jio's small business initiative, with the power of WhatsApp, we can enable people to connect with businesses, shop and ultimately purchase products in a seamless mobile experience.'[8]

This engagement comes on the heels of Jio's ten-year partnership with Microsoft, which was signed in August 2019. On the promise that Jio offers, Satya Nadella notes, 'We have an incredible opportunity to apply advances in technology to help organizations across India innovate and grow.'[9] All this is possible only because Mukesh Ambani intended to systematically scale an idea and then to take it further by inviting complementary players. It shows that a sharp insight or a genius idea alone doesn't qualify for innovation; the whole system must act in concert for the impact to be realized, and it is through scale that the concept achieves sustenance. Further, during the scaling process, it is advisable to adopt Lean and Six Sigma to lower variance and achieve replication.

An emerging field of inquiry in this context is *lean start-up*. It is, according to Stanford's Steve Blank, a 'methodology that favours experimentation over elaborate planning, customer feedback over intuition, and iterative design over traditional "big design up front" development'.[10] Such methods, which originated from the realm of technology start-ups, are fast finding their ways into problem-solving and innovation endeavours at large organizations. Any setup that attempts to solve problems under extreme uncertainty benefits from the application of lean start-up.

In his book *The Lean Startup*, Eric Ries identifies the following principles of a lean approach to problem-solving: creation of a minimum viable product to test the hypothesis, validated learning through rigorous scientific experimentation and rapid iteration of the build-measure-learn feedback loop.[11] A *valuable* outcome is that which benefits the customer and everything else is a waste. And who validates it? The customer. Except that customers seldom know what they want and hence, the importance of scaling through validated learning. However, only a select few ideas can be meaningfully scaled. This is as true for entrepreneurs as for the established enterprises. As Ries notes, 'Only 5 percent of entrepreneurship is the big idea, the business model, the whiteboard strategizing, and the splitting up of the spoils. The other 95 percent is the gritty work that is measured by innovation accounting: product prioritization decisions, deciding which customers to target or listen to, and having the courage to subject a grand vision to constant testing and feedback.' We will discuss innovation accounting later in this chapter.

Keep the main thing as the main thing

Bill Gates's father once asked the young Bill and his close friend, Warren Buffett, to write down a single word to describe their successes. And they both wrote: focus. Gates attributes his success to his ability to remain focused on specific objectives for extended periods of time. Reflecting on his unwavering focus on computer programming, Gates shares, 'An innovator is probably a fanatic, somebody who loves what they do, works day and night, may ignore normal things to some degree and therefore be viewed a bit imbalanced . . . Certainly in my teens and 20s, I fit that model.'

Gates doesn't even shy away from complimenting one of his arch-rivals, stating, 'Steve Jobs' ability to focus in on a few things that count, get people who get user interface right, and market things as revolutionary are amazing things.'[12]

When Jobs returned to Apple in 1997, after an exile of over a decade, he saw a team low on morale and chasing as many as fifteen product platforms. With finite talent, it was impossible to deliver on so many fronts. So Jobs chose to focus on just about four platforms.[13] The team found a new confidence, focusing only on desktops and laptops, and creating meaningful, differentiated products, which could be scaled. Even today, Apple, despite the company's size, has the narrowest range of products, even though the company operates in multiple industries—computing, music, mobile phones, retail, etc.

As one of the most influential coaches of personal productivity and a highly effective person himself, Stephen Covey always reminded leaders, 'The main thing is to keep the main thing the main thing.'[14] You cannot scale in multiple dimensions; you must choose.

Jeff Bezos attributes Amazon's success to an obsessive-compulsive 'focus' on its customers, and not on competitors or products. Talking of his company's strategic choices, Bezos notes, 'I very frequently get the question: "What's going to change in the next 10 years?" And that is a very interesting question; it's a very common one. I almost never get the question: "What's not going to change in the next 10 years?" And I submit to you that that second question is actually the more important of the two—because you can build a business strategy around the things that are stable in time.'[15] Bezos chooses to 'focus' on what won't change, and that is faster delivery, vast selection and low prices. That's the virtue of focus.

It is not enough to be clear with your priorities; they must also be communicated, given every single chance. As LinkedIn CEO, Jeff Weiner, warns leaders: 'When you are tired of saying it, people are starting to hear it.'[16] Along similar lines, General Electric's former CEO, Jack Welch, has noted, 'No vision is worth the paper it's printed on unless it is communicated constantly and reinforced with rewards.'[17] But do not assume that it is only the leader who has to communicate. In fact, the middle management is equally, if not more, responsible in this regard. 'More than anyone, middle management can help you project your message over a distance,' was the incisive observation made by Intel's former chief Andy Grove.[18]

An immensely powerful instance of communicating what matters to employees is the time-tested credo at Johnson & Johnson. Robert Wood Johnson, the company's former chairman, crafted it in 1943, years before terms like customer-centricity, corporate social responsibility, employee diversity and inclusion came into vogue.

I am reproducing the first para of the J&J credo here:

We believe our first responsibility is to the patients, doctors and nurses, to mothers and fathers and all others who use our products and services. In meeting their needs everything we do must be of high quality. We must constantly strive to provide value, reduce our costs and maintain reasonable prices. Customers' orders must be serviced promptly and accurately. Our business partners must have an opportunity to make a fair profit.

Before you go further, I would encourage you to read the credo at www.jnj.com/credo.

Now that you have read it, let the fact sink in that the credo was crafted in 1943. That is how far ahead of his time Robert Wood Johnson was, which explains why J&J has been in business for over 130 years.

There are brilliant insights about design thinking embedded right in the credo. Firstly, it starts with patients and their immediate context, comprising doctors, nurses and families. Instead of focusing very narrowly on the paying customers, the credo expands the definition of customers to all those who are impacted by the company's products and services. Secondly, the credo strives to balance the needs of desirability, technical feasibility and business viability—the trinity of design thinking.

Thirdly, the credo emphasizes the need to experiment, tolerate mistakes and invest in the future, where customers don't yet exist. Finally, the credo makes the order of priority adequately clear to every new employee or value chain partner—customers, employees, communities and, finally, stockholders. This explicit prioritization enables making tough decisions under uncertainty and allows employees to innovate with confidence.

Are you doing enough of it at your organization? If not, here are some specific pointers for business leaders who endeavour to provide a conducive environment for scaling ideas.

Cut some slack

In the nineteenth edition of the 'IBM Global C-suite Study', in which 2,148 CEOs were interviewed, two characteristics were cited as the most instrumental in organizational success: encouraging employees to try out new ideas, and having clear rewards for fast failures and successful innovations.[19] The leaders hinted at the importance of cultivating autonomy and learning to experiment in cross-functional teams, which helps lower the risk of failures and enables employees to anticipate customer needs faster. In short, innovation happens when you encourage employees to try out new things, offer them critical resources and time, and tolerate failure. As Google's Eric Schmidt and Jonathan Rosenberg note, 'The ethos is always to build the prototype as cheaply as possible, and to worry about scaling only after the prototype *fails to fail* [italics mine].'[20] By running numerous experiments across the length and breadth of the company and giving employees the *safety net* to occasionally fail, Google ensures that they have more promising ideas to pursue and put money behind.

Design thinking necessitates a *prototyping mentality*, which is nowhere close to the *efficiency mentality* that most senior executives hone by default. If the ethos of quality is *right the first time*, that of innovation is *wrong the first time*. Being wrong the first time is not easy, as it often comes at the cost of personal reputation, and, as a result, most would happily lowball instead of aiming high. A prototyping mentality also necessitates investments in terms of hard resources, talent and time. Unless the leadership appropriates resources for such efforts, most employees will not venture into even mildly risky bets. The need to cut some slack does not come naturally to efficiency-minded managers, and yet it is the oxygen of creative problem-solving.

Tom Peters and Robert Waterman, in their book *In Search of Excellence*, present some counter-intuitive Japanese management practices, especially around managing new product development and innovation. In stark contrast to typical Western firms, Japanese companies regularly operate at suboptimal resource allocation, allow for duplication of efforts, encourage internal competition and an inefficient division of labour, when it comes to innovation.[21] Apparently, the deliberate inefficiencies in product development are only matched by the fanatic levels of efficiencies in product manufacturing and other operations. New product creation or creative problem-solving is not a setting for demonstrating efficiencies.

Most innovative organizations have policies in place for allocating resources, especially talent and time, on projects with no immediate consequences. Such a provisioning of scarce resources cannot be a one-off practice but must be a part of organizational routines.

Google has the famous *20 per cent time-off* practice, which is borrowed from the legendary 3M, which institutionalized the *15 per cent rule*, way back in 1945. Google's 20 per cent time-off policy, dubbed the 'innovation time off', requires the staff from the engineering and technology functions to spend 20 per cent of their paid time to pursue projects other than their assignments. Managers are also required to spend no more than 70 per cent of their time on the core business, 20 per cent on related but different projects and 10 per cent on entirely new businesses and products. Google has a position of 'Director of Other', to help manage the 10 per cent time requirement.[22] If an employee does not have some sort of a 20 per cent project going on, it is perceived negatively in the Google community. These could be hobby projects, some moonshot assignments, social work or whatever else the employee gets excited about.

As Eric Schmidt confirms, 'Many, many initiatives in the company have come out of 20 percent time ideas . . . And while the rule says you can do anything you want to with your 20 percent time, these people are computer scientists and engineers, they're not going to veer too far away from their core business—and that is the genius of 20 percent time.'[23]

Some of Google's famous projects that resulted from its innovation time-off policy include Orkut, Gmail, Google News, Google Maps and AdSense.

Inspired by Google, Scott Cook, founder of Intuit, rolled out a policy at the company in the mid-2000s, encouraging all employees to spend 10 per cent of their time on unstructured projects. To get first-hand insights about customer issues, the company set in motion a practice where every employee, at the director level and above, would meet with customers and other experts twelve times a year to develop fresh perspectives about the future. Every year, the top 400 leaders of the organization would present their insights, which would keep the creative juices flowing.[24] Does it cost money? Yes. Is it a super-efficient way of utilizing human resources? Perhaps no. But it all pays in the long run.

By not tying up every resource to visible opportunities or to the exploitation of existing avenues, you could bring about the desired mutation in the ways of thinking and doing at your organization. In a design-thinking workshop, you must allow for divergence before converging on specific problem areas or opportunities. Iteration should lead to better results, and you must be willing to start amid uncertainty instead of waiting for full clarity. If an organization is open to provisioning resources for future bets, not monitoring resources tightly and allowing people to go on a tangent once in a while, a design-thinking programme can do wonders, while in a straight-jacketed, efficiency-oriented culture, design thinking has limited chances of survival. But cutting some slack has no meaning if it cannot offer fresh perspectives, which can be garnered when leaders show up and challenge orthodoxies.

Leaders must show up

Woody Allen instructed us that 80 per cent of success is showing up. The idea has gravitas because most people do not show up when the time comes, and especially when the times are difficult. If a leader has done all the hard work in getting the brief right, creating a stretch, bringing in diversity and offering resources to experiment, his or her absence from the scene can lead to a plummeting of morale. How frustrating would it be if your leader leaves you struggling with the problem all by yourself?

Nothing is more critical than the leader being physically and cerebrally involved in a problem-solving exercise. A leader's presence in the room has three remarkable impacts. First, it sends a strong signal that what everyone is here for is not trivial, and my presence signifies that; I am here with you through the journey, just as another participant. Second, it keeps the participants and the trainer/coach oriented towards the true north, or the stated objective of the session; whether it is about new product development, process improvement challenge or cutting down the cost, the leader keeps the endeavour honest. Third, the leader demonstrates the importance of being a continuous learner, which is both humbling and inspiring.

Indra Nooyi, the former chief of PepsiCo, took a more personal approach to popularize design thinking at her company. For Nooyi, 'a well-designed product is one you fall in love with. Or you hate. It may be polarizing, but it has to provoke a real reaction.'[25] It is about rethinking the entire experience, from conception to what is on the shelf to the post-product experience.

Nooyi has been personally driving the agenda for design thinking at the organization across the 'fun for you' and 'good for you' product categories. She has been in the thick of customer engagement and insight generation personally. As the former chief says, 'I visit a market every week to see what we look like on the shelves. I always ask myself—not as a CEO but as a mom—"What products really speak to me?"' She thinks like a mom and not a CEO. That is what is meant by being the customer you wish to serve.

In 2012, to scale the adoption of design thinking at PepsiCo, Nooyi brought in Mauro Porcini, 3M's long-time residential design guru, as PepsiCo's first chief design officer. For Porcini, design is 'more than the aesthetics and artifacts associated with products . . . as a strategic function that focuses on what people want and need and dream of, then crafting experiences across the full brand ecosystem that are meaningful and relevant for customers'.[26] The key contribution Porcini made at PepsiCo was to enable a prototyping mentality among its leaders, for he believes that prototypes help unlock resources like no business plan could. Having been at the organization for eight years now, Porcini says that to create true design culture the organization needs a *shared language*, a structure and, most of all, the right people, and that new culture needs to be 'protected by the CEO or by somebody at the executive level'.

When it comes to change, a leader's commitment makes all the difference.

Let me share two instances from my engagements. In 2011, I was invited to conduct a day-long creativity workshop with the leadership team of Café Coffee Day (CCD). It was the company's heyday, when Starbucks was yet to enter India, and the intense competition from the likes of Chai Point, Hatti Kaapi and others was still awaited. The team was rearing to offer novel experiences to customers across the formats of CCD Lounge, Square and Express, with not just drinks and food but also a whole host of amenities for someone to have a good time at their outlets.

The workshop was attended by the heads of design, marketing, finance, human resources and other key functions. But the most crucial person in the room was the late V.G. Siddhartha, the charismatic, disciplined, eager-to-learn leader of CCD. His keenness to listen to all the ideas was humbling, and so was his insistence that we address the real issues without getting lost in the motions of problem-solving. When such a busy person takes the time to be at a session, imagine the signal it sends to the troops? The leader is saying, 'It is important for me, and so it should be for you all.' Even after almost a decade, I cherish the session for the way the leader showed up.

Another episode happened more recently when I was invited by Professor Vivekanand Khanapuri to my alma mater NITIE, Mumbai, to engage with a batch of students on design thinking. Prof. Khanapuri taught me in 2003–05, when I was studying industrial engineering at the institute. And after all these years, he had reached out to me for delivering a primer on design thinking for a batch of about twenty-five students. After briefly introducing me to those present and setting the context, Prof. Khanapuri sat on the very first bench of the class, with his notebook open, pen at the ready and phone switched off! Most other teachers would have conveniently walked out of the class after handing me the floor, but not Prof. Khanapuri. What was the signal sent to the students? That there is no age, qualification, designation or pedigree that should stop you from learning. It was an extremely humbling experience, and I hope more teachers make a note of that.

In the mid-'90s, when Wipro was embracing the famed Six Sigma approach towards improving quality, its entire top leadership team camped at the Motorola University to understand the principles and practices of Six Sigma from the pioneer. For an entire week, the leaders were in the US, and guess who was sitting in the first row? Wipro's chairman Azim Premji himself. Could he have inspired his commanders any other way? His presence, his attention, his eagerness to learn and embrace change is what made Wipro a pioneer in software and IT services quality, much before quality management became the norm in the industry.

I distinctly remember my induction programme at Wipro in June 2005, as a part of the newly hired MBA batch. The week-long programme saw several top leaders from across functions offering advice, showing us the big picture, motivating and orienting us, but there was one session that was special and most-awaited: with Azim Premji, on the topic of 'integrity'. Could he have delegated this session to anybody else—say, to the CEO, Vivek Paul—and still managed to convey the importance of integrity? I don't think so. After all these years, I still remember his talk more than any other from that eventful week.

It is vital for the leader to be a part of the problem-solving workshop, so that the efforts go in the right direction and important decisions could be made in a timely manner. At IDEO, to effectively facilitate design-thinking programmes, three key leadership roles have been identified: the *explorer*, the *gardener* and the *player-coach*.[27] The explorer leads from the front by asking strategically purposeful questions and reframing questions in a manner that challenge assumptions. The gardener leads from behind by fostering conditions where new ideas could be nurtured, collaboration could happen and new capabilities around creativity could be built, without the organization succumbing to the productivity mindset. Finally, the player-coach leads from the side by helping the team meet and circumvent challenges, keeping the rhythm of experimentation alive and being present during the phases of execution. These different leadership styles could be put to use at different stages of the innovation cycle, but what remains unambiguous is that a leader must 'show up' for innovation to happen.

Provide 'air cover'

As failure is an integral part of innovation, it is imperative that employees are encouraged to experiment and their careers protected from the undesirable fallouts of failed experiments. Effective leaders shape a culture where you are *better off asking for forgiveness afterwards than asking for permission beforehand.* They do not necessarily innovate; rather, they *protect those who innovate.*[28] They do so by offering *psychological safety*, allowing for resource leverage and guiding on the basis of their wisdom. Leaders must inculcate a spirit of experimentation in their organizational culture, and back it up with personal behaviour. As Jeff Bezos likes to put it, 'If you want to have more inventions, you need to do more experiments per week, per month, per year, per decade.'[29] He further underscores the importance of hiring those who like to invent and cautions that often these people can be rebels, mavericks and annoying.

Encouraging dissent is the hallmark of creative leaders and innovative organizations. If employees are not encouraged to challenge assumptions, think about radical concepts, put those to rigorous test and made to feel they can afford to fail, a climate of design thinking would be elusive. Leaders must explicitly seek employees exhibiting nonconformity and be more tolerant of them, as long as they operate within the broad ambit of organizational values and priorities. Original thinkers flourish under such settings, and it is a leader's personal responsibility to encourage variance of thought, aptitude, attitude and worldview.

A brilliant example of encouraging dissent comes from Hewlett-Packard. The company bestowed upon its engineer, Chuck House, the first and only Medal of Defiance, for 'extraordinary contempt and defiance beyond the normal call of engineering duty'.[30] David Packard narrates the story (observe carefully the elements of design thinking intuitively practised by Chuck House):

> Chuck House, was advised to abandon a display monitor he was developing. Instead, he embarked on a vacation to California – stopping along the way to show potential customers a prototype model of the monitor. He wanted to find out what they thought, specifically what they wanted the product to do and what its limitations were. Their positive reaction spurred him to continue with the project even though, on his return to Colorado, he found that I, among others, had requested it to be discontinued. He persuaded his R&D manager to rush the monitor into production.[31]

As it turned out, the company sold over 17,000 display monitors, representing revenues of $35 million.

What do we learn about Chuck from this? That he demonstrated a prototyping mentality, sought early feedback from real customers, thought with his hands, took half chances, sought forgiveness rather than permission, was persuasive and had a thick skin. The story also talks about Chuck's R&D manager who provided him 'air cover'.

'Make dissent one of your organization's core values,' says the psychologist Adam Grant. He cites examples of how, during the early days of Apple, the Mac team gave away awards to anybody challenging Steve Jobs; and how Warren Buffett invited a trader, who had been shorting the stock, to share his criticisms at

Berkshire Hathaway's annual meeting.[32] The key responsibility of a leader is to create an environment where people can openly share critical opinions and are respected for doing so.

Calculated risk-taking is a cultural thing, and a leader must hone that culture with patience and practice.

Google co-founder Larry Page once told an executive who'd made a several-million-dollar blunder, 'I'm so glad you made this mistake. Because I want to run a company where we are moving too quickly and doing too much, not being too cautious and doing too little. If we do not have any of these mistakes, we are just not taking enough risk.'[33] This is how you, as a leader, design a culture of risk-taking, and some of those risks turn out to be breakthroughs. A leader needs to offer the team time, space, budget and a license to make mistakes, for as long as the failing employees *fail forward*.

A remarkable practice that fosters the culture of risk-taking and tolerating failure at an institutional level is Tata Group's Tata Innovista programme. Launched in 2006, Tata Innovista is a unique multi-tier rewards and recognition programme that celebrates the best innovations, both successful and failed, across the Tata Group companies.

Of the several award categories under this programme—such as 'Implemented Innovations', 'Piloted Technologies' and 'Design Honour Award'—there's one called 'Dare to Try'. The Dare to Try award, introduced in 2007, is aimed at recognizing teams that did not initially get the desired results but are raring to go again with new solutions to achieve their goals.[34] The project must demonstrate an exemplary intent, an exemplary effort and an exemplary withdrawal, while offering lessons for future projects.

Some of the recent winning entries for the Dare to Try award include a flavour pill for Tetley tea, a wristwatch for keyless entry into cars, a mechanism for vehicle-to-vehicle audio, video and data sharing, an aluminium diesel engine and a ghost car augmented-reality navigation for the Jaguar Land Rover. The award winners make presentations detailing why and how their ideas failed and what is being done to fix and relaunch the concepts.

Many have suspected whether such awards for failed innovations encourage risk-taking. As an external validation of the impact of the award on shaping a risk-tolerant culture, Phanish Puranam from INSEAD and Redd Kotha from SMU studied the data of 7,642 Implemented Innovations and 801 Dare to Try projects, and concluded that the award only works as a sort of painkiller and doesn't make failures seem more attractive.

One of the architects of Tata Innovista, Ravi Arora reports in his book, *Igniting Innovation*, that Dare to Try awards increase the chance of an employee's participation in successfully completed innovation by 36 per cent. On record, seven Tata Group companies, between themselves, won all the nine Dare to Try awards between 2011 and 2016, and the same took home 70 per cent of the awards meant for successfully completed innovations.[35] In fact, between 2007 and 2015, the number of Tata employees who competed for Dare to Try awards went up fifty-five times! That is Tata's way of encouraging, protecting and celebrating risk-takers.

Another case in point of how offering air cover could make all the difference between wishful thinking and world-class innovation is the very birth of Titan. The Watch Project, as it was referred to in the late 1970s at Tata Group, faced massive resistance from internal leaders, including Ratan Tata at one point in time. However, it was the foresight of J.R.D. Tata and his trust in the leadership team at Titan—comprising Xerxes Desai, Minoo Mody and Anil Mandhanda—that mattered in the end. J.R.D. fought the internal battles and kept the idea alive.

Years after successfully launching the Watch Project into Titan, Desai said, 'There had been times in the intervening years when we felt weary of the effort needed to find a partner, negotiate a know-how contract and get governmental approvals in the teeth of opposition by smugglers and entrenched Indian manufacturers. There were times when Minoo, Anil and I felt like abandoning the effort. But, there was one man who thought that the effort should not slacken. That was J.R.D. Tata!'[36] The same air cover Ratan Tata had provided to Tanishq when the consultants from McKinsey proposed that Tatas close down their loss-making jewellery business.

Cultivate innovation evangelists

In the context of design thinking and creative problem-solving, an innovation evangelist helps people build their creative confidence, so that they can generate meaningful ideas and take those ideas forward. Such evangelists not only have to be deeply knowledgeable on the subject of innovation but also well-connected, with an ability to move people.

Equating ideas or new products to epidemics, Malcolm Gladwell explains how sometimes small changes could have a large and lasting impact, and he calls such change agents *mavens*, *connectors* and *salesmen*. Mavens are the knowledge banks, connectors are like social glue and salesmen are selfless persuaders. Together they can, in an appropriate context, take a seemingly ordinary concept and make it successful. If, as a leader, you wish to scale your ideas and the overall adoption of design thinking, do not try doing it all by yourself; rather, identify, motivate and unleash the innovation evangelists. Some of the evangelists would be the expert mavens, others would be highly effective connectors and the rest would be compelling salesmen or saleswomen.

Some would be knowledge specialists, while others would be people specialists.

As Gladwell writes, 'The success of any kind of social epidemic is heavily dependent on the involvement of people with a particular and rare set of social gifts . . . What Mavens and Connectors and Salesmen do to an idea in order to make it contagious is to alter it in such a way that extraneous details are dropped and others are exaggerated so that the message itself comes to acquire a deeper meaning.'[37] And to scale a concept, you do not need so many of such people either. They could be just a handful, which is enough to cause an epidemic, in a good sense.

Let me share the case of ANAND Group, one of India's leading designers and makers of auto components. They have a robust problem-solving programme, with dedicated innovation evangelists at various levels across the group of companies. But before talking about these evangelists, it would be useful to understand how the leaders at the company have defined innovation and innovation culture.

Sunil Kaul, group president, innovation and technology, ANAND Group, says, 'We define innovation as an introduction of new ideas or new ways of doing things differently, to achieve more than 30 percent improvement. We want our employees to think beyond chasing targets of five to 15 percent improvements with kaizen.' As for innovation culture, Kaul clarifies, 'We attempt to touch at least 30 percent of our people to set in motion the culture of innovation. With such broad definitions, we found that immediately people caught on to that, and we started seeing innovations in almost all spheres of the company—inventory reduction, account receivables, productivity, maintenance, quality, etc.'[38]

An improvement above 30 per cent is innovation, and once you cross the *tipping point* of 30 per cent of your workforce you have an innovation culture, which is elegant and effective, especially in a manufacturing context where continual improvement is often confused with innovation.

Since 2010, the company has been identifying teams like i7@Anand, i5@Gabriel (Gabriel is a group company), FiresStarters@Anand, InnovationStarters@Anand—innovation evangelists who are well-equipped, deeply passionate and connected enough to be able to scale the discipline of problem-solving. M.S. Shankar, a blend of maven, connector and salesman, and the group head of technology and innovation, expresses the core belief of his evangelical efforts: 'Firstly, innovation is not only about technology or inventing clever gadgets; secondly, insights create exponential value propositions; and thirdly, innovation springs from the unlikeliest of people and places.'[39]

Having spent time with Kaul, Shankar and several other evangelists at ANAND Group, I realize how important it is to enable fission of ideas, at multiple levels and by adopting multiple methods. What are the qualities common among those evangelists? They are all deeply passionate and selfless.

In recognition of their efforts at scaling the concept of systematic problem-solving, ANAND Group won the prestigious Golden Peacock Award in the 'Innovation Management' category in 2014. The group was lauded for enrolling and enabling innovators across functions and levels and for achieving a 33 per cent increase in the top line, owing to its innovative style of conducting business.[40]

A relevant question: Does creating job titles like innovation evangelist motivate employees and help foster innovation culture?

While at Wipro, somewhere around 2007, I proposed to my then supervisor, Vikesh Mehta, that I be given the job title of innovation evangelist. I was hugely inspired by Guy Kawasaki, Apple's marketing evangelist. The term innovation evangelist was not much in vogue then, and Vikesh did not think of it as much of a hazard either. So I started using 'Innovation Evangelist' in my e-mail signature and soon got it on my business card. It was a great conversation-starter, both inside and outside Wipro, and thirteen years later, I continue to use the same title at my company.

'Evangelism is not self-promotion,' says Guy Kawasaki. 'It's a responsibility—and an opportunity—that falls to everyone, from HR to IT, finance to operations, the C-suite to the shop floor . . . In the social age, evangelism is everyone's job.'[41] Kawasaki offers three means of evangelism: 1) through schmoozing, which is to build a meaningful professional network; 2) through public speaking, especially by narrating informative and compelling stories; and 3) through social media, by being interesting, offering value and keeping it brief.

Do you get to choose a title like innovation evangelist? Do such titles really move the needle on innovation culture, especially in a traditional organization?

In an empirical research, University of Pennsylvania's Adam Grant and Justin Berg, and London Business School's Daniel Cable, analysed the impact of personalized titles on employees' job satisfaction and emotional exhaustion levels.[42] Adopting inductive, qualitative, and deductive experimental methods, the researchers studied various organizations and came to an understanding that when employees are allowed to choose their own job titles, which uniquely reflect the nature of their work, they are more likely to experience greater self-confidence, psychological safety and establish a good rapport with clients and colleagues.

Encouraging employees to pick up personalized titles, which reflect their true being, won't cost you much but could inspire in them an unprecedented commitment towards the job and a great deal of creativity. I experienced it, at first hand.

Measure for impact

To paraphrase Peter Drucker, you cannot manage what you cannot measure. To ensure enduring success of a design-thinking project, you must put some hard measures in place. Such matrices need not always be about the product, processes or experiences but about ensuring that the overall approach of systematic problem-solving is working and employees are getting disciplined at it. In-process measures are often more important than the outcome measures—the former keep the process of creation ongoing, and then what gets created is *released* someday.

On how a sense of progress can be the motivational cornerstone of creatives, Harvard's Teresa Amabile and Steven Kramer note, 'Of all the things that can boost emotions, motivation, and perceptions during a workday, the single most important is making progress in *meaningful work*. And the more frequently people experience that sense of progress, the more likely they are to be *creatively productive* in the long run [italics mine].'[43] A study of 12,000 diary entries from 238 knowledge workers engaged on twenty-six project teams across seven companies indicated that people are creative when they are intrinsically motivated by the work itself and have a positive perception of their colleagues and organization. It also helps when their managers 'catalyze progress and nourish spirits' by keeping the work meaningful and the progress visible.

OKR (objectives and key results) is a time-tested way to measure and manage progress. The objectives are defined as 'what is to be achieved', *as measured by* the key results, which are 'benchmarks and monitors on how to get to the objective'. While good objectives are always aspirational, effective key results are specific, succinct, time-bound, measurable, verifiable and, mostly, numeric. As the American venture capitalist John Doerr likes to put it, 'Objectives are the stuff of inspiration and far horizon.

Key results are more earth-bound and metric-driven.' The recipe for success, then, is 'to set aggressive goals, achieve most of them, pause to reflect on the achievement, and then repeat the cycle'.[44]

At companies like Google and—even prior to Google—at Intel, OKRs have formed the shared language of aspiration-driven achievements. OKRs can help manage scale. As noted by Larry Page, 'OKRs have helped lead us to 10x growth, many times over. They've helped make our crazily bold mission of "organizing the world's information" perhaps even achievable. They've kept me and the rest of the company on time and on track when it mattered the most.'[45]

As for measuring progress on your design-thinking project, you could think of three parameters: *input*, *in-process*, and *output*. The input stage would comprise the inspire, empathize and define phases; the in-process stage would represent ideate; and the output stage would encompass prototype and test. A sample OKR for a design-thinking programme is presented in Figure 19.

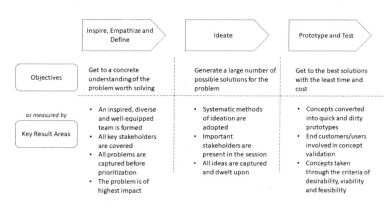

Figure 19: Sample OKR for a design-thinking programme

To make the OKRs more robust, you might add quantitative measures to the key result areas. However, it is advisable to keep the total number of objectives and key result areas as mutually exclusive, as well as collectively exhaustive and few (no less than three, no more than five).

On how OKRs have helped Google achieve difficult targets, Sundar Pichai shares, 'Google is propelled by our moonshot culture. The very ambitious is very hard to do . . . Whenever we invent something new at Google, we're always thinking: How can we scale it to a billion? Early in the process, that number can seem very abstract. But when you set a measurable objective for the year and chunk the problem, quarter by quarter, moonshots become more doable. That's one of the great benefits of OKRs. They give us clear, quantitative targets on the road to those qualitative leaps.'[46]

Scaling an idea is a matter of disciplined execution. As Larry Bossidy, former chief of AlliedSignal, notes, 'Tactics are central to execution, but execution is not tactics. Execution is fundamental to strategy and has to shape it . . . Execution requires a comprehensive understanding of a business, its people, and its environment.' Bossidy, along with the management coach Ram Charan, identified the linking of rewards to performance and making the linkage transparent as crucial enablers of effective execution. With OKRs signifying the 'what' and 'how' of your scaling plan, if you can also add the 'why'—in terms of 'what is in it for the employees'—the execution could be made more robust. Above all, this calls for financial discipline.

Don't confuse empathy with good business sense

What is common between Kingfisher Airlines, Jet Airways and Moser Baer? These were very customer-centric companies and yet went broke. I for one never came across any unhappy customer of Kingfisher Airlines—the king of good times. Did you? Frankly, with their top-of-the-line in-flight services, courteous crew, plush flight interiors and a lot of freebies thrown around, there was not much to complain about. Ditto for Naresh Goyal's Jet Airways, which, after serving Indian and global customers for over twenty-five years, went out of business in April 2019.

These are cases of bad business logic, often under the shadow of great customer service. Regardless of how customer-centric you claim to be, you cannot afford to take your attention away from the basics of business. Unfortunately, this does not seem to go well with the current crop of start-ups, with their enthusiasm artificially fuelled by investors' money. As David Packard famously noted, 'More companies die of indigestion than starvation'.[47]

So far, we have discussed the upsides of customer-centricity and why, going forward, it would be an important business touchstone. But all of this has to be governed by a good and ethical sense of business.

A useful construct to discipline your thinking about scaling your ideas is the business model canvas. The canvas comprises nine inter-linked business elements: 1) Customer segments: the groups of buyers and users your business wishes to serve; 2) Value proposition: bundles of products or services that offer value to your intended customers; 3) Channels: your approach of communicating with and reaching your customer segments; 4) Customer relationships: the kind of relationship you wish to establish with your customers; 5) Revenue streams: the ways through which your company generates cash; 6) Key resources: the most important assets required to compete in the market; 7) Key activities: the most important activities you need to perform to remain competitive; 8) Key partners: the network of suppliers and partners that help you conduct your business; and 9) Cost structure: the cost incurred to operate your business. Together, these nine blocks encourage you to think about how you intend to take your idea forward in a manner that makes sound business logic. Remember, the business model canvas is not about the idea; it's about what you do with the idea and it is possibly the shortest summary of your business plan.

For good business sense, we can look towards one of India's oldest and well-established conglomerates, Aditya Birla Group. The Birla family has been in business for well over seven generations now, starting with Shobharam Birla in the early 1800s. One of the accounting practices followed at this quintessential Marwari business is the *parta* system, which is a daily account of the cash inflows and outflows in any business entity. The system was followed very diligently by Kumar Mangalam Birla's grandfather, Ghanshyam Das Birla, and is one of Kumar's chief means of keeping a pulse on the business at the Aditya Birla Group, which is now worth $45 billion.

Instead of focusing on the balance sheet or profit-and-loss statements, which typical organizations monitor periodically, leaders at the Aditya Birla Group insist that they be presented with a daily parta, so that by the end of workday Kumar Mangalam Birla has an account of the entire group's cash flow on his table.

Some might consider this micromanagement. But Kumar Mangalam Birla is clear about the method's usefulness: 'It is a timeless concept and can be applied even 20 years from now . . . [Managing the environment] is not an area of strength for us. It may mean sacrificing growth, but we are quite happy to do that. It is important that you sleep well at night.'[48]

One of the equivalents of the parta system is the cash value add method, which many companies have adopted over the last few years. However, these financial measures mostly depend on the quality of the data and your ensuing actions.

An organization that has taken the virtue of discipline to its heart and in the process scaled unprecedented heights is

Radhakishan Damani's DMart. Founded in 2000 in Powai, the company (registered as Avenue Supermarts) has stores at 191 locations across eleven states and one union territory. The company closed the financial year 2018–19 with a top line of over Rs 20,000 crore, and a profit after tax of Rs 900 crore, a rarity in the retail industry.[49] The company has never seen a loss-making quarter in its seventeen years of existence. For a start-up in a hypercompetitive industry, that's quite remarkable.

Being an ace investor himself, Damani brought the discipline of long-term investing to his retail venture. For instance, the promoter prefers to purchase properties instead of renting or getting them on long-term lease. As much as 90 per cent of the company's retail space is self-owned and -developed. It helps keep the biggest fixed cost, rentals, from spiralling out. The rental cost at DMart is as low as 0.2 per cent of the total sales, as compared to 8 per cent for a typical Big Bazaar.[50]

DMart's large-format stores (30,000–35,000 sq ft) are typically located in residential areas, as against malls, offering daily-need products and commodities at deep discounts. As for keeping the vendors loyal, the company has a policy of clearing their dues latest by the eleventh day after the purchase, as against the industry practice of around three weeks.[51]

The decision of going slow has also allowed DMart to choose its locations and formats wisely and ensure profitability from the very start of a new store. As for the merchandize, the company has chosen to go for fewer varieties, largely limited to food and groceries, but at a high volume, which allows better margins at scale. Also, the retailer avoids private labels as much as possible. Most food and grocery products would be sold at prices 6–12 per cent cheaper than elsewhere, and in some cases even 10 per cent lower than the MRP.

The following statement summarizes DMart's business ethos: 'Start with low-cost products that consumers need daily and that you can sell for slightly below MRP. This allows you to rack up a great inventory turnover ratio. Then use that quick inventory turnover to negotiate better prices with wholesalers which in turn allows you to support your low prices.'[52] Simple and scalable.

In the online space, a company that has thrived amid external chaos and owing to internal discipline is Bigbasket. During its early days, when the leading investors likes Tiger Global and SoftBank were backing the asset-light grocery delivery models, the founders of Bigbasket stuck to their plans. Their inventory-based business model stemmed from deep consumer insights and aspirations of offering above 99.5 per cent fill rate and 99 per cent on-time delivery, unheard of in the industry.[53]

Eventually, the asset-light models collapsed, and Bigbasket emerged as the winner. Then, in 2018, as a testimony to Bigbasket's strategic choices and execution at scale, Alibaba invested in the company, helping Bigbasket leverage Alibaba's expertise in bulk storage, logistics and distribution.[54] Their insight-driven foresight, conviction, strategic patience and, above all, discipline in the face of agnostic customers and antagonistic investors made Bigbasket India's largest online grocer, with over twelve million customers across twenty-six cities.

Scale validates your ideas and efforts, and whether you are a start-up or a large enterprise, you must plan for scale.

Let us now look at how these principles and practices play out in the real world. In the following chapter, I depict the flow of a typical two-day design-thinking workshop and discuss the enablers that can help institutionalize the design-thinking approach at your organization.

9

Design Thinking in Action

'Innovation isn't about perfection. You've got to shank a few before you swing smooths out. Get out there and observe the market, your customer and products. Brainstorm like crazy and prototype in bursts.'

—Tom Kelley[1]

Design thinking exercises are best done in a workshop format, because learning must be hands-on for it to sustain and translate to real work. In this chapter, we look at some of the best practices of hosting or participating in a design-thinking problem-solving workshop. This would be applicable to any setting, whether you are doing it for your internal teams or for clients.

Jake Knapp and his colleagues from Google Ventures recommend a five-day *design sprint*, with a day dedicated to each of the five stages of design thinking, namely, map, sketch, decide, prototype and test.

Once the team has set aside an entire week to attack the difficult problem of, say, significantly improving the customer experience for an existing product or creating a new service altogether, they go through a disciplined approach, as summarized below.

On Monday, the team sets out to learn everything about the issue and the context to map out the problem and agree on the initial target. Tuesday is dedicated to structured ideation sessions, where participants generate potential solutions and add details by sketching or through other means of visualizing ideas. Come Wednesday, and the team selects the most promising ideas to proceed with, often through a voting process and some quick discussions, instead of resorting to long-winded meetings or presentations. Each shortlisted solution is detailed into a testable hypothesis before being taken to the anvil.

Thursday is spent in giving shape to the selected ideas in the form of working prototypes that highlight different concepts. Finally, on Friday, the prototypes are put up for scrutiny before the target customers, so that the team can get valuable insights for their next sprint. And then the process starts all over again, this time taking them closer to the desired outcome. As Knapp puts it, '[Design sprint] gives our startups a superpower: They can fast-forward into the future to see their finished product and customer reactions, before making any expensive commitments.'[2]

Knapp and his team also share useful techniques of conducting a design sprint: 1) form a team of 7–10 members with diverse skills and temperaments, who are all in agreement about the vital question to be addressed; 2) get the participants to free up their calendar for the entire duration of the sprint, so that they are physically and cerebrally present in the workshop; 3) get the participants to keep aside their laptops, mobile phones or any other devices for the duration of the workshop and plan for well-timed breaks for people to check their devices; 4) have a *decider* in the room, so that critical decisions could be taken on the spot and the team can rapidly progress; 5) keep the workshop venue well-stocked with stationery items, like chart paper, sticky notes, colour sketch pens, markers, tapes, soft-board pins, craft paper, pencils and crayons, and ensure that there are a couple of large white boards available throughout the workshop; 6) seek expert opinion to shorten your learning curve whenever possible, but never miss an opportunity to get a first-hand insight, if time and resources permit; and 7) always sketch out your ideas in as much detail as possible and be ready for lightening demos. An effective workshop mandates an empathetic facilitator, with no vested interest in the problem or in the team.

One limitation with the prescribed five-day design sprint is that it seems to be highly oriented towards technology start-ups, mainly focusing on new product or service development, whereas most real-world organizations are not always looking for new product development; instead, they are looking to solve everyday problems, systematically. Further, an investment of five days may be too much to ask for, especially considering the rhythms of most corporate firms and the myriads of problems they encounter daily. A more practical duration is two days, where a cross-functional team attacks a reasonably well-identified problem space, which, if solved, would result in building creative confidence for the team, generating momentum so that the team can eventually plan a five-day sprint.

A two-day design-thinking workshop

I typically facilitate two-day workshops for problem-solving using design thinking. Anything less than two days is often experienced as rushed, and a duration beyond two days makes the participants restless. So here are the objectives, ground rules and an outline of a typical two-day programme, along with the specific methods employed and a proposed mentoring programme.

Session objectives

The key takeaways from the workshop are as follows:

- Learn about the skill sets, toolsets and mindsets of a systematic approach to problem-solving
- Develop means to understand the unmet and unarticulated needs of the customers (a customer is anyone whose problem you wish to solve)
- Pick up methods of prioritizing, scoping and framing problems worth solving
- Generate high-impact ideas methodically
- Find ways of validating the ideas and demonstrating those to key stakeholders

Ground rules

Some of the means of instilling discipline in the proceedings are:

- A session with 25–30 participants
- Workshop anchored around a few strategic themes or organizational priorities
- Each team of 5–6 participants working on a specific problem area or theme
- No mobile phones or laptops allowed during the workshop
- Eight hours of commitment per day, preferably in an offsite setting
- Handouts provided to each participant, detailing the session flow, tools and techniques of design thinking

Workshop flow

Table 1: Outline of Day 1 of a design-thinking workshop

Theme	Topics covered	Duration
On problem-solving	1. Why a problem fully understood is half-solved? 2. Why not traditional models of problem-solving? 3. A disciplined approach to creativity	1 hour
A primer on design thinking (DT)	1. What is DT and why DT now? 2. The process model of DT 3. Key tenets of DT	1 hour
Inspire	1. Design brief (impact, constraints and equifinality) 2. Team formation and project scoping	1 hour
Empathize	1. Importance of deep listening and empathy 2. Going from symptoms to problems to root causes 3. Probing techniques (problem exploration, stakeholder map, empathy map, customer journey maps, user personas)	3 hours
Define	1. 80/20 rule and MECE 2. Problem canvas	1 hour

Table 2: Outline of Day 2 of a design-thinking workshop

Theme	Topics covered	Duration
Ideate	1. Principles of ideation 2. Ideation techniques (challenging assumptions, across value chain; beyond current users; design for the extreme; analogous design; ideation triggers)	3 hours
Prototype and test	1. Idea shortlisting methods (desirability, feasibility, viability) 2. On quick and dirty prototyping 3. Storytelling, scenarios and storyboarding 4. Customer feedback review	1 hour
Scale	1. Business model canvas 2. Objectives and key results	2 hours
Reflection and closure	1. Summary of key takeaways 2. Personal reflections	1 hour

Mentoring programme

As a trainer and coach, I strongly believe that real learning happens on the job. It is relatively easy to excite an audience with examples and narratives on how design thinking works, but the 'moment of truth' occurs only when they get back to their workplaces, where if they revert to their old ways of problem-solving the entire purpose is defeated. So, in most of my programmes, I insist on follow-up mentoring engagements, where we see to it that the learning, about problem-solving using design thinking, is applied in real contexts. This is one step towards fostering innovation culture.

Here are a few practices that can be followed at mentoring programmes: 1) Have well-defined, well-scoped projects where some preliminary results can be shown in about a quarter's time; 2) Have participants work in teams, which don't have to be the same as the ones for their business-as-usual tasks; 3) Have an internal mentor/supervisor from the business who keeps a pulse on the project's progress; 4) Link the project's success to the participants' fate in the organization, through incentives or performance appraisal; and 5) Showcase the results to the senior management to generate visibility for the team's efforts and bring to notice the importance of design thinking.

You would realize that a mentoring programme would help broaden the application of design thinking in a more enduring manner.

Build your own version of a design-thinking programme

Every company is unique in its own way—different in terms of aspiration levels of its leaders and employees, risk tolerance, comfort with ambiguity, ability of being disciplined and open to external changes. Notwithstanding the discipline that a design-thinking programme can bring to the discourse and practice of creative problem-solving, you must aim at customizing the approach that suits your organizational temperament. Some of the more successful innovators have created a grounds-up model of problem-solving, on the basis of the principles and practices of IDEO's design-thinking approach.

The financial software company Intuit has its own version of design thinking called Design for Delight (D4D). Launched in 2007, the D4D model is based on three tenets: deep customer empathy; go broad to go narrow; and rapid experiments with customers. The D4D programmes are run across the organization by dedicated innovation capabilities teams. The team used to report to the chief of staff in the office of the former CEO, Brad Smith, and this speaks volume about Intuit's seriousness towards design thinking.

The company has created the position of 'innovation catalyst' to identify and run design-thinking projects and evangelize their benefits, in order to make this approach integral to their business. By 2017, over 1,500 innovation catalysts were trained and taken through three, five or fourteen days of design-thinking and leadership-training programmes.[3] Intuit also runs D4D Forums, with around 1,000 participants each, where employees share success stories, listen to experts talking about the power of design thinking and are encouraged to adopt those practices. Their focus on design thinking can be gauged from the fact that between 2006 and 2017, the number of designers at the executive level at Intuit grew from six to thirty-five.

Accenture has its own version of design thinking, called FORM Methodology. This five-stage process comprises a series of 'form' steps, which are about co-discovering problems and co-creating solutions with clients in an iterative fashion. The stages are: 1) Inform: Discover with insight; 2) Formulate: Describe with impact; 3) Freeform: Co-create with agility; 4) Transform: Scale with excellence; and 5) Outperform: Sustain with improvement.[4]

Accenture runs a three-day course called 'Design Thinking Academy', to generate awareness, skills and a common language around the topic of design thinking, and follows it up with ninety days of virtual coaching. These sessions are not only meant for the company's global leaders and senior managers but also for clients. I have been a part of some of the co-innovation sessions at Accenture Bengaluru Innovation Hub and could see the company's commitment towards offering a differentiated client experience by adopting design-thinking principles.

Several organizations that I have engaged with have borrowed the best practices from the likes of IDEO, Stanford d.school and LUMA Institute among others, and have rolled out their own versions. I have personally witnessed this, at companies like Titan, Oracle, Honeywell, Samsung, Deloitte and Asian Paints among others. But all learning is only as good as its implementation.

Offer avenues to practise design thinking

What happens when your excited, trained and primed employees do not get an opportunity to even try out design thinking in a real-world context? Most programmes on design thinking, or any other approach on creative problem-solving, fail because the leaders do not provide avenues for their employees to practise some of these concepts and methods. As a result, it remains business as usual, and soon, disillusionment towards design thinking sets in. If this continues, employees become cynical. Sincere employees always want to actively participate in problem-solving, instead of being passive observers, and as a leader it is your responsibility to make that transition happen. Here is a case on how avenues for practising design thinking can be created and progress can be measured.

Vishal Sikka, former CEO of Infosys, was far more instrumental than any other Indian leader in raising awareness of the concept and importance of design thinking. As a PhD from

Stanford University and a protégé of SAP's Hasso Plattner, Sikka had a deep understanding and appreciation of design thinking.

In his very first quarter at Infosys, he focused on sensitizing his top brass on the importance of customer-centricity, the iterative style of problem-solving and the virtues of prototyping. In late 2014, as a part of the Bringing Innovation Culture in Every Project (BICEP) initiative, the CEO rolled out training programmes on design thinking for Infosys employees. The senior leaders were sent to attend short-term programmes at Stanford University, and those on projects and offshore locations were trained by experts at the various Infosys campuses and training facilities. As of March 2016, over 80,000 Infosys employees and key clients had been trained in the principles and methods of applying an empathetic, human-centric model of problem-solving.[5]

During his brief term at Infosys (2014–17), Sikka made sincere efforts to build avenues for employees to practise creative problem-solving alongside their day job. Two such avenues were the Zero Distance and Zero Bench programmes. The Zero Distance programme, which began in early 2015, was aimed at gaining customer insights for new product launches and continual product improvements. In the words of Sikka: 'Zero-distance has a three-fold emphasis: to reduce the gap between us and the code we write, the gap between us and our clients, and the gap between us and the ultimate end-user.'[6] The programme offered opportunities to improve client projects beyond the scope of work and were monitored by those right at the top.

The Zero Bench programme, launched in July 2015, aimed at eliminating the bench resources (employees between projects) and creating an internal marketplace of talent, so that employees awaiting long-term assignments contribute to Infosys projects. While utilizing the company's learning infrastructure, the unbilled employees, under this programme, could also work on short, internal projects of their own choice, gain exposure, build a network and deliver value to the organization.

By March 2016, over 1,35,000 employees had taken up 16,000 innovation and continuous improvement projects under the Zero Distance initiative; and there had been more than 25,700 small projects completed by over 44,000 Infoscions under the Zero Bench programme.[7]

For its efforts towards training employees in design thinking, Infosys was given the 'Leader in the Winner's Circle – Excellent at Innovation and Execution' title by HFS Research.[8] The report highlighted how Infosys had adopted design thinking as a means to drive a cultural shift in the organization, as well as the company's commitment towards training all employees in design thinking and co-creating with clients using design-thinking sessions.

Though Sikka could not himself witness the fruits of his investments, especially in regard to his drive towards design thinking, his Infosys term did raise the industry's sensitivity towards end-customers, rapid iteration and the significance of problem definition. The key, however, was to offer enough avenues and incentives for employees to exercise these newly acquired skills, and in this department Sikka made a lasting impression.

Think beyond jugaad

Indians instinctively gravitate towards improvisation. People in both rural and urban dwellings, with varying levels of resources, do not shy away from creating and applying quick fixes. Often referred to as jugaad, these good enough, affordable solutions are everywhere in our daily lives, often in unknown ways. In the technology domain, jugaads are also referred to as 'hacks'.

A missed-call based reminder, a Tata Ace doubling up as a portable kitchen or even a school van, inventive ways of squeezing paste out of a tube or creatively preserving and reusing food, are all examples of ingenuity applied amid constraints. These are cases of addressing symptoms without bothering about the underlying problem, without taking pains to get to the root cause and trying to solve the problem permanently. In many cases, getting to the problem is not justified, for the problem may be a one-time event. But not always.

Improvisation has a place in problem-solving, but making it a default is problematic. That is what Indians are guilty of. Improvisation makes sense for as long as it emerges from a genuine scarcity of resources, as demonstrated by ISRO's Mangalyaan team, or when time is at a premium, as was the case with the astronauts on board the Apollo 13 Lunar Module. But it cannot be made into a habit, because if that happens, no one would have incentives to deliberately think of making processes better and outcomes more robust. An improvisation-based approach suffers from three key limitations: such approaches are not reliable, not repeatable and, consequently, not scalable. Think of jugaad as a prototype that got shipped.

Let us understand why Indians are comfortable with improvisation. The reason is cultural as much as economic, for a jugaad-based approach is seen as beneficial even when resources are replete, as in the case of most corporate or elite segments of society.

To understand the cultural context, let us look at the work of social psychologist Geert Hofstede. For over four decades now, Hofstede has been studying various national cultures and scoring countries on the following parameters: power distance index, individualism versus collectivism, masculinity versus femininity, uncertainty avoidance index, long-term orientation versus short-term normative orientation and indulgence versus restraint.[9] For our discussion, the parameters of interest are power distance, individualism and uncertainty avoidance.

Power distance index is the extent to which the less powerful members of organizations and institutions (like the family) accept and expect that power to be distributed unequally. Individualism versus collectivism is the degree to which individuals are integrated into groups. Uncertainty avoidance index deals with a society's tolerance for uncertainty and ambiguity.

As per Hofstede's analysis, where does India stand on these parameters? Power Distance: 77; individualism: 48; and uncertainty avoidance: 40. Please note that these are generalized scores and they don't take into account India's sheer diversity.

At 77, India scores high on power distance index (PDI), which means an appreciation for hierarchy and top-down structure in society and organizations. The hierarchies are observed in both personal and professional settings and typically, the line of command is clear and often unquestioned. To get a better picture, compare this with Mexico and Malaysia, whose PDI is as high as 81 and 100 respectively. On the other hand, you have Israel, with a PDI of 13, and Australia at 38.

India's score on individualism (IDV) is average: 48. It suggests a mix of individualistic and collectivistic behaviour, indicating that individuals retain their identity and thought process while complying with the larger group norms. Australia (90) and the United States (91) are among the countries that have a high IDV level, whereas the low-IDV countries include Venezuela (12) and Colombia (13).

On the uncertainty avoidance index (UAI), India scores 40. This one is interesting. 'In India,' notes Hofstede, 'there is acceptance of imperfection; nothing has to be perfect nor has to go exactly as planned . . . People generally do not feel driven and compelled to take action-initiatives and comfortably settle into established rolls and routines without questioning.'[10] Which countries score high on UAI? Belgium is at 94, Japan at 92 and Israel at 81.

Do you see any relation between the tendencies of uncertainty avoidance and innovation? There is a clear link, and Hofstede mentions about India that, 'Rules are often in place just to be circumvented and one relies on innovative methods to "bypass the system". A word used often in India is "adjust" and means a wide range of things, from turning a blind eye to rules being flouted to finding a unique and inventive solution to a seemingly insurmountable problem.'[11] What he is referring to here is nothing but jugaad.

If comfort with ambiguity or uncertainty is combined with low levels of individualism and high power distance, you have a perfect recipe for frugal improvisation. For radical product innovation, you would need a low power distance, which encourages defiance and dissent, as well as a more individualistic culture, where you do not feel the urge to comply with the group. On a more formal institutional dimension, India's high transaction cost, poor regime of intellectual property rights and weak law enforcement don't encourage product innovation either. Why would you risk an intellectual property-based product innovation when you are not sure of your state's capacity to back you up? You would rather gravitate towards process improvements, business model improvements, improvisation and clever imitation to keep going. Would you not 'hack' your way through the market instead of taking pains to build something elegant?

Another key reason Indians have not produced the innovations that do justice to the country's higher-education system and its sheer market size is that knowledge and skills are often treated as separate compartments here. The 'know-how' does not always come with the 'know-why', and vice versa. Let me explain. I am an engineer, but every time I have an electrical issue at my home or an electric device misbehaving, I resort to an electrician. Similarly, a mechanical engineer would pretty much know how an internal combustion engine works but would rely on a mechanic whenever his car breaks down. A mechanical engineer has knowledge and a mechanic has skills, the former has the know-why whereas the latter has the know-how, and in an Indian context they seldom co-exist.

That is not typically the case in the West, where most take pride in fixing their homes, mending their lawns, washing their dishes and repairing their cars. As Walter Isaacson writes in his book *The Innovators*, most of the pioneers of the computer era used to be very much hands-on from early childhood. They would build mechanical and electrical contraptions, operate ham radios, perform experiments in their garages, make and break stuff apart and learn through practice. Recollecting his childhood days, Robert Noyce, co-founder of Fairchild Semiconductor and later of Intel, said: 'Dad always managed to have some sort of workshop in the basement . . . I grew up in small town America, so we had to be self-sufficient. If something was broke you fix it yourself.'[12]

Because of cheap labour in India—a division of labour that owes a lot to *varna vyavastha* (caste system)—the ones who know do not feel the urge to practise, while the ones who practise seldom feel like they need to know much beyond getting through the problem. A jugaad typically comes from someone with skills or knowledge, but an elegant innovation calls for both know-how *and* know-why for it to be robust and reliable. Unless this artificial and ancient chasm between knowledge and skills is bridged, particularly in the minds of youngsters, we would have fewer innovations and more improvisations.

Rishikesha Krishnan, who has extensively studied innovation at national, sectoral and organizational levels, attributes India's overall lack of 'systematic innovation' to 'poor teamwork, the enduring importance of upward hierarchical progression, a Brahminical attitude that gives brainwork a superior position over physical work, a weak systems and strategic orientation, low tolerance of failure, a lack of confidence in innovation capabilities coupled with a failure to positively reinforce innovation efforts, and a strong need for control'.[13] These factors make individuals and organizations gravitate towards jugaad-style improvisations and improvements.

So, what is the solution? I would propose that more people adopt design thinking. Design thinking puts a premium on empathy and getting to the core of the problem, something that jugaad skips entirely. To add to this, rigorous prototyping and iterative development bring the solution closer to the desirable outcome. In an Indian context, design thinking can lend the necessary discipline to problem-solving, making the approach more reliable, repeatable and scalable.

Pay attention to the physical space

Do you wonder why Google spends so much money in making its offices so amazing? The company's headquarters, the Googleplex, located in Mountain View, California, boasts nap pods for overworked employees, massage rooms, slides connecting different floors, three free gourmet meals a day for the staff, complimentary campus bikes, Android bots, organic gardens for the veggies and herbs used in the cafeteria, meditation spots, plenty of electric car charging stations, large playgrounds and recreational areas, and a lot more which you only get to experience as an employee. As Eric Schmidt puts it, 'We invest in our offices because we expect people to work there, not from home. A serendipitous encounter (with a colleague) would never happen when you are working from home.'[14]

Google is among the top ten in the ranks of the world's highest R&D spenders, of companies with the highest number of US patents granted and of the world's most innovative companies. Many universities and company campuses have imitated Google's workplace design to encourage a free flow of ideas, a spirit of collaboration, a balance of personal and open spaces, and other frills to foster innovation.

To create and maintain such huge spaces, you require foresight and commitment to look at the not-so-obvious aspects of innovation culture. An innovation culture thrives only in the right context. On the power of context, Malcolm Gladwell reminds us, 'Non-verbal clues are as or more important than verbal clues . . . Simple physical movements and observations can have a profound effect on how we feel and think.'[15] A culture of systematic problem-solving, just as epidemics, says Gladwell, 'are sensitive to the conditions and circumstances of the times and places in which they occur'. As a leader, you need to design such environments painstakingly, for they might speak louder than you ever could.

Steven Johnson, author of *Where Good Ideas Come From*, builds a compelling case of how physical spaces shape our thinking and possibilities of idea generation. Open, high-density, randomizing environments that maintain a delicate balance between private and public spaces encourage people to spontaneously connect and cobble together concepts to generate yet more powerful ideas. Our physical environments shape our brain's ability to explore new possibilities along multiple unpredictable paths.

Citing the case of eighteenth-century English coffeehouses, which sparked and nurtured numerous Enlightenment-era ideas and innovations, Johnson comments: 'The collisions that happen when different fields of expertise converge in some shared physical or intellectual space. That's where the true sparks fly. The modernism of the 1920s exhibited so much cultural innovation in such a short period of time because the writers, poets, artists, and architects were all rubbing shoulders at the same cafés. They weren't off on separate islands, teaching creative writing seminars or doing design reviews.'[16]

That is why cities, as they grow, give rise to new ideas, as do the workplaces that are carefully crafted to strike a balance between chaos and order. They allow for greater possibilities of connections between hitherto disparate people, insights, hunches, knowledge domains, concepts and ideas.

Take the example of IIM Bangalore. The faculty blocks are designed in such a way that the professor of marketing would have an office adjacent to that of the professor of business strategy and right opposite could be where the professor of economics sits, with his office door wide open. At IIMB, the space isn't divided on the basis of departments or, worse still, designations. The campus is designed to encourage serendipitous encounters, academic collaborations and joint authorship of research papers.

When it comes to brainstorming sessions, the physical space plays a crucial role. As John Seely Brown, former director of Xerox PARC, observes: 'If you can design the physical space, the social space, and the information space together to enhance collaborative learning, then that whole milieu turns into a learning technology.'[17] Of all the companies in the computer era, PARC has had a profound impact on the way we interact with computers, and this could well be attributed to how the place was designed. Creative teams not only need to be able to share their ideas verbally but also visually and physically, and a well-designed space can enable multiple forms of expression, essential to design thinking. One of the emerging trends is coworking spaces.

University of Michigan's Gretchen Spreitzer, Peter Bacevice and Lyndon Garrett have extensively studied coworking spaces, looking at why people feel more productive and motivated in such environments as compared to in typical offices.[18] The researchers cite two reasons for the growing popularity of coworking spaces. First, people who use coworking spaces see their work as more meaningful, because there is little direct competition or internal politics and the members don't feel impelled to adopt a work persona; they also get more opportunities to contribute to others' work in a non-threatening way. Second, the setting allows office workers to have more control on their work. The 24/7 operations, various seating arrangements, mix of public and private spaces, and recreational and refreshment facilities allow members to choose their own rhythm to work. The community further brings discipline to the work routine, especially for freelancers and solo entrepreneurs.

I have been working out of a coworking space for the last three years now and have managed to write a substantial part of this book sitting at one—91springboard in Bangalore. I do see the value of such spaces.

An open work environment is a requisite for an effective problem-solving workshop. Instead of resorting to a classroom seating, break up the pattern and see if you can make participants sit in clusters of 5–6 diverse individuals—though a team might be working on a specific theme, a diversity of perspectives is much required to break the deeply entrenched patterns of thinking. Leave enough space for participants to move around. Hang charts on the walls and provide your participants with sticky notes, markers, sketch pens, white boards and Lego blocks or synthetic clay to play with. All these objects go a long way in fostering a climate of creativity, because now you are engaging the whole being, and especially the hands.

As a moderator or participant in such sessions, you need to pay attention to the interaction between physical space and human behaviour. Think carefully of ambient lighting, room temperature, personal space, free space and other props, so that the participants feel like giving their best to the problem on hand.

Stanford d.school, which has hosted more design-thinking projects than probably any other place on earth, has some best practices to offer on how to design a space that can inspire creativity. David Kelley, the founder of d.school, identifies the standout characteristics of such a space as follows: Keep people together but not too close, so that their privacy is maintained; ensure that noise is managed well, as brainstorming sessions can get quite noisy; have a mix of flexible and rigid spaces, so that the setting does not become disorienting; allow the teams to tailor the spaces and create their own 'micro environments'; leave sufficient rough spaces and rough material for people to experiment with; and celebrate when a project moves from a prototype to scale or when an experiment succeeds.[19] Simple, but not easy.

One of the most thoughtfully created workspaces that I have been to is the Titan Integrity Campus. The new head office of Titan, the Integrity Campus was opened in 2017 in the Electronic City area of Bangalore. The biophilic campus, spread over 6.5 acres, has a natural lake in it and another man-made lake right at the centre where the office buildings are. The three low-rise, stone-clad buildings on the campus are designed to bring in maximum sunlight and allow for continuous movement of breeze. There are cascading terrace gardens at every level, offering enough space for employees to walk around and work in open areas.

The entire campus has been made with natural materials. Although the various departments are colour-coded and housed in separate buildings and on different floors, they are connected through large open atriums, which mix private and public spaces. These have been equipped with wide steps, courtyards, product-display walls, seating areas, a section for visitors and another for hosting informal meetings.[20]

On how the office architecture encourages creativity, Revathi Kant, Titan's chief design officer, shares: 'In a natural environment, everyone feels comfortable, thinks differently, it leads to more constructive discussion, better insights. The energy, vibe, motivation levels—all have gone up.'[21] There's little doubt that like Titan, more companies are moving towards adopting open-office architecture in a big way. So do not let the workspace be the weakest link in your innovation effort.

Trust the process

Finally, it comes down to discipline. Most people find it difficult to believe that creativity and discipline can coexist. For them, creativity is possible *only if* there are few constraints, fewer rules, more resources and a lot more liberty. This notion is nothing more than an excuse for not being disciplined. True creativity comes through a process, where a few well-laid-out rules are followed and a meticulous approach is taken, as exemplified by ace sportspeople and innovators alike. On the benefits of discipline, Google's co-founder Larry Page says, 'As much as I hate process, good ideas with great execution is how you make magic.'[22]

You need not look any further than the US Navy SEALs to understand how discipline enables creativity and the way real constraints push ordinary people towards achieving extraordinary results. As Jocko Willink, the famous Navy SEAL officer who led various missions to Iraq, notes, *discipline equals freedom*. In the book *Extreme Ownership*, Willink and Leif Babin talk about various missions in Ramadi city where they had to devise and communicate standard operating procedures (SOPs) for activities ranging from search and rescue to carrying out surgical strikes. These SOPs not only saved precious time but also saved lives and helped the team gather more actionable intelligence from the field.

'Instead of making us more rigid and unable to improvise, discipline actually made us more flexible, more adaptable, and more efficient. It allowed us to be creative,' Willink says in the book.[23] If people in a war can be creative while being extremely disciplined, do you think yours is a more precarious situation?

In contrast to the commonly held belief, innovative companies are highly process-oriented. Take, for instance, Pixar Animation Studios, one of the leading producers of animation movies for all ages. The studio has delighted us over the years with films like *Toy Story*, *Up*, *Finding Nemo* and other deeply moving narratives. The co-founder of Pixar, Ed Catmull writes in *Creativity, Inc.* that one of the most memorable lessons he learnt over the years at Pixar and, later, at Disney, is that when it comes to creativity, one must trust the process.

At Pixar, every animation movie is different, in terms of its characters, storyline and even its emotional tone, and yet its making follows, by and large, the same well-regimented processes, which have evolved over the years.

But do not assume that following a process is an end in itself, and that the process alone would magically lead you to results. Disciplined creativity is enabled by living, ever-adapting processes. Remember, without a process it is all chaos, but with an inflexible and unadaptable process there is no progress either. As Catmull explains, 'When we trust the process, we remember that we are resilient, that we've experienced discouragement before, only to come out the other side. When we trust the process – or perhaps more accurately, when we trust the people who *use* the process – we are optimistic but also realistic. The trust comes from knowing that we are safe, that our colleagues will not judge us for failures but will encourage us to keep pushing the boundaries.'[24]

In my experience, when it comes to creativity, most people err on the side of not following a process at all, rather than getting completely subsumed under one. The entire notion of 'processes killing creativity' is largely unfounded. Some of the most creative teams and innovative companies are far more disciplined than what meets the eye. Christopher Nolan, one of the most successful film directors of the twenty-first century, puts it nicely, 'Breaking rules isn't interesting. It is making up new ones that keeps things exciting.'[25] While you don't need discipline to break the rules, you certainly do to create new ones.

So far, our discussion has largely been limited to organizations and teams. In the next chapter, we talk about individuals and identify some of the personal traits that can help you become a better problem-solver and unleash your creativity.

10

How to Be a Design Thinker

'Go for a walk; cultivate hunches; write everything down, but keep your folders messy; embrace serendipity; make generative mistakes; take on multiple hobbies; frequent coffeehouses and other liquid networks; follow the links; let others build on your ideas; borrow, recycle, reinvent.'

—Steven Johnson[1]

By now you must be convinced that design thinking can be cultivated as a skill, by adopting suitable toolsets and honing the appropriate mindsets. But how about being a design thinker? Can you be one? Do innovative companies actively seek certain specific skill sets and mindsets? The answer to all of the above is yes.

According to Tim Brown, IDEO looks at the following five traits in a design thinker: empathy, integrative thinking, optimism, experimentalism and willingness to collaborate.[2] Empathy to look at the world from others' perspectives; integrative thinking to go beyond the either/or choices; optimism to continuously seek better solutions; experimentalism to validate assumptions systematically; and collaboration across disciplines and organizational boundaries.

The real question is: can problem-solving be routinized? Yes, it can be. In fact, some of the most creative individuals and innovative companies credit their consistently high performance to practising robust routines. The researcher Martha Feldman defines routines as, 'Repeated patterns of behaviour that are bound by rules and customs and that do not change very much from one iteration to another.'[3] Routines are a source of both stability and change—stability by laying out rules and customs, and change by allowing the agent (read problem-solver) to exercise autonomy. In the absence of a robust routine, you would have to start from first principles to solve every problem, every single time, whereas if your routine is cast in stone, your approach to problem-solving would never improve. An example of non-routinized problem-solving is jugaad or improvisation, and as we discussed in the previous chapter, improvisation is not always desirable, since it lacks repeatability, reliability and scalability.

Routines for an organization are akin to *habits* for an individual. As Mihaly Csikszentmihalyi, one of the leading authorities on research on creativity, notes, creative individuals have well-built habits. 'Most creative individuals,' he states, 'find out early what their best rhythms are for sleeping, eating, and working, and abide by them even when it is tempting to do otherwise. They wear clothes that are comfortable, they interact only with people they find congenial, they do only things they think are important . . . But personalizing patterns of action helps to free the mind from the expectations that make demands on attention and allows intense concentration on matters that count.'[4]

Design thinking is about getting into a routine of systematic and systemic problem-solving. In the following section, I offer pointers on the skill sets and mindsets that could help you become a better (design) thinker.

Live curious

'Live curious' is the tag line of National Geographic. Their website says, 'Where knowledge ends, curiosity begins.' This is so true in the realm of creativity. Thanks to Google, there is not as much value in knowing stuff anymore as in applying what's known, exploring the unknown and creating new knowledge in the process—the knowledge that can help solve complex problems faster than the rate at which new problems get created.

On the importance of living curious, Christopher Nolan, one of the finest minds today in movie-making, observes, 'You're never going to learn something as profoundly as when it's purely out of curiosity.'[5] And another genius filmmaker of our generation, Quentin Tarantino, admits, 'Taking what you like from what already exists and putting it into your own work. And by the way you do it, the way you frame it, creating something that didn't exist before. It has taken a while for that to be respected, all right. But that's always kind of where I've been coming from.'[6] Interestingly, neither of the two went to a film school. Perhaps that explains their creativity.

Curiosity is the hallmark of great scientists, inventors, artists and successful entrepreneurs—curiosity to not just seek ideas but also sniff out problems worth solving. Unless you cultivate and respond to your inbuilt urge to know more, there is no way you can go from information to insight, from the spoken to the unarticulated, and from knowledge to imagination.

In support of curiosity over passion, author Elizabeth Gilbert proposes, 'I am a big advocate for the pursuit of curiosity . . . Passion is rare; curiosity is everyday. Curiosity is therefore a lot easier to reach at times than full-on passion – and the stakes are lower, easier to manage. The trick is to just follow your small moments of curiosity.'[7]

Francesca Gino of the Harvard Business School suggests that a curious mind is a more creative mind. Her empirical work shows that curiosity in adults helps them overcome confirmation biases, generating alternatives to problems, lowering group conflicts, encouraging more open communication and leading to visible gains in overall performance, on both creative and routine tasks.[8]

Notwithstanding the business benefits of curiosity, most employees feel that often they are not encouraged by their employers to be inquisitive at work. In a survey of 3,000 employees across industries, Gino found that 70 per cent of the respondents faced barriers in asking more questions and just about 25 per cent could say they could regularly indulge their curiosity on the job. A follow-up survey of 520 chief learning officers and chief talent development officers revealed that managers fear too much curiosity may hamper business productivity. So what is the solution? Gino recommends organizations to hire for curiosity and then model inquisitiveness by cultivating listening skills, encouraging a questioning attitude in employees, setting learning goals and offering avenues for broadening one's interests.

IBM's former CEO Ginni Rometty identifies curiosity as one of the most important traits the company seeks in a new hire. In an interview with *Fortune* magazine, Rometty says, 'We receive 7,000 job applications a day, and our managers and HR teams are geared to look for people who are curious and committed to constantly advancing what they know.' As for her personal strength, she is quick to note, 'A constant thirst to learn has served me well my entire career, especially in the tech industry.'[9]

The prerequisite for being a good design thinker is to seek inspiration in the ordinary. It is to not wait for a problem to surface but seek an opportunity when none exists in plain sight. The case of Bangalore-based iD Fresh Food demonstrates just how opportunities can be created and backed with a disciplined approach to build a market from scratch.

Imagine selling idli/dosa batter to South Indian households, where the typical practice is to make the fermented mix of parboiled rice and urad dal at home and consume it over days. Buying this stuff from the market was out of the question for many, and even if one did, it was a choice among a limited bunch of unhygienic, small-scale producers. Then along came P.C. Mustafa, who, together with his cousins, spotted the opportunity of selling fresh, ready-to-consume, preservative-free batter. Soon, iD Fresh Food became a household name in India and the Middle East.

From a humble beginning in 2005, with an initial investment of Rs 50,000 and a fifty-square-feet kitchen, iD Fresh Food today sells over 50,000 kg of batter daily, available at 30,000 retail stores in thirty-five cities. Along the way, the company secured funds from Helion Venture Partners and Premji Invest, at a time when, and in a market where, investors avoided brick-and-mortar businesses.

An acute sense of curiosity led Mustafa to launch vada batter and traditional filter coffee decoction packs, categories which were not thought suitable for packaged products. The innovative vada-making mechanism took the team three years to design, manufacture and perfect. Explaining the prototype-driven approach adopted to make the contraption, Mustafa says, 'We consulted industry experts and engineering consultants but no one had a solution. Finally, my cousin and co-founder went to a welding shop and created a mock-up using a hammer and pipe. It took him a year to have a working model. Finding the right food-grade material took another year. It paid off: One simply has to squeeze the pouch and the batter comes from all sides of the spout and you cut to get the shape.'[10] You have to use the product to believe its intuitiveness.

The story of iD Fresh Food has all the ingredients of design thinking: inspiration, empathy, ideas, prototypes and scale. And what knits it all together is the unfailing curiosity of the team. The next stop? The team wants to get rid of plastic in food packaging and make 'the world's best breakfast' without adding to the world's plastic burden.

Companies like MTR Foods, iD Fresh Food, Paper Boat have scripted a new story in Indian business on what it means to uphold tradition and be modern at the same time. These brands have succeeded because they have been able to combine an intense sense of empathy with disciplined execution.

One way of developing curiosity is to travel and read widely. Both these activities cost money, but with today's technological and commercial disruptions, like no-frills airlines, Airbnb and Oyo Rooms, travelling is not that prohibitive. On how travelling and staying at foreign locations profoundly influence creativity, the social psychologist Donald Campbell reminds us, 'Persons who have been uprooted from traditional culture, or who have been thoroughly exposed to two or more cultures, seem to have an advantage in the range of hypotheses they are apt to consider, and through this means, in the frequency of creative innovation.'[11]

A telling example of how travelling to and living at different places can help you become more creative and resilient is Julie Sweet. The first-ever female CEO of Accenture reflects, 'I have often pursued paths that were not well-trodden . . . Starting with my decision to learn Chinese and live in Taiwan and China in 1987 and 1988, before it was commonplace.' On how such experiences have shaped her thinking, Sweet adds, 'It has helped me become a continuous learner and to understand that it is often from unexpected sources and places that you learn the most.'[12]

So never give away a chance to move around.

Listen with intent

When David Rubenstein asked Sir Richard Branson about the most important attribute of a good leader, the latter responded with, 'Listening, and then choosing the words carefully.'[13] If you shift the spotlight, you would see how good a listener Rubenstein himself is, which is what makes him so sharp at quizzing some of the most powerful people in the world and so capable of surprising his listeners.

Though good listening is one of the twenty-first century's most significant skills, it is not just a skill; it is also a matter of attitude. While you listen with intent, you must also cultivate the humility to be genuinely surprised. A sense of surprise can only emerge from deliberate listening, which is called *listening with intent* or *empathic listening.*

Identifying listening as one of the core means of transforming Microsoft's culture, Satya Nadella says, 'Listening was the most important thing I accomplished each day because it would build the foundation of my leadership for years to come.'[14]

John Chambers, the former CEO of Cisco and one of the longest-serving leaders in the fast-paced technology industry, credits Cisco's stellar performance to the listening skills of its leaders. Having served at IBM and Wang Corporation, Chambers is quick to note that the technology industry is punishing if you do not listen to your customers in advance and are ready to have your thinking disrupted. Several of the successful acquisitions that Cisco made over the years were triggered by its customers. As Chambers says, 'Customers helped us spot a market shift and pointed us toward a new technology that would be useful in making the leap. That's one reason I spend so much time listening to CIOs, CTOs, and CEOs during sales calls.'[15] If a busy CEO can take time out to listen, what stops you?

But unfortunately, we are all becoming poor listeners. As author Stephen Covey quipped, 'Most people do not listen with the intent to understand; they listen with the intent to reply.'[16] So how do we develop listening skills? Remember, just like any other skill, listening with intent can be cultivated. Let me offer you a few avenues.

Julian Treasure, in his TED Talk, '5 Ways to Listen Better', offers a host of approaches for improving one's conscious listening.[17] One particularly useful tool is RASA, which stands for receive, appreciate, summarize and ask. The process begins with receiving information without any biases or judgements, then appreciating the problems or the concerns of the other party, followed by summarizing or paraphrasing what you have understood and finally, asking for clarification. Only when you have listened with intent can you start to understand the issue and then, possibly, address it.

In our attempt to develop good listening skills, perhaps the most difficult thing is to appreciate or have a genuine sense of gratitude towards the speaker. Think of it—how can you solve somebody's problem without appreciating the person facing that problem? You need to do that before thinking or acting on the problem. So says Oprah Winfrey, 'I've talked to nearly 30,000 people on this show and all 30,000 had one thing in common . . . They all wanted validation.'[18] That is why scores of celebrities let their guards down before Oprah and let out their deepest, often ugliest truths. She has mastered Julian's RASA technique, and so can you, with practice.

To add to this technique, I would propose the '1:5 Rule of Listening'. The heuristics, more of a best practice, states that for every single word that you speak, try listening to five; or for every minute that you speak for in a conversation, listen for five minutes. I have been trying it, to moderate success, and find myself becoming more empathetic as a result.

Observe with purpose

Acute observations can yield remarkably different insights that mere listening will not. You could listen to what is stated, but a lot remains non-verbal, which can only be observed and experienced. Our memories cannot always be trusted, for the simple reason that we all are liable to make errors of omission and commission. So for real insights to emerge, good listening must be complemented with skilful observation.

The Japanese are masters of good observational skills, and that is why continuous improvement and waste reduction are like second nature to them. According to Akio Morita, Sony's co-founder, the observational skills of Japanese people can be traced to the meticulousness with which they must learn to read and write the complicated script of their language.[19]

Honda, one of the world's most innovative automobile companies, owes its success to the well-honed practice of *sangen shugi*, which means seeing it with your own eyes by going to the spot before making a decision. Sangen shugi comprises three realities: *Gen-ba* (the real spot), *Gen-butsu* (the real part) and *Gen-jitsu* (the real facts). Honda trains its employees in the art and science of making first-hand observations and gaining knowledge by being close to the problem, in its real context. As the author Jeffrey Rothfeder notes, 'No decision is made at Honda without firsthand information, and no Honda manager or employee would dare try to offer a point of view, make a recommendation, or challenge an existing process or system unless he or she had "gone to the *gen-ba*," a term that is heard at Honda factories and offices everywhere in the world, no matter what language is spoken locally.'[20]

Good observational skills don't come easy. They mostly require painstaking practice. You need to step out of the routine, look at the world from a fresh perspective and then continue getting amazed without making conclusions too soon. To paraphrase the famous Indian philosopher Jiddu Krishnamurti, the ability to observe without evaluating is the highest form of intelligence.

Can observational skills be sharpened? Of course. Anthropologists do it all the time. The famous American cultural anthropologist and folklorist Ruth Benedict says that the purpose of anthropology is to make the world safe for human differences. The real insights come not from similarities but from differences, and such nuances often escape an untrained eye. Good anthropologists have a beginner's mind—they listen with intuition, park their judgements and embrace human behaviour with all its surprises. The key is to not look for perfection but authenticity.

The idea is not to fit the data into your preconceived framework but to look at the outliers—those who are using a washing machine to make lassi, or a pressure cooker to make espresso. Interact with the misfits, the creative types, and get comfortable with their worldview. The counter-intuitive practices are embedded in a culture and they are impossible to make sense of in the absence of a cultural context. The aforementioned examples of alternative uses of washing machines and pressure cookers are perfectly legitimate in the improvisation-oriented, frugality-celebrating culture of rural India. But elsewhere, they may evoke utter surprise.

Observing users in their cultural habitats would not only help you to understand the nuances of human behaviour but would also, occasionally, lead you to infer the motivations and emotions behind their actions. Deep observations offer surprising insights from the ground, enabling you to reframe the problems. For instance, if there is a significant market of people who are using washing machines for making lassi, would it not make sense to design a large mixer as part of your home appliances business?

That's what Haier did, seeing that Chinese customers were using washing machines for washing vegetables.

While observing, try to maintain a diary of your observations and ideas, much like Charles Darwin did on board the *HMS Beagle*, or Leonardo da Vinci while wandering around the Italian countryside. The practice of maintaining a 'commonplace notebook' was prevalent in Europe during the Renaissance period, and it contributed to an avalanche of scientific discoveries and inventions. Over time, the insights and hunches preserved in your notes and in your memory start to form patterns, which were never available before. Often the faintest pencil marks are far more powerful than the strongest memory.

But conscious listening and observing are only as good as your ability to park your biases and accept new insights while letting go of your preconceived notions and assumptions.

Defer your judgement

In Oscar Wilde's play *A Woman of No Importance*, one of the characters, Lord Illingworth, says, 'The only difference between the saint and the sinner is that every saint has a past, and every sinner has a future.' Nothing summarizes the true spirit of being non-judgemental better than this statement. Genuine empathy comes from looking at the world as *how it is* and not *how it is supposed to be*, and to do so you need to defer your judgement. The very expertise that makes you capable of addressing a problem often comes in the way of understanding the problem empathetically.

If you want empathy to seep in, intuition to take shape and new ideas to emerge, learn to suspend analysis. Jeff Bezos admits that his best decisions, in business and life, have been made with heart, intuition, taste and guts, and not with analysis.[21] And remember,

Bezos runs a company which is one of the largest creators of general-purpose AI.

In his book *Originals*, Adam Grant builds a case for procrastination, stating that the advantages of acting quickly and being first are often outweighed by their disadvantages.[22] Highlighting numerous cases—from the famous 'I Have a Dream' speech of Martin Luther King, Jr, to the works of great thinkers and artists like Benjamin Franklin and Bob Dylan—Grant argues how deferring judgement promotes divergent thinking, provided that you are thinking about the task in the back of your mind. The author claims that procrastination, which is otherwise a productivity killer, allows for greater cognitive flexibility and improvisation, enables people to overcome functional fixedness and results in a superior quantity and quality of ideas.

On why deferring judgment is crucial for synthesizing insights and connecting them in new ways, author Steven Johnson offers, 'Most hunches that turn into important innovations unfold over much longer time frames. They start with a vague, hard-to-describe sense that there's an interesting solution to a problem that hasn't yet been proposed, and they linger in the shadows of the mind, sometimes for decades, assembling new connections and gaining strength . . . But that long incubation period is also their strength, because true insights require you to think something that no one has thought before in quite the same way.'[23] In this sense, there are no real epiphanies or eureka moments. Most genuine ideas take shape slowly but appear as though they have sprung from nowhere, and they take time. As Google's former CEO Eric Schmidt says, 'One of the hallmarks of an innovative company is that it gives good ideas plenty of time to gestate.'[24]

By consciously deferring your judgement, you get in a daydreaming-like state of mind, and this enables you to make surprising connections between insights, ideas, experiences and knowledge. The reason daydreaming—or activities like walking or taking a shower—is a highly fertile period of idea generation is that in this state your sense of judgement is not heightened. You are in a state of *relaxed attention*, allowing your mind to work on *task-unrelated ideas* and establish connections that would be otherwise difficult to even think of.

Maintaining a running inventory of your observations, ideas and questions is also helpful, so that you can refer to those as the patterns emerge. On the importance of taking down notes, writer and entrepreneur Frans Johansson shares, 'Probably the best insurance against prejudging ideas is to write them down or diagram them when they occur to you. This will allow you to return to the ideas at frequent intervals. Then, if an idea suddenly seems more attractive, you can examine it more closely.'[25]

Judgement is the unwanted side effect of expertise. The more one becomes an expert in a certain domain, the higher one's latent inhibition becomes, the shorter the time taken to arrive at a decision and the stronger the biases once they are formed. Expertise, for all its strengths, makes it harder for one to come out of established patterns and make associations across disciplines. The associative barriers often are a consequence of deep expertise, which further traps us within our value networks of co-workers, friends, associates and acquaintances, and limit our worldview. Science historian Thomas Kuhn once famously observed, 'Almost always the men who achieve these fundamental inventions of a new paradigm have been either very young or very new to the field whose paradigm they change.'[26]

So learn to defer your judgement as much and for as long as possible, and do not just limit this advice to the area of creative problem-solving.

Hone multiple affiliations

Several years back, I met this amazing person named Douglas Solomon, who also happens to be the former chief technology officer of IDEO. I had the privilege of interviewing him during one of his trips to India. One of my questions was: What do you look for in a new hire at IDEO?' In response, Douglas took out a small piece of paper from his pocket and drew the following:

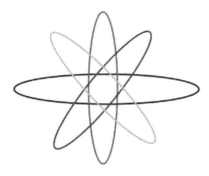

Figure 20: Honing multiple affiliations

Looking at Figure 20, at first, I thought he was referring to nuclear physics, but he soon clarified that the drawing was suggesting something different: *multiple affiliations.*

What matters is not who you are but who *all* you are and how many interests you pack in your life. IDEO and scores of other innovative companies look for individuals with multiple skills, multiple hobbies and not those who focus only on the activity they get paid for, their day job. If you are only XYZ at the ABC organization, even the CEO of a Fortune 500 company, the big question is: Who else are you? What else makes up your life?

If you define yourself narrowly in terms of your professional affiliations, it would severely limit your learning. And if that one key affiliation goes down for some reason, you are left with nothing. So it is critical that you broaden your horizons by doing various other things, such as taking music lessons, teaching kids how to code, playing badminton over the weekends, writing short stories, learning to cook some new dishes on your own, and then also making time for your day job. That's the approach of a creative person.

The easiest way to hone multiple affiliations is to pick up new hobbies. Don't think that hobby classes are meant only for kids, and don't worry if you aren't able to make something great out of that hobby. If the idea of picking up a hobby sounds too much at first, try picking up a side project, one where you are not judged even if you fail but which nonetheless keeps you stimulated.

It was one of Tim Berners-Lee's side projects, of keeping track of his colleagues and their work, that eventually became the World Wide Web. Since this wasn't his day job, he could look at things a lot differently as compared to those entrusted with inventing something new. In his own words, the low-profile genius admits, 'Most of the technology involved in the web, like the hypertext, like the Internet, multifont text objects, had all been designed already. I just had to put them together. It was a step of generalization, going to a higher level of abstraction.'[27] Berners-Lee's *relaxed attention* allowed him to connect those dots, seemingly intuitively. After working for almost ten years on his own, in 1990 he was officially appointed by CERN to work on the Hypertext project, which later led to the creation of the World Wide Web. (It should be mentioned that Berners-Lee's comment clearly shows how ideas are like Lego blocks and you must put them together in new combinations to create new stuff.)

For lessons on how side projects, hobbies and lifelong interests can help in creative problem-solving, look at the lives of the Nobel laureates. According to Adam Grant, Nobel Prize winners are twice as likely, as compared to their peers, to play a musical instrument, seven times as likely to draw or paint, twelve times as likely to write fiction or poetry, and twenty-two times as likely to perform as actors, dancers or, even, magicians. Grant concludes, 'This unique combination of broad and deep experience is critical for creativity . . . People who are open to new ways of looking at science and business also tend to be fascinated by the expression of ideas and emotions through images, sounds, and words.'[28]

The history of the technology industry is replete with examples of stalwarts who existed at the intersection of science and humanities. The same would be true in the future too. As Walter Isaacson writes, '[I]nnovation will come from people who are able to link beauty to engineering, humanity to technology, and poetry to processors.'[29]

If someone can maintain hobbies and yet go on to bag a Nobel Prize, are you saying that you are too busy? Maybe you need to learn to protect your hobbies from your profession.

Several outstanding achievers were real polymaths. But there has been none greater than Leonardo da Vinci. In his sixty-seven years of life, Da Vinci was driven by two powerful forces—*curiosity* and *observation*. And he packed his life with all possible affiliations he could lay hands on. He was proficient in metalworking, leather arts, carpentry, drawing, painting, sculpting and was a mathematician, an inventor, architect and amateur anatomist.

Describing the genius of Da Vinci, Walter Isaacson writes:

There have been, of course, many other insatiable polymaths, and even the Renaissance produced other Renaissance Men. But none painted the *Mona Lisa*, much less did so at the same time as producing unsurpassed anatomy drawings based on multiple dissections, coming up with schemes to divert rivers, explaining the reflection of light from the earth to the moon, opening the still-beating heart of a butchered pig to show how ventricles work, designing musical instruments, choreographing pageants, using fossils to dispute the biblical account of the deluge, and then drawing the deluge.[30]

We live in a more connected world, enjoy a better life expectancy than the previous generations and are endowed with powerful institutions. So if we choose to live unidimensional lives, we shouldn't wonder why new ideas don't occur to us that often. Ideas come when you expose yourself to the unfamiliar, the uncertain, and this does not happen by accident.

One of the hobbies that Satya Nadella nurtured was playing and following cricket. Having been a proficient cricketer in his early days in India, Nadella remains in touch with the sport. The Microsoft CEO says that playing cricket has taught him a lot about working in teams and leadership—lessons that have stayed with him throughout his career. He drew three core lesson from the world of cricket: first, to compete vigorously and with passion in the face of uncertainty and intimidation; second, to put the team first, ahead of your personal statistics and recognition; and third, that leadership plays a big role in bringing out the best in everyone.[31]

Piyush Pandey, the quintessential ad man of India, also owes a lot of his creativity to his passion for cricket. A Ranji Trophy player himself, Pandey writes:

It was due to my relative success at cricket that I got to travel the length and breadth of India, participating in various tournaments, seeing an India which most young men my age didn't have the opportunity to do. Travel exposed me to various cultures, sounds, colours, music, food and languages. Travel exposed me to the spectacular variety of terrains, the variety in villages, towns and cities that form India . . .

Cricket helped me meet, literally, hundreds of people, many of whom would turn out to be mentors in my life.[32]

Both Nadella and Pandey *played* the sport. It was through their actual involvement with cricket—going through the motions of failure and triumph, breaking ice with strangers, getting out of difficult situations, controlling emotions, setting eyes on the big picture and taking those emotional and physical blows—that their thinking got designed.

Be a T-shaped person

Your multiple affiliations in life directly translate to your becoming a *T-shaped* personality in the work sphere. A T-shaped person is one who has a significant depth of understanding in a subject along with an ability to relate to several other domains. The stem of the 'T' represents expertise, while the bar indicates empathy (Figure 21).

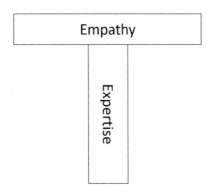

Figure 21: Being a T-shaped personality is key to creativity

McKinsey popularized the concept of T-shaped consultants—those with deep expertise in one domain as well as perspective on several others to draw rich insights from. Bain & Company seek *expert-generalists,* those who work at the intersections of multiple disciplines while being specialists in only a few areas. Explaining the logic of expert-generalists, Orit Gadiesh, Bain's chairperson, shares, 'To me the modern Renaissance man is curious, interested in different things. You have to be willing to "waste time" on things that are not directly relevant to your work because you are curious. But then you are able to, sometimes unconsciously, integrate them back into your work.'

On promoting T-shaped consultants, Gadiesh notes, 'We make people switch areas and fields. It is fundamental at Bain, a core reason for our success. You become better at your area of expertise when you actually take a chance and do something else.'[33]

Why is a T-shaped person essential to creative problem-solving? Important ideas are born at the intersections of disciplines, as they must exhibit both utility (typically grounded in the depth of one discipline) and novelty (which often comes from the breadth across disciplines). It is not recommended to be a 'jack of all trades', but you must certainly be a master of one or two and reasonably appreciative of others, so you can build upon their knowledge and contribute meaningfully. A T-shaped person is adept at freely moving between radically different fields, and some of these associations can offer surprising insights, which elude even the experts in these fields.

The key to creativity, it seems, is to strike a balance between depth and breadth of knowledge, and this is indeed effortful because depth always comes at the cost of breadth (or at least that is what we are made to believe during, say, a PhD programme). Still, too much depth in a subject is not without its drawbacks.

In a qualitative research involving expert toy designers, Kimberly Elsbach, of the University of California, Davis, and

Francis Flynn, of Stanford University, studied how artistic creativity and design expertise often hamper collaboration.[34] The researchers identified that though creative individuals would be productive *idea givers*, they may not necessarily be good *idea takers*. The domain experts perceive their identity as artists being threatened when somebody offers them an idea. Further, because of their passionate involvement in a project, they would want to have their own stamp on it and resist passing on the baton. As a solution, experts must develop empathy, a willingness and ability to listen to others and look at the world from other people's perspectives. Walter Isaacson makes a similar observation: 'Computer innovators, like other pioneers, can find themselves left behind if they get stuck in their ways. The same traits that make them inventive, such as stubbornness and focus, can make them resistant to change when new ideas come along.'[35] A T-shaped personality helps overcome such biases and makes one receptive to contrarian views.

A T-shaped person would be far more proficient at solving complex problems than an I-shaped (deep expert) or a dash-shaped (pure generalist) person. By virtue of your work, most of the problems you face would stem from your discipline, but you will not be able to find a novel answer by going any deeper in your discipline, because you are stuck to the *paradigm* or to 'normal science' in the words of Thomas Kuhn. A better approach would be to look across disciplines and draw inspiration from how others have solved the same problem elsewhere. Borrowing from other disciplines, or cross-pollinating, would not only help you attack your problem more efficiently but also bring freshness to your core discipline. 'This is the way that good ideas often blossom,' writes Isaacson. 'A bumblebee brings half an idea from one realm, and pollinates another fertile realm filled with half-formed innovations.'[36]

It was through such cross-pollination—between biomimicry and design—and insights from their T-shaped engineers that Japan's bullet train designers could learn from the kingfisher bird in overcoming the sonic boom problem and achieve a 30 per cent greater efficiency for their trains.[37] At an individual level, too, being T-shaped helps one address difficult problems by learning from unrelated domains, provided you have deliberately exposed yourself to diverse domains and have the ability to do some *associative thinking* and draw useful insights. Remember, you get paid for your depth, but get promoted for your breadth.

Innovative companies actively seek T-shaped people, for what they bring to the table far exceeds what they ought to. Take the case of Apple. Ken Kocienda worked as a software developer at Apple and is the author of *Creative Selection*. His author biography on the dust jacket reads as follows:

> Ken Kocienda was a software engineer and designer at Apple for over fifteen years. After graduating from Yale [Bachelor of Arts], he fixed motorcycles, worked in the editorial library of a newspaper, taught English in Japan and made fine art photographs. Eventually, he discovered the internet, taught himself computer programming and made his way through a succession of dot-com-era start-ups, before landing at Apple in 2001, where he worked on the software teams that created the Safari web browser, iPhone, iPad and Apple Watch.

You may think, 'What is a fine-arts guy doing at Apple?' This self-taught programmer was a part of the core team that wrote the software for the iPhone. Steve Jobs was a master of attracting and retaining T-shaped talent. He eagerly looked for the misfits, the round pegs in square holes, and Kocienda was not an exception in that way. Jobs knew how to get the most out of such multiple-affiliation types by showing them the big picture and pushing them towards the seemingly improbable. Jobs's successor, Tim Cook, is of the same view: 'I feel very strongly that the better products we produce the more diverse the team that produces them . . . A diverse team is more than academic, they bring life experience.'[38]

Often, as an expert, you would approach a situation from your position of expertise, and this may lead you to be blindsided by the weak signals, the stuff that really matters. So instead of doing that, learn to start with empathy. Learn to listen with intent, observe with purpose and defer your judgement, so that you can appreciate the problem in totality, in its context, and then deploy your expertise to address it. Remember, expertise often comes at the cost of empathy and it should be your constant endeavour to manage the tension between the two without giving in to either. In his 2017 MIT commencement address, Tim Cook warned graduates, 'People will try to convince you that you should keep empathy out of your career. Don't accept this false premise.'[39] His deep sense of empathy and his embrace of diversity have helped Cook to fit comfortably into the big shoes of Steve Jobs and enabled him to keep Apple at the top of the list of the world's leading innovators.

So next time you are looking for a new hire, do not just look at the relevant domain expertise but also at the person's exposure to other domains and their ability to draw useful insights from those. Problems are increasingly becoming cross-functional and so should the problem-solvers.

Develop failure tolerance

Innovation is inevitably a surprise, and for you to create something innovative it is important that you believe in your idea at a time when many others are not willing to. The urban legends associated with Richard Drew and Art Fry, the creators of masking tape and Post-it Note respectively, often obscure the fact that they were enormously thick-skinned people, known for their propensity for insubordination. None of the internal or external forces could deter them from taking their ideas forward.

There is a very thin line between becoming a hero and getting fired, but it is only through relentless prototyping and testing, often at a personal expense, that ideas become realities. As Pixar's Ed Catmull reminds us, 'When it comes to creative endeavours, the concept of zero failures is worse than useless. It is counterproductive.'[40] The key is to uncouple the willingness to experiment from the fear of failure.

Tolerating failure, error and occasional ridicule is essential to creativity. Ken Robinson, one of the biggest proponents of creativity in early education, says, 'If you're not prepared to be wrong, you'll never come up with anything original.'[41] If you are too worried about what others are going to think of your idea, you would seldom conceive anything radical, let alone take the effort to pursue it.

Having multiple affiliations, developing a T-shaped personality and cultivating a tolerant attitude towards failure would allow you to connect more dots—some will make beautiful patterns out of those, while others would not, but the experience in both cases would be highly instructive. What might be seemingly irrelevant in one context could be surprisingly useful in another, and if you are not too critical about such apparently irrelevant information, you significantly up your chances of making novel connections between the familiar.

One's ability to be comfortable with errors and failures and one's openness to seemingly irrelevant information are intricately linked to low latent inhibition and this, in turn, is perceived as the hallmark of original thinking. Psychologists from the

University of Toronto and Harvard University have proposed that low levels of latent inhibition—defined as 'an animal's unconscious capacity to ignore stimuli that experience has shown are irrelevant to its needs'—might also, hypothetically, contribute to original thinking, particularly in combination with high IQ.[42]

Low latent inhibition is generally associated with tendency towards psychosis, where the brain weakens on its capacity to screen from conscious stimuli previously experienced as irrelevant. However, in terms of creativity, lower states of mental alertness can allow disparate information to flow in more freely and potentially offer avenues for making novel connections.

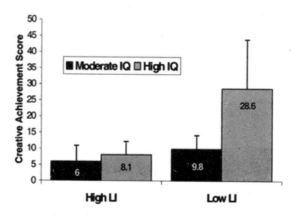

Figure 22: Creative Achievement Questionnaire (CAQ) scores against high and low latent inhibition (LI) levels, and high and moderate IQ. (Source: Shelley Carson, Jordan Peterson and Daniel Higgins)

Figure 22 offers much-needed clarity on the moderating role latent inhibition plays in the relation between a person's IQ score and their creative achievement. I am not going into the technicalities of the research or the chart here. Suffice it to say that even a person with high IQ does not exhibit high levels of creativity if their latent inhibition is acute. The corollary is that a person with moderate IQ can have a high creativity score, provided they keep their inhibitions at bay. Unlike in psychotic cases, low levels of latent inhibition can be engineered through practice, allowing for more lucid associations between apparently distinct disciplines.

Low latent inhibition also translates to low *associative barriers*. Most original connections are made at a subconscious level and only occasionally do they spring up to the conscious mind when you begin to apply your thinking to specific problems. There is not much value in honing multiple affiliations or being curious about things if your associative barriers are heightened. Multiple stimuli are valuable only to the extent that you make them work for you, and they typically do not work in a linear, predictable manner.

Can inhibitions be lowered? Certainly. One approach is to get drunk. Seriously. In a study of how drinking affects creativity, a research team of the University of Illinois at Chicago, comprising Andrew Jarosz, Gregory Colflesh and Jennifer Wiley, noticed that mild intoxication increased people's creative abilities.[43] A group of twenty male subjects was served with vodka-cranberry cocktails, until their blood alcohol levels neared the legal intoxication limit (BAC = .075 per cent), and then they were asked to answer fifteen questions from a creative problem-solving assessment called the Remote Associates Test (RAT). The intoxicated individuals solved more RAT items, in less time, than the sober ones and were more likely to perceive their solutions as the result of a sudden insight rather than of prior knowledge. The researchers inferred that alcohol helped slip seemingly irrelevant stuff into the users' brains, which otherwise would be blocked to such stimuli during phases of heightened levels of alertness, say when the subjects were on caffeine. But being drunk is certainly not the most advisable way of becoming creative, because like most stuff in science, there is an inverted-U relationship here as well, in the sense that intoxication makes you creative only up to a point, after which the effect on creativity could be adverse.

One way of developing failure tolerance is by organizing your life as a *portfolio of ventures*, so that you can compensate for those areas where you play boringly safe with other, more important endeavours where you can take disproportionate levels of risk. Seeking excitement on all fronts of life can be exhausting. That is what Edwin Land, one of the greatest innovators of the previous century, reminded us of. 'No person could possibly be original in one area unless he were possessed of the emotional and social stability that comes from fixed attitudes in all areas other than the one in which he is being original,' he said.[44]

It must, however, be remembered that you are declared as a creative individual only retrospectively. Till proven otherwise, most creatives are considered lunatics. Moses Judah Folkman, who persevered for several years with his radical treatment of tumour angiogenesis, reflects: 'If your idea succeeds, everybody says you are persistent. If it fails, you are stubborn.'[45] So, be prepared to be ridiculed, and try developing a thick skin.

Here is one way to know if you are thick-skinned: Can you take criticism from your subordinates? Constructive criticism from subordinates can make a supervisor far more creative, says Yeun Joon Kim, of the University of Cambridge, and Junha Kim, of the Ohio State University. In a field experiment that involved employees at a Korean health-food company, the researchers studied the impact of top-down, bottom-up and lateral feedback, and observed that while negative feedback from both supervisors and peers can negatively impact creativity, it has the opposite effect if the criticism comes from a lower-ranked employee.[46] The researchers explained their counter-intuitive findings thus, 'In reality, most supervisors are willing to receive negative feedback and learn from it. It's not that they enjoy criticism—rather, they are in a natural power position and can cope with the discomfort of negative feedback better.' However, employees would offer a critical feedback to their supervisors only if the latter have fostered a climate of psychological safety.

As Peter Thiel says, 'If you're less sensitive to social cues, you're less likely to do the same things as everyone else around you.'[47] That is not just true for start-ups but also for life in general.

The key attributes of a design thinker or an expert problem-solver could be summarized into three core characteristics: a clear head, a deep heart and a thick skin. A clear head would help you think through a complex problem, a deep heart makes you more empathetic and a thick skin is necessary for failure tolerance. Figure 23 represents these attributes in the form of a Venn diagram.

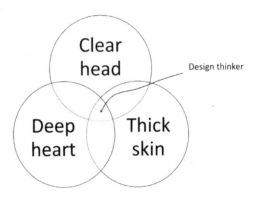

Figure 23: Core attributes of a design thinker

I sincerely hope that you would be able to hone some of the aforementioned skills to become a better problem-solver and teach others by demonstrating such skills at your next design-thinking workshop.

Appendix A

Key Toolsets, Skill Sets and Mindsets

This book offers pointers on the skill sets, mindsets and toolsets that would enable you to become a more disciplined problem-solver. Here is a summary of those elements, identified across the various stages of design thinking.

Stages	Toolsets (What?)	Skill sets (How?)	Mindsets (Why?)
Inspire	• Design thinking vision • Metaphors and analogies • Perpetual sense of crisis	• Crafting a design brief • Widening the aperture	• Creating a stretch • Encouraging diversity • Living curious
Empathize and define	• Problem exploration • Stakeholder map • Customer journey map • Empathy map • Unfocus Group • Hybrid-analytics • 80/20 rule • Problem framing rules	• Listening with intent • Observing with purpose • Deferring judgement • Prioritization • Problem-framing/ sandboxing	• Empathizing • Embracing constraints • Practising mindfulness

Stages	Toolsets (What?)	Skill sets (How?)	Mindsets (Why?)
Ideate	• Challenging assumptions • Across value chain • Beyond current users • Design for the extreme • Analogous design • Ideation triggers	• Hybrid brainstorming • Honing multiple affiliations • Deferring judgement	• Quantity over quality of ideas • Embracing imitation
Prototype and test	• Paper prototypes • Storyboarding • Scenarios • Plays and skits • Dogfooding	• Storytelling • Validating hypothesis • Thinking with your hands • Collaborating across borders	• Being quick and dirty • Developing failure tolerance • Failing faster to succeed sooner • Doing the last experiment first
Scale	• Lean start-up methods • Business model canvas • Objectives and key results	• Cutting some slack • Providing air cover • Showing up personally • Innovation evangelism	• Keeping the main thing as the main thing • Having a good business sense • Thinking beyond jugaad

Appendix B

Frequently Asked Questions

In this section, I share some of the questions I have received over the years as an innovation evangelizer and as someone who conducts design-thinking workshops. The questions are followed by my responses. These would be useful in your own endeavours of practising and propagating design thinking.

Is design thinking limited to product design and development, or to the world of technology?

Though design thinking has its roots in the disciplines of product design, industrial design and architecture, the technique has come a long way as a new approach to problem-solving that builds on the tenets of the design sphere. The first to embrace this expansive view of design thinking were technology companies, as it was intuitive for them to relate software development and hardware creation to the principles of design. That is one reason why popular media coverage on design thinking is replete with the cases of tech development and clever consumer products. However, the emerging view of design thinking offers it as a human-centric approach of designing experiences, and from that vantage point, design thinking is industry-, domain- and function-agnostic. Far from the world of technology, we see the tenets and practices of design thinking applied to creating better patient care at hospitals, enabling NGOs serve their communities better, teachers engage with special-needs kids, companies rework their brand identities and talent managers devise new means for engaging with their workforce. The scope of design thinking goes well and truly beyond the tech space, and I encourage you to script your own adoption story here.

If there is a paucity of time, what should be the focus of your design-thinking process?

Of the five stages of design thinking—namely, inspire; empathize and define; ideate; prototype and test; and scale—I find the second (empathize and define) to be the weakest link in most organizations. On the basis of my research, my reading of popular literature and my corporate exposure, I have found that most firms have a lot of ideas in search of important problems. Thanks to idea campaigns, hackathons, innovation contests and various other means, companies do manage to generate ideas, but they often don't know what to do with those ideas. This happens because not enough attention is paid to discovering and defining the problems thoroughly. So if you must pick up specific stages of the design-thinking process to focus on, owing to paucity of time or funds, you are better off focusing on the empathize and define stage.

Where should a design-thinking intervention begin? Top-down or bottom-up?

I believe that change always flows top-down. You must sensitize the leaders before going down the rung. Imagine a situation where you have motivated, trained and equipped grassroots employees of an organization and that they are eager to go about applying design thinking, but in the absence of top management's support, all that enthusiasm goes to waste. Instead, if you first sensitize the top management and demonstrate the power of design thinking, you could set an avalanche in motion. The senior management would become champions of design thinking; they would nominate their team members for the programme, create avenues for employees to practise design thinking and, more importantly, release funds. So, always start from the top if you want your efforts to have a lasting impact.

What problems are best suited to be solved using design thinking?

Design thinking is not a universally suitable or even advisable approach for problem-solving. It is highly recommended in the context of high uncertainty and when human emotions are involved. If both the problem and its possible solutions are reasonably well-known, the adoption of design thinking might be overkill. However, some of the tenets of design thinking, especially empathy and visual thinking, could be adopted while solving any problem. Even if there is no involvement of humans, it is still worthwhile to consider the impact a solution would have on its users, for technology alone cannot offer you a winning solution.

How can one leverage design thinking towards fostering an innovation culture?

An innovation culture is typified by three attributes: first, a wide-scale participation of people from across functions and levels in generating ideas; second, a well-governed mechanism to take the ideas through to their logical conclusions; and third, the supporting incentive mechanisms to ensure continued engagement of employees. Design thinking, with its human-centric, systematic approach of problem-solving can help on furthering each of these dimensions of innovation culture. The emphasis on empathy, stakeholder management and visual artefacts can further enable wide-scale participation; the five-stage process model can offer the discipline of channelizing ideas from insights to implementation; and the associated skills and tools can offer sufficient learning incentives to employees so that they stay committed. Companies such as IBM, Microsoft, Amazon, Intuit, PepsiCo, 3M and Dr. Reddy's among others have harnessed the power of design thinking to shape an innovation culture for their respective employees.

How do children gain from learning design thinking?

As discussed throughout this book, design thinking is more about thinking than designing; or, to put it differently, it is about designing your thinking. Have children been taught how to think? When I was growing up, there weren't any courses or discourses on thinking clearly or systematically, as everyone assumed that thinking skills are acquired through experience. But that is not true. If children are taught how to think systematically and approach their problem-solving endeavours in a more methodical manner, they would certainly grow up to become more confident and productive. Tools such as mind maps, stakeholder maps, journey maps and general methods of root-cause analysis would serve children very well in short-term tasks, like school assignments, as well as long-term ones, like crafting a career for themselves. Especially, the skills of listening with intent, observing with purpose and being less judgemental can help children become better problem-solvers. As for thinking clearly, the earlier the better.

How do I apply design thinking to my work when my role offers limited avenues to do so?

Even with extensive interest in and appreciation for design thinking, there are hardly roles titled 'Design Thinkers' or 'Chief of Design' at corporate firms, including tech companies. Boxing design thinking into a job title would kill the spirit of what the method has to offer. If you understand design thinking as a human-centric, systematic approach of problem-solving, a wider canvas will open for the application of its tools and techniques. Every role or job could gain from adopting a systematic approach of problem solving. Whether it be supply-chain management, talent sourcing or managing network security, the application of design-thinking tools for problem diagnosis, ideation and idea validation would help the cause. Remember, you are not required to apply the entire process of design thinking and use all the prescribed tools and skills, but rather pick the ones most relevant to your job. I reckon there is no task that cannot be improved by being a little more mindful and methodical, which is all the more urgent and important for an economy like India.

What aspects of design thinking are most suitable for start-ups and small enterprises?

The popular discourse on design thinking might make one mistakenly conclude that the method is most suited for tech companies that are into consumer products. The narratives from Apple, Amazon, Nike, Ikea, Starbucks, Google, Samsung, Netflix and Microsoft have led many to believe that design thinking belongs only to the world of the fast and nimble. As a result, non-tech start-ups and small enterprises find the approach too complex. However, if one distils design thinking into its constituent toolsets, skill sets, and relevant mindsets, it becomes apparent that some of these are universally applicable to problem-solving, on any scale and of any complexity. Especially for small enterprises, the virtue of empathizing with the end-customers and listening to their unstated concerns, performing quick and dirty prototyping, generating and validating hypotheses before scaling solutions and engaging in emphatic storytelling could offer significant value. Similarly, firms in their early stages of development can teach their scarce workforce to systematically conduct root-cause analysis, be more methodical while ideating and adopt storyboard to validate promising ideas—and some of these techniques can take away a lot of guesswork from the growth equation.

What is a good starting point to learn about design thinking?

There are several useful books on creative problem-solving in general and design thinking in particular that could serve as a good starting point. I would recommend *The Art of Innovation* by Tom Kelley and Jonathan Littman; *The Ten Faces of Innovation* by Tom Kelley and Jonathan Littman; *Creative Confidence* by David Kelley and Tom Kelley; *Change by Design* by Tim Brown; *Sprint* by Jake Knapp; *The Design of Everyday Things* by Don Norman; and *Business Model Generation* by Alexander Osterwalder and Yves Pigneur. You would also find a lot of useful reading material and case studies on the IDEOU (www.ideou.com) and Stanford d.school (https://dschool.stanford.edu/resources) websites. Further, TED Talks by David Kelley and Tim Brown offer insights on how design thinking can be applied in real-world contexts, beyond product design.

Acknowledgements

This book is an outcome of the influence several people had on my thinking, knowingly and unknowingly. The toolsets, skill sets and the appropriate mindsets discussed in this book around creative problem-solving are the ones I got to understand during my years of working, learning, researching and teaching. This is in gratitude to all those who have designed the way I think.

It was at NITIE Mumbai where Prof. H.V. Bhasin, Prof. Hema Date, Prof. Vivekanand Khanapuri and Prof. Teegalapelly Prasad kindled my interest in technology management. My internship at Titan was a turning point in my career, where I got a crash course on innovation under the head of design and development, B.V. Nagaraj, who taught me the virtue of perseverance. At Wipro, I was lucky to work with Sangita Singh, a leader who personifies perfection and who taught me the importance of thinking big and chasing down those goals with grit. In her team, I met G.S. Nathan, a father figure, who gave me the mantra of 'being a foot soldier'—a mindset that has served me well through my years at the PhD programme and in my entrepreneurial journey.

My abode at Wipro was the CTO Office, where I imbibed the company's hallmark entrepreneurial spirit, and the credit for this goes to Vikesh Mehta. I have not come across a person more empathetic than Vikesh. He taught me how to appreciate the value of empathy in creativity. The two CTOs that I was privileged to work with, Mangalath Divakaran (MD) and Vijaya Kumar Ivaturi (IVK), had assembled creative geniuses from across Wipro and beyond to help the firm foster an innovation culture. From MD I learnt the virtue of disciplined risk-taking, and IVK taught me the power of knowledge and networks. I was privileged to be surrounded by several T-shaped connectors—Ramprasad K., Malay Das, Raghuraman K., Karthikeyan Iyer, Ashim Ghosh, Hrishi Mohan, Pravin Hungund, Vikesh and Nathan. The CTO Office offered me the freedom to learn at my own pace, experiment, make mistakes, engage far and wide, and then move on to the next orbit—the PhD programme at IIM Bangalore.

It was Prof. Rishikesha Krishnan, my PhD adviser and a role model, who has had the most significant impact on my attitude towards and aptitude for innovation. I always wish to have more of his pragmatism, work ethics and efficiency as a researcher and teacher. Apart from Prof. Krishnan, the other influencers at IIM Bangalore were Prof. Mathew Manimala, Prof. Rejie George, Prof. Ganesh Prabhu, Prof. K. Kumar, Prof. Kanchan Mukherjee, Prof. Manoj Chakravarti, Prof. Abhoy Ojha, Prof. P.D. Jose, Prof. Mukta Kulkarni, Prof. Sourav Mukherji and Prof. Ramadhar Singh. As I attended their classes, wrote term papers and discussed my ideas with them, I got to appreciate the significance of rigour coupled with relevance. I have attempted to strike the very same balance in this book.

The idea of starting a consulting company and writing for practitioners was further fuelled by my IIMB colleagues Vipul Mathur, Amol Agrawal, Kshitij Awasthi and Kishore Gangwani.

Off campus, I was constantly in contact with L.R. Natrajan, Eswaran Narasimhan, Ved Prakash, Mahesh Venkataraman, Pinkesh Shah, Madan Mohan Rao, Dr Pankaj Gupta, Dr Anil Rao, Navyug Mohnot, David Wittenberg, William Miller, Naveen Lakkur, Shivakumar Venkateswaran, Col Shashi Kohli, Prof. Charles Dhanaraj, Bose Nair, Balaram Menon, Navratan Katariya, Sanjeev Malhotra, Khyati Shah, Sakyasingha Mahapatra, Yogesh Agiwal, Ravi Arora, Jilani M.H.K.K., Rajiv Upadhyay, Vinay Dabholkar and Narendra Pratap Singh (Nandu). They ensured that I never lost touch with the practice of entrepreneurship, innovation and creativity. These are all stalwarts in their own fields and offer a constant reminder of the rewards of working for the long haul.

This book on design thinking would not have been possible without the trust my corporate partners have shown in me while giving me opportunities to engage with their teams on real-life projects and workshops. I would like to place on record my immense gratitude towards Maclean Raphael and Aparna Sardar from 3M; Anupama Nithyanand and Fenal Shah from Accenture; Kalyan Ram and Chandra Bhattacharjee from Aditya Birla Group; Sathish Parameshwara and Spencer McKeown from American Express; M.S. Shankar and Sampada Inamdar from ANAND Group; Akanksha Agarwal, Shruti Joshi and Aniruddha Soman from Asian Paints; Suresh Subramanian, Srinivas S., Bindu Ajit and Ramgopal Sajjalaguddam from Biocon; Sri Krishnan and Rajeev Devasthali from Bosch; Balachandar N. and the late V.G. Siddhartha and from Café Coffee Day; Selvan Dorairaj and Madheswaran N. from Capgemini; Anushka Bose and Murali Krishna from Dell; Vishal Karad from Emcure; and Shahnawaz Khan and Nidhi Malhotra from Flipkart.

I am also grateful to Yogesh Potdar and Rahul Wagh from GE; Uma Shankar and Aarti Rai from Infosys; Dr Rajendra Srivastava and Reema Gupta from ISB; Partha Pratim and Rafiqul Islam from ISRO; Vivek Gupta and Sanjay Kumar from ITC; Raushan Rishu and Murugan Pugalenthi from Johnson & Johnson; Imtiyaz Tinmaker from Merck; Lakshmi Bellave from NHRD Bangalore Chapter; Vivek Jha from Novartis; Prabhu Pantula and Manjiri Joshi from Oracle; Nikita Doshi and Varun Salaria from Publicis Sapient; Sundara Raghavan from Reliance; Vinay Baijal and Lalit Wadhwani from Siemens; Amit Khare from Société Générale; Yogesh Aphale, Sanjay Ranawade, Sumant Sood and Ritika Gandhi from Titan; Ashish Joshi and Sugam Kumar from Unilever. At Wipro my gratitude goes out to Saurabh Govil, K.R. Sanjiv, Prithviraj Nath, Muralidharan S., Shriraj Nagarhalli and Saksham Khandelwal, for their untiring support during my research, teaching and consulting endeavours. As all attempts at writing down acknowledgements, this too suffers from recency bias, and I am certain I have missed out on many names, of those who have been instrumental in designing what has gone into this book.

I would like to thank Lohit Jagwani from Penguin Random House for reaching out to me for the book proposal, and Radhika Marwah and Rachna Pratap for helping me put this book in shape and in time. But it is the brilliance of Vineet Gill, the book's editor, that should get maximum credit for making the book more readable.

I would also like to acknowledge the support various media partners have extended in helping me validate some of the ideas around design thinking. Gratitude goes to Seema Chowdhry and Shalini Umachandran from *Mint*; Saira Sayani, Shikha Dave, Suma Ramachandran and Akashy Bhaskar from YourStory.com; Suparna Chawla Bhasin, Neelanjana Mazumdar and Mastufa Ahmed from People Matters; Meha Agarwal from Inc42; and Aastha Singal and Saurabh Kumar from Entrepreneur India.

I would like to profoundly thank David Kelley, Tom Kelley, Tim Brown and Roger Martin for establishing the discipline of design thinking. With this book, I wish to make a humble contribution to their legacy.

Finally, and most importantly, tribute goes to my parents for supporting me unconditionally; to my mother-in-law for being a pillar of support; to my wife, Nimisha, for keeping me grounded; and to my daughter, Avnira, for teaching me how to cherish simple joys of life. This book would not have been possible without their countless sacrifices.

Bangalore   Pavan Soni
April 2020

Notes

Introduction

1. Richard Watson, *Digital Vs Human: How We'll Live, Love, and Think in the Future* (Melbourne: Scribe, 2016).
2. John Dewey, *How We Think* (Boston: DC Heath & Company, 1933).

Chapter 1: What is Design Thinking?

1. Kishore Biyani, *It Happened in India: The Story of Pantaloons, Big Bazaar, Central and the Great Indian Consumer* (New Delhi: Rupa Publications, 2007).
2. Vasundhara Sawhney, 'The Skills Every Founder Needs: An Interview with Ritesh Agarwal', *HBR Ascend*, 27 October 2017, https://hbrascend.org/topics/ritesh-agarwal-skills-every-founder-needs/
3. Eric Schmidt and Jonathan Rosenberg, *How Google Works* (New York: Grand Central Publishing, 2014).
4. Gerard J. Tellis, *Unrelenting Innovation: How to Build a Culture for Market Dominance* (San Francisco: Jossey-Bass, 2013).
5. Stefan Thomke and Donald Reinertsen, 'Six Myths of Product Development', *Harvard Business Review*, May 2012, https://hbr.org/2012/05/six-myths-of-product-development

6. Ibid.

7. Jon Kolko, 'Design Thinking Comes of Age', *Harvard Business Review*, September 2015, https://hbr.org/2015/09/design-thinking-comes-of-age

8. Tom Kelley with Jonathan Littman, *The Art of Innovation: Lessons in Creativity from IDEO, America's Leading Design Firm* (New York: Currency/Doubleday, 2001).

9. David M. Kelley and Tom Kelley, *Creative Confidence: Unleashing the Creative Potential within Us All*, (London: William Collins, 2013).

10. Tim Brown, *Change by Design: How Design Thinking Transforms Organizations and Inspires Innovation* (New York: HarperCollins, 2009).

11. Tim Brown, 'Designers—think big!', TED.com, July 2009, https://www.ted.com/talks/tim_brown_urges_designers_to_think_big

12. Kelley with Littman, *The Art of Innovation: Lessons in Creativity from IDEO, America's Leading Design Firm*.

13. Source: https://www.ideou.com/pages/design-thinking

14. David Kelley, 'Why Design Thinking is Relevant', IDEOU.com, 30 July 2017, https://www.ideou.com/blogs/inspiration/david-kelley-on-design-thinking

15. Bill Burnett, 'Design Thinking = Method, Not Logic' , YouTube.com, 13 April 2016, https://www.youtube.com/watch?v=vSuK2C89yjA

16. Peter Thiel in conversation with Reid Hoffman, Darryl Woodson and Natasha Hastings, Mastersofscale.com, 10 November 2017, https://mastersofscale.com/peter-thiel-escape-the-competition/

17. 'Design Thinking', Ideou.com, https://www.ideou.com/pages/design-thinking

18. For more information, see https://dschool.stanford.edu/resources

19. W. Chan Kim and Renée Mauborgne, *Blue Ocean Strategy: How to Create Uncontested Market Space and Make the Competition Irrelevant* (Boston: Harvard Business School Press, 2005).

20. Darshan Devaiah B.P., 'Bengaluru Traffic Police to implement "No Helmet, No Fuel" rule soon', *The Indian Express*, 26 July 2019, https://indianexpress.com/article/cities/bangalore/bengaluru-traffic-police-to-implement-no-helmet-no-fuel-rule-soon/

21. James de Vries, 'PepsiCo's Chief Design Officer on Creating an Organization Where Design Can Thrive', *Harvard Business Review*, 11 August 2015.

22. Ken Robinson, 'Do schools kill creativity?', TED.com, February 2006, https://www.ted.com/talks/sir_ken_robinson_do_schools_kill_creativity?language=en

23. Jon Kolko, 'Design Thinking Comes of Age', *Harvard Business Review*, September 2015, https://hbr.org/2015/09/design-thinking-comes-of-age

24. Jeanne Liedtka, 'Why Design Thinking Works', *Harvard Business Review*, September–October 2018, https://hbr.org/2018/09/why-design-thinking-works

25. Brown, *Change by Design: How Design Thinking Transforms Organizations and Inspires Innovation.*

26. Regina E. Dugan and Kaigham J. Gabriel, '"Special forces" Innovation: How DARPA Attacks Problems', *Harvard Business Review,* October 2013, https://hbr.org/2013/10/special-forces-innovation-how-darpa-attacks-problems

27. Donald E. Stokes, *Pasteur's Quadrant: Basic Science and Technological Innovation* (Washington, DC: Brookings Institution Press, 1997).

28. Regina E. Dugan and Kaigham J. Gabriel, '"Special forces" Innovation: How DARPA Attacks Problems', *Harvard Business Review,* October 2013, https://hbr.org/2013/10/special-forces-innovation-how-darpa-attacks-problems

Chapter 2: Why Design Thinking Now?

1. Jeff Bezos in an interview with Charlie Rose, CharlieRose.com, 28 July 2010, https://charlierose.com/videos/15732

2. Daniel Kahneman, 'The riddle of experience vs. memory', TED.com, February 2010, https://www.ted.com/talks/daniel_kahneman_the_riddle_of_experience_vs_memory

3. Boston Consulting Group, 'Innovation 2005: BCG Senior Management Survey', BCG.com, 2005, https://www.bcg.com/documents/file14520.pdf

4. Boston Consulting Group, 'Innovation in 2019', BCG.com, 21 March 2019, https://www.bcg.com/en-us/publications/2019/most-innovative-companies-innovation.aspx

5. Satya Nadella, *Hit Refresh: The Quest to Rediscover Microsoft's Soul and Imagine a Better Future for Everyone* (New York: Harper Business, 2017).

6. Abhijit V. Banerjee and Esther Duflo, *Poor Economics: A Radical Rethinking of the Way to Fight Global Poverty* (New York: PublicAffairs, 2011).

7. Vinay Kamath and K. Giriprakash, 'Formalising informal sectors is what we have done best: Bhaskar Bhat', *The Hindu BusinessLine*, 10 September 2019, https://www.thehindubusinessline.com/companies/formalising-informal-sectors-is-what-we-have-done-best-bhaskar-bhat/article29385216.ece

8. Rob Walker, 'The Guts of a New Machine' *New York Times Magazine*, 30 November 2003, https://www.nytimes.com/2003/11/30/magazine/the-guts-of-a-new-machine.html

9. Jon Kolko, 'Design Thinking Comes of Age', *Harvard Business Review*, September 2015, https://hbr.org/2015/09/design-thinking-comes-of-age

10. Varun Singh, 'Honda Activa is largest selling two-wheeler in H1 FY20, nearly 14 lakh units sold', *India Today*, 24 October 2019, https://www.indiatoday.in/auto/bikes/story/honda-activa-is-largest-selling-two-wheeler-in-first-half-of-financial-year-2019-20-nearly-14-lakh-units-sold-1612546-2019-10-24

11. Dina Gerdeman, 'Clayton Christensen: The Theory of Jobs To Be Done', Harvard Business School's *Working Knowledge*, 3 October 2016, https://hbswk.hbs.edu/item/clay-christensen-the-theory-of-jobs-to-be-done

12. Source: http://www.studiofiveb.com/we-believe

13. BS Reporter, 'Dr Reddy's launches new logo and brand', *Business Standard*, 1 July 2015, https://www.business-standard.com/article/companies/dr-reddy-s-launches-new-logo-and-brand-115070100900_1.html

14. Tim Brown, *Change by Design: How Design Thinking Transforms Organizations and Inspires Innovation* (New York: HarperCollins, 2009).

15. See https://www.ted.com/tedx/events

16. Surojit Gupta, 'India may be the most active country in terms of TEDx events: Chris Anderson', *The Times of India*, 15 November 2018, https://timesofindia.indiatimes.com/india/india-may-be-the-most-active-country-in-terms-of-tedx-events-chris-anderson/articleshow/66627734.cms

17. Peter Thiel and Blake Masters, *Zero to One: Notes on Startups, or How to Build the Future* (New York: Crown Business, 2014).

18. Monthly report retrieved from MIT OpenCourseWare, December 2019, https://ocw.mit.edu/about/site-statistics/monthly-reports/

19. Satya Nadella, *Hit Refresh: The Quest to Rediscover Microsoft's Soul and Imagine a Better Future for Everyone* (New York: Harper Business, 2017).

20. Steve Blank, 'What's A Startup? First Principles.', SteveBlank.com, 25 January 2010, https://steveblank.com/2010/01/25/whats-a-startup-first-principles/

21. 'CNBC Transcript: SpaceX CEO Elon Musk Speaks with CNBC's "Closing Bell"', CNBC.com, 18 June 2014, https://www.cnbc.com/2014/06/18/first-on-cnbc-cnbc-transcript-spacex-ceo-elon-musk-speaks-with-cnbcs-closing-bell.html

22. Suneera Tandon, 'Male grooming in India moves beyond shaving creams and shampoos', *Mint*, 13 November 2019, https://www.livemint.com/companies/news/male-grooming-in-india-moves-beyond-shaving-creams-and-shampoos-11573645189201.html

23. Richa Naidu and Soundarya J., 'P&G posts strong sales, takes $8 billion Gillette writedown', Reuters.com, 30 July 2019, https://in.reuters.com/article/proctergamble-results/pg-posts-strong-sales-takes-8-billion-gillette-writedown-idINKCN1UP1FT

24. Drake Baer, 'People are psychologically biased to see bald men as dominant leaders', *Independent*, 2 August 2017, https://www.independent.co.uk/news/business/people-are-psychologically-biased-to-see-bald-men-as-dominant-leaders-a7872761.html

25. Pritish Raj, 'Year of SUVs: Of 20 possible car launches in 2019, 15 are utility vehicles', *Financial Express*, 13 January 2019, https://www.financialexpress.com/industry/year-of-suvs-of-20-possible-car-launches-in-2019-15-are-utility-vehicles/1441860/

26. 'Volkswagen to drive in 4 SUVs in India by 2021', *Times of India*, 8 December 2019, https://timesofindia.indiatimes.com/business/india-business/volkswagen-to-drive-in-4-suvs-in-india-by-2021/articleshow/72407736.cms

27. Arpit Sharma, 'Over 20 Million DTH Subscribers Quit on Their Connections After Trai Tariff Regime', TelecomTalk.info,

7 October 2019, https://telecomtalk.info/20million-dth-subscribers-quit-trai/221765/

28. Malcolm Gladwell, *The Tipping Point: How Little Things Can Make a Big Difference* (New York: Little, Brown and Company, 2000).

Chapter 3: Key Tenets of Design Thinking

1. Louis V. Gerstner, Jr, *Who Says Elephants Can't Dance?: Leading a Great Enterprise Through Dramatic Change* (New York: Harper Business, 2003).

2. Josh Catone, 'Jeff Bezos Gives Advice on Long Term Success', Sitepoint.com, 22 November 2008, https://www.sitepoint.com/jeff-bezos-gives-advice-on-long-term-success/

3. Mihir Dalal, 'The rise and rise of Amazon', *Mint*, 20 May 2016, https://www.livemint.com/Companies/zs1JqXLNTv7ML2xeE9joRL/The-rise-and-rise-of-Amazon.html

4. Vijay Govindarajan and Ravi Venkatesan, '3 Reasons Global Firms Should Keep Investing in India', *Harvard Business Review*, 16 February 2018, https://hbr.org/2018/02/3-reasons-global-firms-should-keep-investing-in-india

5. Omkar Joshi, 'Amazon Chai Cart: Winning sellers' hearts and now a GOLD award, all over a cup of tea', Amazon's Seller Blog, 7 April 2016, https://services.amazon.in/resources/seller-blog/amazon-chai-cart-won-gold.html

6. Swati Bucha and Jobin Sam Varghese, 'Amazon Tatkal – Route planner 2017', Amazon's Seller Blog, 3 August 2017, https://services.amazon.in/resources/seller-blog/amazon-tatkal-route-planner-2017.html

7. For more information, visit https://www.amazon.in/b?ie=UTF8&node=13939285031

8. Daniel Aloi, 'Ratan Tata says inspiration for Nano was safety', *Cornell Chronicle*, 16 March 2011, https://news.cornell.edu/stories/2011/03/safety-first-ratan-tata-reveals-origins-nano

9. 'Preterm Birth', WHO.int, 19 February 2018, https://www.who.int/news-room/fact-sheets/detail/preterm-birth

10. Shilpa Kannan, 'The low cost technology saving premature babies' lives', BBC.com, 26 August 2013, https://www.bbc.com/news/business-23817127

11. Lora Perry and Robert Malkin, 'Effectiveness of medical equipment donations to improve health systems: How much medical equipment is broken in the developing world?', *Medical & Biological Engineering & Computing* (49), 2011.

12. Steven Johnson, 'The Genius of the Tinkerer', *Wall Street Journal*, 25 September 2010, https://www.wsj.com/articles/SB100014240527487 03989304575503730101860838

13. 'Global Health: Innovation Insight Series', Stanford.edu, 11 April 2012, https://www.gsb.stanford.edu/sites/gsb/files/publication-pdf/dtm-designing.pdf

14. For more information, visit https://www.embraceinnovations.com/#home

15. Tim Brown, *Change by Design: How Design Thinking Transforms Organizations and Inspires Innovation* (New York: HarperCollins, 2009).

16. Vilayanur Ramachandran and Eric Altschuler, 'The use of visual feedback, in particular mirror visual feedback, in restoring brain function', *Brain*, 2009.

17. Mileha Soneji, 'Simple hacks for life of Parkinson's', TED.com, February 2015, https://www.ted.com/talks/mileha_soneji_simple_hacks_for_life_with_parkinson_s

18. Eric Schmidt and Jonathan Rosenberg, *How Google Works* (New York: Grand Central Publishing, 2014).

19. R.C. Bhargava with Seetha, *The Maruti Story: How a Public Sector Company Put India on Wheels* (New Delhi: HarperCollins, 2010).

20. Ibid.

21. 'Maruti Suzuki hits double century: Over 200 new service workshops added', MarutiSuzuki.com, 22 May 2019, https://www.marutisuzuki.com/corporate/media/press-releases/2019/maruti-suzuki-hits-double-century-over-200-new-service-workshops-added

22. 'Maruti Suzuki now offers car service at customers' doorsteps, Launches "Service on Wheels"', MarutiSuzuki.com, 28 August 2019, https://www.marutisuzuki.com/corporate/media/press-releases/2019/maruti-suzuki-now-offers-car-service-at-customers-doorsteps--launches-service-on-wheels

23. 'Maruti Suzuki's new True Value now 250 outlets strong in two years', MarutiSuzuki.com, 13 August 2019, https://www.marutisuzuki.com/

corporate/media/press-releases/2019/maruti-suzukis-new-true-value-now-250-outlets-strong-in-two-years#

24. 'Aiming to train 15 lakh people via driving school network by 2020: Maruti', *Economic Times*, 30 July 2018, https://economictimes. indiatimes.com/news/company/corporate-trends/aiming-to-train-15-lakh-people-via-driving-school-network-by-2020-maruti/ articleshow/65196130.cms

25. 'Maruti Suzuki launches NEXA: A New Premium Automotive Experience', MarutiSuzuki.com, 23 July 2015, https://www. marutisuzuki.com/corporate/media/press-releases/2015/maruti-suzuki-launches-nexa-a-new-premium-automotive-experience

26. Nabeel A. Khan and Pratishtha Nangia, 'Is Nexa treading on the right path?', *Economic Times*, 25 November 25 2019, https://auto. economictimes.indiatimes.com/news/aftermarket/why-are-partners-losing-interest-in-nexa-and-whats-the-road-ahead/72182245

27. 'Maruti Suzuki stands tall with 20 Million sales in India', MarutiSuzuki.com, 30 November 2019, https://www.marutisuzuki.com/corporate/media/ press-releases/2019/maruti-suzuki-stands-tall-with-20-million-sales-in-india

28. Tim Brown, *Change by Design: How Design Thinking Transforms Organizations and Inspires Innovation.*

29. Linda Geddes, 'Chaos is Good for You', *Slate*, 2 December 2012, https://slate.com/technology/2012/12/antifragile-book-interview-nassim-nicholas-taleb-on-how-chaos-and-disaster-can-build-antifragile-systems.html

30. David M. Kelley and Tom Kelley, *Creative Confidence: Unleashing the Creative Potential within Us All* (London: William Collins, 2013).

31. Jennifer Mueller, Shimul Melwani and Jack Goncalo, 'The Bias Against Creativity: Why People Desire But Reject Creative Ideas', *Psychological Science*, 2011.

32. For more information, visit https://www.itcportal.com/businesses/ agri-business/e-choupal.aspx

33. Ken Robinson, 'Do schools kill creativity?'

34. R.R. McCrae, 'Creativity, divergent thinking, and openness to experience', *Journal of Personality and Social Psychology*, 1987.

35. Adam Grant, *Originals: How Non-conformists Move the World* (New York: Viking, 2016).

36. Roger Martin, *The Opposable Mind: Winning Through Integrative Thinking* (Boston: Harvard Business Review Press, 2007).

37. Roger L. Martin, 'How Successful Leaders Think', *Harvard Business Review*, June 2007, https://hbr.org/2007/06/how-successful-leaders-think

38. 'A Year of Creative Debates', *The New Indian Express*, 31 December 2014, https://www.newindianexpress.com/cities/bengaluru/2014/dec/31/A-Year-of-Creative-Debates-699976.html

39. Jenna Goudreau, 'Malcolm Gladwell Shares the Single Most Important Factor of a Person's Success', BusinessInsider.in, 8 October 2014, https://www.businessinsider.in/Malcolm-Gladwell-Shares-The-Single-Most-Important-Factor-Of-A-Persons-Success/articleshow/44718895.cms

40. '"Fast And Slow": Pondering The Speed Of Thought', NPR.org, 19 October 2011, https://www.npr.org/2011/10/27/141508854/fast-and-slow-pondering-the-speed-of-thought

41. Daniel Goleman, *Emotional Intelligence: Why It Can Matter More Than IQ* (New York: Bantam Books, 1995).

42. Thomas Wedell-Wedellsborg, 'Are You Solving the Right Problems?' *Harvard Business Review*, January–February 2017, https://hbr.org/2017/01/are-you-solving-the-right-problems

43. N. Madhavan, 'Small Is Dominant', *Business Today*, 25 May 2014, https://www.businesstoday.in/magazine/cover-story/biggest-indian-innovation-tata-ace/story/205824.html

44. Ketan Thakkar, 'Tata Ace to come in a new avatar, crosses 2-million-milestone in 12 years', *Economic Times*, 20 December 2017, https://economictimes.indiatimes.com/industry/auto/lcv-hcv/tata-ace-crosses-2-million-milestone-in-12-years/articleshow/62134644.cms?from=mdr

45. For 'Dropbox Intro Video', visit https://www.youtube.com/watch?v=w4eTR7tci6A

46. Barbara Minto, *The Pyramid Principle: Logical Writing, Thinking and Problem Solving* (London: Prentice Hall, 2002).

47. Tim Brown, *Change by Design: How Design Thinking Transforms Organizations and Inspires Innovation* (New York: HarperCollins, 2009).

48. Stanford Biodesign, 'IDEO: Medtech Prototyping', Youtube.com, 6 February 2015, https://www.youtube.com/watch?v=Ii1rcNJU0io

49. Ibid.

50. Robert Youmans, 'The effects of physical prototyping and group work on the reduction of design fixation', *Design Studies*, 2011.

51. Inbal Arieli, 'Can playing with junk lead to creativity and innovation?', *Israel 21C*, 20 March 2017, https://www.israel21c.org/can-playing-with-junk-lead-to-creativity-and-innovation/

52. Dan Senor and Saul Singer, *Start-up Nation: The Story of Israel's Economic Miracle* (New York: Grand Central Publishing, 2009).

53. Walter Isaacson, *Leonardo Da Vinci: The Biography* (New York: Simon & Schuster, 2017).

54. *The Codex Arundel* can be accessed at http://www.bl.uk/turning-the-pages/?id=cb4c06b9-02f4-49af-80ce-540836464a46&type=book

55. Jennifer Reingold, 'Hondas in Space', *Fast Company*, 1 February 2005, https://www.fastcompany.com/52065/hondas-space

56. George Anders, 'Jeff Bezos's Top 10 Leadership Lessons', *Forbes*, 4 April 2012, https://www.forbes.com/sites/georgeanders/2012/04/04/bezos-tips/#7ae6323d2fce

57. Tom Kelley, *The Art of Innovation: Lessons in Creativity from Ideo, America's Leading Design Firm* (New York: Currency, 2001).

Chapter 4: Inspire

1. 'Biocon Annual Report 2019', Biocon.com, 2020, https://www.biocon.com/docs/Biocon_Annual_Report_2019.pdf

2. David Packard, *The HP Way: How Bill Hewlett and I Built Our Company* (New York: Harper Business, 1995).

3. Benedict Sheppard, Hugo Sarrazin, Garen Kouyoumjian and Fabricio Dore, 'The business value of design', *McKinsey Quarterly*, 25 October 2018, https://www.mckinsey.com/business-functions/mckinsey-design/our-insights/the-business-value-of-design

4. Brad Smith, 'Intuit's CEO on Building a Design-Driven Company', *Harvard Business Review*, January–February 2015, https://hbr.org/2015/01/intuits-ceo-on-building-a-design-driven-company

5. John Doerr, *Measure What Matters: OKRs: The Simple Idea That Drives 10x Growth* (New York: Penguin Portfolio, 2018).

6. Schmidt and Rosenberg, *How Google Works*.

7. Jaeyong Songh and Kyungmook Lee, *The Samsung Way: Transformational Management Strategies from the World Leader in Innovation and Design* (New York: McGraw-Hill Education, 2014).

8. For more information on Samsung's CDC, visit http://www.design.samsung.com/global/m/contents/seoul_office/

9. Youngjin Yoo and Kyungmook Kim, 'How Samsung Became a Design Powerhouse', *Harvard Business Review*, September 2015, https://hbr.org/2015/09/how-samsung-became-a-design-powerhouse

10. Mihir Dalal, 'The untold story of Flipkart, the big billion ecommerce startup', YourStory.com, 8 October 2019, https://yourstory.com/2019/10/flipkart-story-big-billion-startup-ecommerce

11. Mihir Dalal, *Big Billion Startup: The Untold Flipkart Story* (New Delhi: Pan Macmillan, 2019).

12. Emily Lakdawalla, 'India prepares to take flight to Mars with the Mars Orbiter Mission (MOM)', *Planetary Society*, 31 October 2013, https://www.planetary.org/blogs/emily-lakdawalla/2013/10311230-india-prepares-to-take-flight-faq.html

13. Press Trust of India. 'Planned for 6 months, India's Mars mission Mangalyaan completes 5 years', *India Today*, 25 September 2019, https://www.indiatoday.in/science/story/mangalyaan-mission-isro-completes-5-years-orbiting-mars-1602933-2019-09-25

14. Teresa M. Amabile, Constance N. Hadley and Steven J. Kramer, 'Creativity Under the Gun', *Harvard Business Review*, 1 August 2002, https://store.hbr.org/product/creativity-under-the-gun/R0208C

15. Adi Ignatius, 'How Indra Nooyi Turned Design Thinking Into Strategy: An Interview with PepsiCo's CEO'. *Harvard Business Review*, September 2015, https://hbr.org/2015/09/how-indra-nooyi-turned-design-thinking-into-strategy

16. Brown, *Change by Design: How Design Thinking Transforms Organizations and Inspires Innovation*.

17. Walter Isaacson, *The Innovators: How a Group of Hackers, Geniuses and Geeks Created the Digital Revolution* (New York: Simon and Schuster, 2014).

18. Piyush Pandey, *Pandeymonium: Piyush Pandey on Advertising*, (Gurugram: Penguin Random House India, 2015).

19. Kishore Biyani, *It Happened in India: The Story of Pantaloons, Big Bazaar, Central and the Great Indian Consumer*.

20. The IndiGo commercial can be accessed here: https://www.youtube.com/watch?v=svOyqe2xWSo

21. 'InterGlobe Aviation Limited Annual Report 2018–19', GoIndiGo.in, https://www.goindigo.in/information/investor-relations/annual-report.html

22. Data from https://www.goindigo.in/information/investor-relations.html

23. Aneesh Phadnis, 'Indigo flaunts on-time performance muscle', *Business Standard*, 20 January 2013, https://www.business-standard.com/article/management/indigo-flaunts-on-time-performance-muscle-112032300012_1.html

24. 'Most Innovative Companies 2015', *Fast Company*, 9 February 2015, https://www.fastcompany.com/most-innovative-companies/2015

25. Doerr, *Measure What Matters: OKRs: The Simple Idea That Drives 10x Growth*.

26. Ikujiro Nonaka, 'The Knowledge-Creating Company', *Harvard Business Review*, July–August 2007, https://hbr.org/2007/07/the-knowledge-creating-company

27. 'Mahindra XUV500: Making of the XUV500 – *Inside Out* on Discovery Channel', YouTube.com, 18 October 2013, https://www.youtube.com/watch?v=q5-7ZeORixk

28. Anisha Motwani, *Storm the Norm: Untold Stories of 20 Brands That Did It Best* (New Delhi: Rupa Publications, 2016).

29. Lijee Philip and Ketan Thakkar, 'Ramkripa Ananthan: Ruggedness of M&M's SUV XUV500 has feminine dash', *Economic Times*, 2 October 2011, https://economictimes.indiatimes.com/ramkripa-ananthan-ruggedness-of-mms-suv-xuv500-has-feminine-dash/articleshow/10190873.cms

30. 'Mahindra XUV500: Making of the XUV500 – *Inside Out* on Discovery Channel'.

31. Biyani, *It Happened in India: The Story of Pantaloons, Big Bazaar, Central and the Great Indian Consumer*.

32. Purvita Chatterjee, 'Chief Belief Officer at Future to employ "alternative" methods of doing business', *The Hindu BusinessLine*,

29 July 2011, https://www.thehindubusinessline.com/companies/
Chief-Belief-Officer-at-Future-to-employ-lsquoalternative-methods-
of-doing-business/article20312026.ece

33. Thomas A. Stewart and Anand P. Raman, 'Finding a Higher Gear',
    Harvard Business Review, July–August 2008, https://hbr.org/2008/07/
    finding-a-higher-gear

34. 'Voices @ InStep', InfosysBlogs.com, 24 March 2014, https://www.
    infosysblogs.com/voices-instep/

35. See https://www.infosys.com/instep/internship.html

36. Sylvia Ann Hewlett, Melinda Marshall and Laura Sherbin, 'How
    Diversity Can Drive Innovation', *Harvard Business Review*, December
    2013, https://hbr.org/2013/12/how-diversity-can-drive-innovation

37. Ed Catmull and Amy Wallace, *Creativity, Inc.: Overcoming the Unseen
    Forces That Stand in the Way of True Inspiration* (New York: Random
    House, 2014).

38. Robert Iger, *The Ride of a Lifetime: Lessons Learned from 15 Years as
    CEO of the Walt Disney Company* (New York: Bantam Press, 2019).

39. Biz Stone, 'Twitter's Cofounder on Creating Opportunities', 1 June
    2015, *Harvard Business Review*, https://store.hbr.org/product/twitter-
    s-cofounder-on-creating-opportunities/R1506A

40. Andrew S. Grove, *Only the Paranoid Survive: How to Exploit the Crisis
    Points That Challenge Every Company* (New York: Currency, 1999).

41. Nadella, *Hit Refresh: The Quest to Rediscover Microsoft's Soul and
    Imagine a Better Future for Everyone*.

42. Pandey, *Pandeymonium: Piyush Pandey on Advertising*.

43. Amy Kazmin, 'Lemon Tree Hotels hires "opportunity-deprived" people
    as a key part of its workforce', *Financial Times*, 16 March 2018, https://
    www.ft.com/content/4257b9bc-e4e0-11e7-a685-5634466a6915

44. David M. Kelley and Tom Kelley, *Creative Confidence: Unleashing the
    Creative Potential within Us All* (London: William Collins, 2013).

45. Linda A. Hill, Greg Brandeau, Emily Truelove and Kent Lineback,
    'Collective Genius', *Harvard Business Review*, June 2014, https://hbr.
    org/2014/06/collective-genius

46. Martine Haas and Mark Mortensen, 'The Secrets of Great Teamwork',
    Harvard Business Review, June 2016, https://hbr.org/2016/06/the-
    secrets-of-great-teamwork

47. Tom Kelley and Jonathan Littman, *The Ten Faces of Innovation: IDEO's Strategies for Beating the Devil's Advocate and Driving Creativity throughout Your Organization* (New York: Currency/Doubleday, 2005).

Chapter 5: Empathize and Define

1. Sneha Jha, 'Two Qualities Anand Mahindra Looks for in a Business Leader' *Economic Times*, 20 April 2016, https://cio.economictimes.indiatimes.com/news/strategy-and-management/two-qualities-anand-mahindra-looks-for-in-a-business-leader/51857154

2. David and Tom Kelley, *Creative Confidence: Unleashing the Creative Potential within Us All.*

3. Nadella, *Hit Refresh: The Quest to Rediscover Microsoft's Soul and Imagine a Better Future for Everyone.*

4. IBM Institute of Business Value, 'Global C-suite Study 19th edition', IBM.com, 10 February 2020, https://www.ibm.com/downloads/cas/NJYY0ZVG

5. Akio Morita, Edwin M. Reingold and Mitsuko Shimomura, *Made in Japan: Akio Morita and Sony* (Boston: E.P. Dutton, 1986).

6. Christian Madsbjerg and Mikkel B. Rasmussen, 'An Anthropologist Walks into a Bar . . .', *Harvard Business Review*, March 2014, https://hbr.org/2014/03/an-anthropologist-walks-into-a-bar

7. Piyush Pandey, *Pandeymonium: Piyush Pandey on Advertising.*

8. Malcolm Gladwell, *Blink: The Power of Thinking without Thinking* (Boston: Little, Brown and Company, 2005).

9. Vinay Kamath and Aarati Krishnan, 'HUL's school for leadership', *Hindu BusinessLine*, 12 March 2018, https://www.thehindubusinessline.com/specials/new-manager/huls-school-for-leadership/article20340255.ece1

10. V. Kasturi Rangan and Mona Sinha, 'Hindustan Unilever's "Pureit" Water Purifier', a Harvard Business School case study, 1 February 2011.

11. Ibid.

12. Vijaya Rathore, 'HUL to take water purifiers to villages', *Mint*, 17 September 2008, https://www.livemint.com/Companies/pdJYwSbK8RvIXhHUxg7AOP/HUL-to-take-water-purifiers-to-villages.html

13. 'Providing safe drinking water', Unilever.com, https://www.unilever.com/sustainable-living/improving-health-and-well-being/health-and-hygiene/providing-safe-drinking-water/index.html

14. Jake Knapp, John Zeratsky and Braden Kowitz, *Sprint: How to Solve Big Problems and Test New Ideas in Just Five Days* (New York: Simon & Schuster, 2016).

15. Tom Kelley and Jonathan Littman, *The Ten Faces of Innovation: IDEO's Strategies for Beating the Devil's Advocate and Driving Creativity throughout Your Organization* (New York: Currency, 2005).

16. Madsbjerg and Rasmussen, 'An Anthropologist Walks into a Bar . . .'

17. Yoo and Kim, 'How Samsung Became a Design Powerhouse'.

18. Nadella, *Hit Refresh: The Quest to Rediscover Microsoft's Soul and Imagine a Better Future for Everyone.*

19. Grove, *Only the Paranoid Survive: How to Exploit the Crisis Points That Challenge Every Company.*

20. 'A Platform for New Ideas – Shadow Board', ExperienceMahindra.com, 5 December 2019, https://www.experiencemahindra.com/a-platform-for-new-ideas-shadow-board

21. Lijee Philip and Kala Vijayraghavan, 'Mahindra group follows management practice of shadow boards', *Economic Times*, 15 July 2010, https://economictimes.indiatimes.com/news/company/corporate-trends/mahindra-group-follows-management-practice-of-shadow-boards/articleshow/6169552.cms

22. Morita, Reingold and Shimomura, *Made in Japan: Akio Morita and Sony.*

23. Ken Kocienda, *Creative Selection: Inside Apple's Design Process during the Golden Age of Steve Jobs* (New York: St Martin's Press, 2018).

24. Walter Isaacson, *Steve Jobs* (New York: Simon & Schuster, 2011).

25. Dan Schulman, 'Paypal's CEO on Creating Products for Underserved Markets', *Harvard Business Review*, December 2016, https://hbr.org/2016/12/paypals-ceo-on-creating-products-for-underserved-markets

26. Lijee Philip, 'How Siddhartha Lal turned Royal Enfield into a global brand', *Economic Times*, 6 November 2017, https://economictimes.indiatimes.com/industry/auto/two-wheelers-three-wheelers/how-siddhartha-lal-turned-royal-enfield-into-a-global-brand/every-indians-bike/slideshow/61531010.cms

27. Siddhartha Lal, 'My Himalayan Adventure', RoyalEnfield.com, 21 January 2016, https://www.royalenfield.com/in/en/motorcycles/himalayan/sid-speak/

28. Pandey, *Pandeymonium: Piyush Pandey on Advertising*.

29. Biyani, *It Happened in India: The Story of Pantaloons, Big Bazaar, Central and the Great Indian Consumer*.

30. Emma K. Macdonald, Hugh N. Wilson and Umut Konuş, 'Better Customer Insight—in Real Time', *Harvard Business Review*, September 2012, https://hbr.org/2012/09/better-customer-insight-in-real-time

31. Marc Randolph, *That Will Never Work: The Birth of Netflix and the Amazing Life of an Idea* (New York: Little, Brown and Company, 2019).

32. Tom Vanderbilt, 'The Science Behind the Netflix Algorithms That Decide What You'll Watch Next', *Wired*, 8 July 2013, https://www.wired.com/2013/08/qq-netflix-algorithm/

33. M.S. Subramanian and T.N. Hari, *Saying No to Jugaad: The Making of Bigbasket* (New Delhi: Bloomsbury India, 2019).

34. Ibid.

35. Ibid.

36. Nikhar Aggarwal, 'Here's how ML and analytics have transformed Bigbasket into Smartbasket', *Economic Times*, 17 December 2019, https://cio.economictimes.indiatimes.com/news/business-analytics/heres-how-ml-and-analytics-have-transformed-bigbasket-into-smartbasket/72809278

37. Morita, Reingold and Shimomura, *Made in Japan: Akio Morita and Sony*.

38. Clayton M. Christensen, Taddy Hall, Karen Dillon and David S. Duncan, 'Know Your Customers' "Jobs to Be Done"', *Harvard Business Review*, September 2016, https://hbr.org/2016/09/know-your-customers-jobs-to-be-done

39. Amrit Raj, 'Still a long way to go to match Hero MotoCorp, says Honda's Noriaki Abe', *Mint*, 4 April 2017, https://www.livemint.com/Companies/KASkrVmMywriAwEaOiRzEP/Still-a-long-way-to-go-to-match-Hero-MotoCorp-says-Hondas.html

40. 'Honda Activa Reaches 1.5 Crore Cumulative Unit Sales', BikeDekho.com, 20 March 2019, https://www.bikedekho.com/news/honda-activa-reaches-15-crore-cumulative-unit-sales

41. Pradeep Shah, 'Royal Enfield Interceptor, Continental GT 650 waiting period now 6 months: Check on road prices', *Financial Express*, 18 April 2019, https://www.financialexpress.com/auto/bike-news/royal-enfield-interceptor-continental-gt-650-waiting-period-now-6-months-check-on-road-prices/1551843/

42. Gwen Moran, '4 ways Google looks for emotional intelligence in job candidates', *Fast Company*, 9 March 2020, https://www.fastcompany.com/90471177/4-ways-google-looks-for-emotional-intelligence-in-job-candidates

43. Raymond Bickson, 'Our Hotel Was Attacked', *New York Times*, 7 February 2009, https://www.nytimes.com/2009/02/08/jobs/08boss.html

44. Rohit Deshpande and Anjali Raina, 'The Ordinary Heroes of the Taj', *Harvard Business Review*, December 2011, https://hbr.org/2011/12/the-ordinary-heroes-of-the-taj

45. Source: https://www.titancompany.in/corporate-social-responsibility-initiative

46. Harish Bhat, *Tanishq Sets the Gold Standard* (New Delhi: Penguin Portfolio, 2013).

47. Harish Bhat, *Tata Log: Eight Modern Stories from a Timeless Institution* (New Delhi: Penguin Portfolio, 2012).

48. Daniel Goleman, *Emotional Intelligence: Why It Can Matter More Than IQ.*

49. Ibid.

50. Ibid.

51. Thich Nhat Hanh, *The Miracle of Mindfulness: A Manual on Meditation* (Boston: Beacon Press, 1996).

52. Catmull and Wallace, *Creativity, Inc.: Overcoming the Unseen Forces That Stand in the Way of True Inspiration.*

53. His Holiness the Dalai Lama, *My Spiritual Autobiography* (London: Rider, 2012).

54. Nadella, *Hit Refresh: The Quest to Rediscover Microsoft's Soul and Imagine a Better Future for Everyone.*

55. Bloomberg Markets and Finance, 'Nadella Says Children's Challenges Taught Him Empathy', YouTube.com, 25 October 2017, https://www.youtube.com/watch?v=SbAPmVoWVZs

56. Tony Buzan and Barry Buzan, *The Mind Map Book: How to Use Radiant Thinking to Maximize Your Brain's Untapped Potential* (New York: Plume, 1993).

57. Roger L. Martin and Tony Golsby-Smith, 'Management Is Much More Than a Science', *Harvard Business Review*, September–October 2017, https://hbr.org/2017/09/management-is-much-more-than-a-science

58. Jon Kolko, 'Design Thinking Comes of Age', *Harvard Business Review*, September 2015, https://hbr.org/2015/09/design-thinking-comes-of-age

59. Adam Waytz, 'The Limits of Empathy', *Harvard Business Review*, January–February 2016, https://hbr.org/2016/01/the-limits-of-empathy

60. J. D. Hattula, C. Schmitz, M. Schmidt and S. Reinecke, 'Is more always better? An investigation into the relationship between marketing influence and managers' market intelligence dissemination', *International Journal of Research in Marketing*, 2015.

61. 'Letter from the Founders', *New York Times*, 29 April 2004, https://www.nytimes.com/2004/04/29/business/letter-from-the-founders.html

62. Robert Simons, 'Choosing the Right Customer', *Harvard Business Review*, March 2014, https://hbr.org/2014/03/choosing-the-right-customer

63. Stephen King, *On Writing: A Memoir of the Craft* (New York: Scribner, 2000).

64. Source: https://www.apple.com/newsroom/2003/01/07Apple-Unveils-Safari/

65. Bhat, *Tata Log: Eight Modern Stories from a Timeless Institution*.

66. Martin and Golsby-Smith, 'Management Is Much More Than a Science'.

67. Joseph L. Bower and Clayton M. Christensen, Disruptive Technologies: Catching the Wave, *Harvard Business Review*, January–February 1995, https://hbr.org/1995/01/disruptive-technologies-catching-the-wave

68. Vinay Kamath, *Titan: Inside India's Most Successful Consumer Brand* (New Delhi: Hachette, 2018).

69. Ibid.

70. Source: Titan Company's 2018–19 annual report.

Chapter 6: Ideate

1. Kevin Ashton, *How to Fly a Horse: The Secret History of Creation, Invention, and Discovery* (New York: Doubleday, 2015).

2. Randolph, *That Will Never Work: The Birth of Netflix and the Amazing Life of an Idea.*

3. Brian Lucas and Loran Nordgren, 'People underestimate the value of persistence for creative performance', *Journal of Personality and Social Psychology*, 2015.

4. PTI, 'Average purity of gold lower than 22 carat: Survey', *Economic Times*, 19 June 2003, https://economictimes.indiatimes.com/average-purity-of-gold-lower-than-22-carat-survey/articleshow/30921.cms

5. Isaacson, *The Innovators: How a Group of Hackers, Geniuses and Geeks Created the Digital Revolution.*

6. Stuart Brown, 'Play is more than just fun', TED.com, May 2008, https://www.ted.com/talks/stuart_brown_play_is_more_than_just_fun

7. Ibid.

8. Bijoy Venugopal, 'Vinoth Poovalingam, the Flipkart Fresher Who Built EKart', Flipkart.com, 12 May 2017, https://stories.flipkart.com/vinoth-poovalingam-ekart/

9. 'No Cost EMI from Flipkart Makes Your Dreams Affordable', Flipkart.com, 31 May 2016, https://stories.flipkart.com/flipkart-no-cost-emi/

10. Thomas Kuhn, *The Structure of Scientific Revolutions* (Chicago: University of Chicago Press, 1962).

11. Kelley and Littman, *The Ten Faces of Innovation: IDEO's Strategies for Beating the Devil's Advocate and Driving Creativity throughout Your Organization.*

12. Michael Diehl and Wolfgang Stroebe, 'Productivity Loss in Brainstorming Groups: Toward the Solution of a Riddle', *Journal of Personality and Social Psychology*, 1987.

13. Paul Paulus and Huei-Chuan Yang, 'Idea Generation in Groups: A Basis for Creativity in Organizations', *Organizational Behavior and Human Decision Processes*, 2000.

14. Jake Knapp, John Zeratsky and Braden Kowitz, *Sprint: How to Solve Big Problems and Test New Ideas in Just Five Days* (New York: Simon & Schuster, 2016).

15. Robert Sutton and Andrew Hargadon, 'Brainstorming Groups in Context: Effectiveness in a Product Design Firm', *Administrative Science Quarterly*, 1996.

16. Isaacson, *The Innovators: How a Group of Hackers, Geniuses and Geeks Created the Digital Revolution*.

17. Ibid.

18. Ibid.

19. Doerr, *Measure What Matters: OKRs: The Simple Idea That Drives 10x Growth*.

20. Isaacson, *The Innovators: How a Group of Hackers, Geniuses and Geeks Created the Digital Revolution*.

21. Frans Johansson, *The Medici Effect: What Elephants and Epidemics Can Teach Us About Innovation* (Boston: Harvard Business Publishing, 2004).

22. Neil Cybart, 'Apple Isn't a Tech Company', AboveAvalon.com, 26 April 2017, https://www.aboveavalon.com/notes/2017/4/26/apple-isnt-a-tech-company

23. Isaacson, *The Innovators: How a Group of Hackers, Geniuses and Geeks Created the Digital Revolution*.

24. Brent Lang, 'Marvel's Kevin Feige on *Spider-Man*'s Future and Why Brie Larson Was Perfect for *Captain Marvel*', *Variety*, 22 November 2016, https://variety.com/2016/film/news/marvel-kevin-feige-interview-spider-man-captain-marvel-diversity-1201923851/

25. Spencer Harrison, Arne Carlsen and Miha Škerlavaj, 'Marvel's Blockbuster Machine: How the Studio Balances Continuity and Renewal', *Harvard Business Review*, 2019.

26. 'Distinguished architect Dr. Balkrishna Doshi, whose oeuvre includes the IIMB campus, has become the first Indian to win the Pritzker Prize, widely considered to be the "Nobel" of architecture', IIMB.ac.in, 10 November 2018, https://www.iimb.ac.in/node/4670

27. Morita, *Made in Japan: Akio Morita and Sony*.

28. Howard Schultz with Joanne Gordon, *Onward: How Starbucks Fought for Its Life without Losing Its Soul* (New York: Rodale Books, 2011).

29. Ashton, *How to Fly a Horse: The Secret History of Creation, Invention, and Discovery*.

30. Randolph, *That Will Never Work: The Birth of Netflix and the Amazing Life of an Idea*.

31. Biyani, *It Happened in India: The Story of Pantaloons, Big Bazaar, Central and the Great Indian Consumer.*

32. David Ogilvy, *Confessions of an Advertising Man* (London: Southbank Publishing, 1963).

33. Jacob W. Getzels and Philip W. Jackson, 'Creativity and intelligence: Explorations with gifted students', *Wiley*, 1962.

34. F. Scott Fitzgerald, *The Crack-Up* (New York: New Directions, 1945).

35. 'Lifebuoy spreads the handwashing message at the Maha Kumbh Mela', HUL.co.in, 11 February 2013, https://www.hul.co.in/news/news-and-features/2013/lifebuoy-spreads-the-handwashing-message-at-the-maha-kumbh-mela.html

36. Mohanbir Sawhney and Sanjay Khosla, Managing Yourself: Where to Look for Insight', *Harvard Business Review*, 2014.

37. Hal Gregersen, 'Better brainstorming', *Harvard Business Review*, March–April 2018 https://hbr.org/2018/03/better-brainstorming.

38. Roberto Verganti, 'The Innovative Power of Criticism', *Harvard Business Review*, January–February 2016, https://hbr.org/2016/01/the-innovative-power-of-criticism

39. Renée Mauborgne and W. Chan Kim, *Blue Ocean Strategy: How to Create Uncontested Market Space and Make the Competition Irrelevant* (Boston: Harvard Business Review, 2004).

40. Edward de Bono, *Lateral Thinking: A Textbook of Creativity* (London: Ward Lock Educational, 1970).

41. Drew Boyd and Jacob Goldenberg, *Inside the Box: A Proven System of Creativity for Breakthrough Results* (New York: Simon & Schuster, 2013).

42. Boudreau, K. J., and Lakhani, K. R. (2013). Using the crowd as an innovation partner. *Harvard Business Review*, 91(4), 60-69.

Chapter 7: Prototype and Test

1. Ravi Arora, *Igniting Innovation: The Tata Way* (New Delhi: Harper Business, 2019).

2. Grant, *Originals: How Non-conformists Move the World.*

3. James Newton, *Uncommon Friends: Life with Thomas Edison, Henry Ford, Harvey Firestone, Alexis Carrel & Charles Lindbergh* (San Diego: Harcourt, 1987).

4. Ashton, *How to Fly a Horse: The Secret History of Creation, Invention, and Discovery.*

5. Kocienda, *Creative Selection: Inside Apple's Design Process during the Golden Age of Steve Jobs.*

6. Mihir Dalal and Shrutika Verma, 'Flipkart apologizes to customers for Big Billion Day sale glitches', *Mint*, 7 October 2014, https://www.livemint.com/Industry/t5UDgJyzPcvF7vK7j7M62O/Flipkart-apologizes-to-customers-for-mega-sale-glitches.html

7. 'Flipkart apologizes to customers for mega sale glitches', *Economic Times*, 7 October 2014, https://economictimes.indiatimes.com/industry/services/retail/flipkart-apologizes-to-customers-for-mega-sale-glitches/articleshow/44627746.cms?from=mdr

8. Malavika Velayanikal, 'It's official: Flipkart's app-only experiment with Myntra was a disaster', TechInAsia.com, 28 March 2016, https://www.techinasia.com/flipkart-myntra-app-only-disaster

9. Digbijay Mishra and Shalina Pillai, 'Flipkart drops its plan to go app-only', *Times of India*, 12 November 2015, https://timesofindia.indiatimes.com/business/india-business/Flipkart-drops-its-plan-to-go-app-only/articleshow/49751060.cms

10. Schmidt and Rosenberg, *How Google Works.*

11. Ben Bold, 'Words of design wisdom: Apple's Jony Ive on failure, problem-solving and Blue Peter', *Campaign*, 26 May 2015, https://www.campaignlive.co.uk/article/words-design-wisdom-apples-jony-ive-failure-problem-solving-blue-peter/1348500?DCMP=ILC-SEARCH

12. Kocienda, *Creative Selection: Inside Apple's Design Process During the Golden Age of Steve Jobs.*

13. Thiel and Masters, *Zero to One: Notes on Startups, or How to Build the Future.*

14. Biyani, *It Happened in India: The Story of Pantaloons, Big Bazaar, Central and the Great Indian Consumer.*

15. 'Richard Branson on The David Rubenstein Show', YouTube.com, 25 July 2018, https://www.youtube.com/watch?v=lFchP5bLzM0

16. Stefan Thomke, 'Building a Culture of Experimentation', *Harvard Business Review*, March–April 2020, https://hbr.org/2020/03/productive-innovation

17. CNBC Television, 'Amazon's Bezos says you can't invent without experimenting', YouTube.com, 19 September 2018, https://www.youtube.com/watch?v=97h6ECZnf9o

18. Knapp, Zeratsky and Kowitz, *Sprint: How to Solve Big Problems and Test New Ideas in Just Five Days.*

19. 'Edison and Innovation Series', Rutgers.edu, http://edison.rutgers.edu/inventionfactory.htm

20. Kocienda, *Creative Selection: Inside Apple's Design Process during the Golden Age of Steve Jobs.*

21. Ibid.

22. Stefan Thomke and Jim Manzi, 'The Discipline of Business Experimentation', *Harvard Business Review*, December 2014, https://hbr.org/2014/12/the-discipline-of-business-experimentation

23. David A. Garvin, 'How Google Sold Its Engineers on Management', *Harvard Business Review*, December 2013, https://hbr.org/2013/12/how-google-sold-its-engineers-on-management

24. Jemima Kiss, 'Google CEO Sundar Pichai: "I don't know whether humans want change that fast"', *Guardian*, 7 October 2017, https://www.theguardian.com/technology/2017/oct/07/google-boss-sundar-pichai-tax-gender-equality-data-protection-jemima-kiss

25. Randolph, *That Will Never Work: The Birth of Netflix and the Amazing Life of an Idea.*

26. 'Paytm Wallet crosses 100 million users', Paytm.com, 11 August 2015, https://blog.paytm.com/paytm-wallet-crosses-100-million-users-f069248cb7ed

27. Digbijay Mishra, 'Paytm sets up 3,000 member team to advise sellers', GadgetsNow.com, 18 January 2016, https://www.gadgetsnow.com/tech-news/Paytm-sets-up-3000-member-team-to-advise-sellers/articleshow/50620968.cms

28. 'JOURNEY TO 1 MILLION MERCHANTS — Bringing in the cashless revolution!', Paytm.com, 26 November 2016, https://blog.paytm.com/journey-to-1-million-merchants-bringing-in-the-cashless-revolution-adce3ae9221

29. Pratik Bhakta, 'Paytm logs 400 million transactions a month', *Economic Times*, 31 May 2019, https://economictimes.indiatimes.com/

small-biz/startups/newsbuzz/paytm-logs-400-million-transactions-a-month/articleshow/69590478.cms

30. Navneet Dubey, 'How to buy FASTag, recharge it using Paytm', *Economic Times*, 4 December 2019, https://economictimes.indiatimes.com/wealth/save/how-to-buy-fastag-recharge-it-using-your-paytm-wallet/articleshow/72252316.cms?from=mdr

31. Paytm Blog, 'Introducing Paytm FASTag, the end of travel delays', Paytm.com, 21 September 2016, https://blog.paytm.com/introducing-paytm-fastag-the-end-of-travel-delays-bc25fd4f3379

32. Jan Carlzon, *Moments of Truth: New Strategies for Today's Customer-Driven Economy* (New York: Ballinger Publishing Company, 1987).

33. Brittany Gibson, 'The 3 Words Disney Employees Aren't Allowed to Say', *Reader's Digest*, 13 December 2019, https://www.rd.com/article/disney-employees-arent-allowed-say/

34. Daniel Goleman, *Emotional Intelligence: Why It Can Matter More Than IQ*.

35. Chip Heath and Dan Heath, *Made to Stick: Why Some Ideas Survive and Others Die* (New York: Random House, 2007).

36. Malcolm Gladwell, *The Tipping Point: How Little Things Can Make a Big Difference* (New York: Little, Brown and Company, 2000).

37. Bhat, *Tata Log: Eight Modern Stories from a Timeless Institution*.

38. 'Ameen Haque: "The Art of Business Storytelling" | Talks At Google', YouTube.com, 12 January 2017, https://www.youtube.com/watch?v=77FUr6ZsWjY

39. Ron Miller, 'How AWS came to be', *Tech Crunch*, 2 July 2016, https://techcrunch.com/2016/07/02/andy-jassys-brief-history-of-the-genesis-of-aws/

40. Ramprasad K.R., 'Making of Wipro HOLMES™', Wipro.com, July 2015, https://www.wipro.com/en-IN/blogs/ramprasad-k-r/making-of-holmes---ai-here-and-now/

41. PTI, 'Wipro redeployed about 12,000 people in 2015, says CEO Abidali Z Neemuchwala', *Economic Times*, 20 July 2017, https://economictimes.indiatimes.com/tech/ites/wipro-redeployed-about-12000-people-in-2015-says-ceo-abidali-z-neemuchwala/articleshow/59688152.cms

42. Catmull and Wallace, *Creativity, Inc.: Overcoming the Unseen Forces That Stand in the Way of True Inspiration.*

43. Jake Knapp, John Zeratsky, and Braden Kowitz, *Sprint: How to Solve Big Problems and Test New Ideas in Just Five Days* (New York: Simon & Schuster, 2016).

44. Kelley and Littman, *The Art of Innovation: Lessons in Creativity from IDEO, America's Leading Design Firm.*

45. Grant, *Originals: How Non-conformists Move the World.*

Chapter 8: Scale

1. Doerr, *Measure What Matters: OKRs: The Simple Idea That Drives 10x Growth.*

2. Isaacson, *The Innovators: How a Group of Inventors, Hackers, Geniuses and Geeks Created the Digital Revolution.*

3. 'Guiding strategy & vision', RIL.com, https://www.ril.com/OurCompany/Leadership/Chairman-And-Managing-Director.aspx

4. 'Highlights of Telecom Subscription Data as on 31st December 2019', Trai.gov.in, 25 February 2020, https://main.trai.gov.in/sites/default/files/PR_No.17of2020.pdf

5. 'Reliance Jio posts loss of Rs 271 crore; Mukesh Ambani says Jio has positive EBIT contribution to RIL Q2 results', *Financial Express*, 13 October 2017, https://www.financialexpress.com/industry/reliance-jio-posts-loss-of-rs-271-crore-mukesh-ambani-says-jio-has-positive-ebit-contribution-to-ril-q2-results/893451/

6. Vidhi Choudhary, 'Reliance Jio initial investment at Rs 150,000 crore: Mukesh Ambani', *Mint*, 31 March 2016, https://www.livemint.com/Companies/ncT04NLRTtEMDEHAWdMPGN/Reliance-Jio-initial-investment-at-Rs150000-crore-Mukesh-A.html

7. Schmidt and Rosenberg, *How Google Works.*

8. David Fischer and Ajit Mohan, 'Facebook Invests $5.7 Billion in India's Jio Platforms', Fb.com, 21 April 2020, https://about.fb.com/news/2020/04/facebook-invests-in-jio/

9. 'Jio and Microsoft announce alliance to accelerate digital transformation in India', Microsoft.com, 12 August 2019, https://news.microsoft.com/

2019/08/12/jio-and-microsoft-announce-alliance-to-accelerate-digital-transformation-in-india/

10. Steve Blank, 'Why the Lean Start-up Changes Everything', *Harvard Business Review*, May 2013, https://hbr.org/2013/05/why-the-lean-start-up-changes-everything

11. Eric Ries, *The Lean Startup: How Today's Entrepreneurs Use Continuous Innovation to Create Radically Successful Businesses* (New York: Crown Publishing Group, 2011).

12. 'The strange love-hate relationship between Bill Gates and Steve Jobs', BusinessInsider.com, 19 August 2017, https://www.businessinsider.in/enterprise/the-strange-love-hate-relationship-between-bill-gates-and-steve-jobs/slidelist/51347248.cms

13. David B. Yoffie and Michael A. Cusumano, *Strategy Rules: Five Timeless Lessons from Bill Gates, Andy Grove, and Steve Jobs* (New York: Harper Business, 2015).

14. Stephen Covey, *The 7 Habits of Highly Effective People* (New York: Free Press, 1989).

15. Jeff Haden, '20 Years Ago, Jeff Bezos Said This 1 Thing Separates People Who Achieve Lasting Success From Those Who Don't', Inc.com, 6 November 2017, https://www.inc.com/jeff-haden/20-years-ago-jeff-bezos-said-this-1-thing-separates-people-who-achieve-lasting-success-from-those-who-dont.html

16. Doerr, *Measure What Matters: OKRs: The Simple Idea that Drives 10x Growth.*

17. Jack Welch and Suzy Welch, *Winning* (New York: HarperCollins, 2011).

18. Grove, *Only the Paranoid Survive: How to Exploit the Crisis Points That Challenge Every Company.*

19. 'IBM C-suite Study: 19th edition', IBM.com, 18 February 2020, https://www.ibm.com/downloads/cas/NJYY0ZVG

20. Schmidt and Rosenberg, *How Google Works.*

21. Thomas J. Peters and Robert H. Waterman, Jr., *In Search of Excellence: Lessons from America's Best-Run Companies* (New York: Harper Business, 1982).

22. Bala Iyer and Thomas H. Davenport, 'Reverse Engineering Google's Innovation Machine', Harvard Business Review, April 2008, https://hbr.org/2008/04/reverse-engineering-googles-innovation-machine

33 33 333

3333333333333333333

23. 'Innovation = Managed Chaos', MastersofScale.com, 2018, https://mastersofscale.com/eric-schmidt-innovation-managed-chaos/

24. Thomas Lockwood and Edgar Papke, 'How Intuit Used Design Thinking To Boost Sales By $10M In A Year', *Fast Company*, 31 October 2017, https://www.fastcompany.com/90147434/how-intuit-used-design-thinking-to-boost-sales-by-10m-in-a-year

25. Adi Ignatius, 'How Indra Nooyi Turned Design Thinking Into Strategy: An Interview with PepsiCo's CEO', *Harvard Business Review*, September 2015, https://hbr.org/2015/09/how-indra-nooyi-turned-design-thinking-into-strategy

26. James de Vries, 'PepsiCo's Chief Design Officer on Creating an Organization Where Design Can Thrive', *Harvard Business Review*, 11 August 2015, https://hbr.org/2015/08/pepsicos-chief-design-officer-on-creating-an-organization-where-design-can-thrive

27. Tim Brown, 'Leaders Can Turn Creativity into a Competitive Advantage', *Harvard Business Review*, 2 November 2016, https://hbr.org/2016/11/leaders-can-turn-creativity-into-a-competitive-advantage

28. Pavan Soni, 'Effective leaders don't innovate, they protect those who do!', PeopleMatters.in, 2019, 23 April 2019, https://www.peoplematters.in/article/leadership/effective-leaders-dont-innovate-they-protect-those-who-do-21483

29. 'Amazon's Bezos says you can't invent without experimenting', https://www.youtube.com/watch?v=97h6ECZnf9o&t=17s

30. David Packard, *The HP Way: How Bill Hewlett and I Built Our Company* (New York: Harper Business, 1995).

31. Ibid.

32. Adam Grant, 'How to Build a Culture of Originality', *Harvard Business Review*, March 2016, https://hbr.org/2016/03/how-to-build-a-culture-of-originality

33. Bala Iyer and Thomas H. Davenport, 'Reverse Engineering Google's Innovation Machine', *Harvard Business Review*, April 2008, https://hbr.org/2008/04/reverse-engineering-googles-innovation-machine

34. Source: https://www.tatainnovista.com

35. Arora, *Igniting Innovation: The Tata Way*.

36. Kamath, *Titan: Inside India's Most Successful Consumer Brand*.

37. Gladwell, *The Tipping Point: How Little Things Can Make a Big Difference.*

38. Based on author's interview with Sunil Kaul, conducted on 18 February 2016 at MAHLE Behr Pune headquarters.

39. Based on author's interview with M.S. Shankar, conducted on 18 February 2016 at Spicer India's Pune headquarters.

40. Source: https://www.anandgroupindia.com/who-we-are/history/

41. Guy Kawasaki, 'The Art of Evangelism', *Harvard Business Review*, May 2015, https://hbr.org/2015/05/the-art-of-evangelism

42. Adam M. Grant, Justin M. Berg and Daniel M. Cable, 'Job Titles as Identity Badges: How Self-Reflective Titles Can Reduce Emotional Exhaustion', *Academy of Management*, 27 July 2013.

43. Teresa Amabile and Steven J. Kramer, 'The Power of Small Wins', *Harvard Business Review*, May 2011, https://hbr.org/2011/05/the-power-of-small-wins

44. Doerr, *Measure What Matters: OKRs: The Simple Idea That Drives 10x Growth.*

45. Ibid.

46. Ibid.

47. Packard, *The HP Way: How Bill Hewlett and I Built Our Company.*

48. Suveen K. Sinha, 'Chip off the Birla block', *Business Today*, 28 September 2011, https://www.businesstoday.in/opinion/columns/kumar-mangalam-birla-parta-cash-management/story/18967.html

49. 'Annual Report 2018–19', retrieved from https://www.dmartindia.com/investor-relationship

50. Anuj Srivas, 'What Explains the Success of Damani's D-Mart, India's Walmart in the Making?', *Wire*, 21 March 2017, https://thewire.in/business/indian-walmart-making-explains-d-mart-success

51. Sourav, 'The Rise and Rise of D-Mart – Building Supermarts the Right way', NextBigBrand.in, 16 May 2019, https://www.nextbigbrand.in/the-rise-and-rise-of-d-mart-building-supermarts-the-right-way/

52. Srivas, 'What Explains the Success of Damani's D-Mart, India's Walmart in the Making?'

53. Subramanian and Hari, *Saying No to Jugaad: The Making of Bigbasket.*

54. Smita Balram, 'More preferring online grocery shops: BigBasket', *Economic Times*, 9 November 2019, https://economictimes.indiatimes.com/small-biz/startups/newsbuzz/more-preferring-online-grocery-shops-bigbasket/articleshow/71978380.cms

Chapter 9: Design Thinking in Action

1. Kelley, *The Art of Innovation: Lessons in Creativity From IDEO, America's Leading Design Firm.*
2. Knapp, Zeratsky and Kowitz, *Sprint: How to Solve Big Problems and Test New Ideas in Just Five Days.*
3. Thomas Lockwood and Edgar Papke, 'How Intuit Used Design Thinking to Boost Sales by $10M in a Year', *Fast Company*, 31 October 2017, https://www.fastcompany.com/90147434/how-intuit-used-design-thinking-to-boost-sales-by-10m-in-a-year
4. Jen Sheahan, 'What is Design Thinking anyway?', Accenture.com, 13 March 2018, https://www.accenture.com/ie-en/blogs/blogs-design-thinking
5. 'Infosys Annual Report 2015-16', Infosys.com, https://www.infosys.com/investors/reports-filings/annual-report/annual/documents/infosys-ar-16.pdf
6. Ibid.
7. 'Sustainability Report 2016–17', Infosys.com, https://www.infosys.com/sustainability/documents/infosys-sustainability-report-2016-17.pdf
8. 'Infosys is the Market Leader for Design Thinking Services Execution', Infosys.com, 26 January 2016, https://www.infosys.com/newsroom/press-releases/2016/leader-design-thinking-services.html
9. You can read more about Geert Hofstede's work at www.hofstede-insights.com.
10. 'Country Comparison', Hofstede Insights, https://www.hofstede-insights.com/country-comparison/india/
11. Ibid.
12. Isaacson, *The Innovators: How a Group of Inventors, Hackers, Geniuses and Geeks Created the Digital Revolution.*
13. Rishikesha T. Krishnan, *From Jugaad to Systematic Innovation: The Challenge for India* (Bangalore: The Utpreraka Foundation, 2010).

14. Schmidt and Rosenberg, *How Google Works*.

15. Gladwell, *The Tipping Point: How Little Things Can Make a Big Difference*.

16. Steven Johnson, *Where Good Ideas Come From: The Seven Patterns of Innovation* (London: Penguin, 2010).

17. John Seely Brown and Paul Duguid, *The Social Life of Information* (Boston: Harvard Business Press, 2000).

18. Gretchen Spreitzer, Peter Bacevice and Lyndon Garrett, 'Why People Thrive in Coworking Spaces', *Harvard Business Review*, September 2015, https://hbr.org/2015/05/why-people-thrive-in-coworking-spaces

19. David Kelley and Tom Kelley, *Creative Confidence: Unleashing the Creative Potential within Us All*.

20. 'Titan Integrity Campus / Mindspace', Archdaily.com, 24 December 2018, https://www.archdaily.com/908221/titan-integrity-campus-mindspace

21. Aparna Piramal Raje, 'When an office becomes a people's home', *Mint*, 3 December 2018, https://www.livemint.com/Leisure/9I4MxLkSQeK9myy0YsBxhM/When-an-office-becomes-a-peoples-home.html

22. Doerr, *Measure What Matters: OKRs: The Simple Idea That Drives 10x Growth*.

23. Jocko Willink and Leif Babin, *Extreme Ownership: How U.S. Navy SEALs Lead and Win* (New York: St Martin's Press, 2015).

24. Catmull and Wallace, *Creativity, Inc.: Overcoming the Unseen Forces That Stand in the Way of True Inspiration*.

25. Robbie Collin, 'Christopher Nolan interview: "I'm completely invested in every project I do"', *Telegraph*, 31 December 2014, https://www.telegraph.co.uk/culture/film/11317410/Christopher-Nolan-interview-Im-completely-invested-in-every-project-I-do.html

Chapter 10: How to Be a Design Thinker

1. Johnson, *Where Good Ideas Come From: The Seven Patterns of Innovation*.

2. Tim Brown, 'Design Thinking', *Harvard Business Review*, June 2008, https://hbr.org/2008/06/design-thinking

3. Martha S. Feldman, 'Organizational Routines as a Source of Continuous Change', *Organization Science*, 2000.

4. Mihaly Csikszentmihalyi, *Creativity: Flow and the Psychology of Discovery and Invention* (New York: HarperCollins Publishers, 1996).

5. Ken Miyamoto, 'Screenwriting Wisdom from Christopher Nolan', ScreenCraft.org, 16 December 2019, https://screencraft.org/2019/12/16/screenwriting-wisdom-from-christopher-nolan/

6. Quentin Tarantino interviewed by Charlie Rose, CharlieRose.com, 21 December 2012, https://charlierose.com/videos/17441

7. Elizabeth Gilbert, 'One of the greatest quotes on creativity ever . . . I am a big advocate for the purs . . .', ElizabethGilbert.com, 8 February 2014, https://www.elizabethgilbert.com/one-of-the-greatest-quotes-on-creativity-ever-i-am-a-big-advocate-for the-purs/

8. Francesca Gino, 'The Business Case for Curiosity', *Harvard Business Review*, September– October 2018.

9. '15 powerful women share the personality trait that's key to their success', *Fortune*, 8 March 2020, https://fortune.com/2020/03/08/15-powerful-women-share-the-personality-trait-thats-key-to-their-success/

10. Ranjani Ayyar, 'Opportunity is everywhere, you need common sense to spot it', *The Times of India*, 18 February 2018, https://timesofindia.indiatimes.com/people/musthafa-pc-id-interview/articleshow/62961602.cms

11. D.T. Campbell, 'Blind variation and selective retention in creative thought as in other knowledge processes', *Psychological Review*, 1960.

12. '15 powerful women share the personality trait that's key to their success', *Fortune*.

13. 'Richard Branson on The David Rubenstein Show', YouTube.com, 25 July 2018, https://www.youtube.com/watch?v=lFchP5bLzM0

14. Nadella, *Hit Refresh: The Quest to Rediscover Microsoft's Soul and Imagine a Better Future for Everyone*.

15. John Chambers, 'Cisco's CEO on Staying Ahead of Technology Shifts', *Harvard Business Review*, May 2015, https://hbr.org/2015/05/ciscos-ceo-on-staying-ahead-of-technology-shifts

16. Covey, *The 7 Habits of Highly Effective People*.

17. Julian Treasure, '5 ways to listen better', TED.com, July 2011, https://www.ted.com/talks/julian_treasure_5_ways_to_listen_better

18. Melanie Curtin, 'According to Oprah, All Your Arguments Come Down to These 3 Questions', Inc.com, 30 June 2018, https://www.inc.com/melanie-curtin/according-to-oprah-all-your-arguments-come-down-to-these-3-questions.html

19. Morita, *Made in Japan: Akio Morita and Sony.*

20. Jeffrey Rothfeder, *Driving Honda: Inside the World's Most Innovative Car Company* (New York: Portfolio, 2015).

21. 'Amazon CEO Jeff Bezos on The David Rubenstein Show', YouTube.com, 19 September 2018, https://www.youtube.com/watch?v=f3NBQcAqyu4&t=1720s

22. Grant, *Originals: How Non-Conformists Move the World.*

23. Johnson, *Where Good Ideas Come From: The Seven Patterns of Innovation.*

24. Schmidt and Rosenberg, *How Google Works.*

25. Johansson, *The Medici Effect: What Elephants and Epidemics Can Teach Us about Innovation.*

26. Kuhn, *The Structure of Scientific Revolutions.*

27. 'Connecting All Humanity', Academy of Achievement, 22 June 2007, http://54.198.197.222/autodoc/page/ber1int-1

28. Grant, *Originals: How Non-Conformists Move the World.*

29. Isaacson, *The innovators: How a Group of Inventors, Hackers, Geniuses and Geeks Created the Digital Revolution.*

30. Isaacson, *Leonardo Da Vinci: The Biography.*

31. Nadella, *Hit Refresh: The Quest to Rediscover Microsoft's Soul and Imagine a Better Future for Everyone.*

32. Pandey, *Pandeymonium: Piyush Pandey on Advertising.*

33. Johansson, *The Medici Effect: What Elephants and Epidemics Can Teach Us about Innovation.*

34. Kimberly Elsbach and Francis Flynn, 'Creative Collaboration and the Self-concept: A Study of Toy Designers', *Journal of Management Studies*, 2013.

35. Isaacson, *The Innovators: How a Group of Inventors, Hackers, Geniuses and Geeks Created the Digital Revolution.*

36. Ibid.

37. 'How a kingfisher helped reshape Japan's bullet train', BBC.com, 26 March 2019, https://www.bbc.com/news/av/science-environment-47673287/how-a-kingfisher-helped-reshape-japan-s-bullet-train

38. John Kennedy, 'Apple CEO Tim Cook says diversity leads to better products', SiliconRepublic.com, 11 November 2015, https://www.siliconrepublic.com/companies/apple-ceo-tim-cook-says-diversity-leads-to-better-products

39. TIME, 'Apple CEO Tim Cook Delivers The 2017 MIT Commencement Speech | TIME', YouTube.com, 9 June 2017, https://www.youtube.com/watch?v=3NXjUpo-1q8

40. Catmull and Wallace, *Creativity, Inc.: Overcoming the Unseen Forces That Stand in the Way of True Inspiration.*

41. Ken Robinson, 'Do Schools Kill Creativity?', TED.com, February 2006, https://www.ted.com/talks/sir_ken_robinson_do_schools_kill_creativity?language=en

42. Shelley H. Carson, Jordan B. Peterson and Daniel M. Higgins, 'Decreased latent inhibition is associated with increased creative achievement in high-functioning individuals', *Journal of Personality and Social Psychology*, 2003.

43. Andrew F. Jarosz, Gregory J.H. Colflesh and Jennifer Wiley, 'Uncorking the muse: Alcohol intoxication facilitates creative problem solving', *Consciousness and Cognition*, March 2012.

44. Grant, *Originals: How Non-Conformists Move the World.*

45. Ivan Oransky, 'Moses Judah Folkman', *The Lancet*, 2 February 2008, https://www.thelancet.com/journals/lancet/article/PIIS0140-6736(08)60191-9/fulltext

46. 'To keep the creative juices flowing, employees should be receptive to criticism', ScienceDaily.com, 4 April 2019, www.sciencedaily.com/releases/2019/04/190404132534.htm

47. Peter Thiel and Blake Masters, *Zero to One: Notes on Startups, or How to Build the Future* (New York: Crown Business, 2014).

Index